WOMEN, WORKPLACE PROTEST AND POLITICAL IDENTITY IN ENGLAND, 1968–85

⇌ Jonathan Moss ⇌

Manchester University Press

Copyright © Jonathan Moss 2019

The right of Jonathan Moss to be identified as the author of this work has been asserted by him in accordance with the Copyright, Designs and Patents Act 1988.

Published by Manchester University Press
Oxford Road, Manchester M13 9PL
www.manchesteruniversitypress.co.uk

British Library Cataloguing-in-Publication Data
A catalogue record for this book is available from the British Library

ISBN 978 1 5261 2488 3 hardback
ISBN 978 1 5261 6043 0 paperback

First published 2019
Paperback published 2021

The publisher has no responsibility for the persistence or accuracy of URLs for any external or third-party internet websites referred to in this book, and does not guarantee that any content on such websites is, or will remain, accurate or appropriate.

Typeset by Deanta Global Publishing Services

GENDER IN HISTORY

Series editors:
Lynn Abrams, Cordelia Beattie, Pam Sharpe and Penny Summerfield

The expansion of research into the history of women and gender since the 1970s has changed the face of history. Using the insights of feminist theory and of historians of women, gender historians have explored the configuration in the past of gender identities and relations between the sexes. They have also investigated the history of sexuality and family relations, and analysed ideas and ideals of masculinity and femininity. Yet gender history has not abandoned the original, inspirational project of women's history: to recover and reveal the lived experience of women in the past and the present.

The series Gender in History provides a forum for these developments. Its historical coverage extends from the medieval to the modern periods, and its geographical scope encompasses not only Europe and North America but all corners of the globe. The series aims to investigate the social and cultural constructions of gender in historical sources, as well as the gendering of historical discourse itself. It embraces both detailed case studies of specific regions or periods, and broader treatments of major themes. Gender in History titles are designed to meet the needs of both scholars and students working in this dynamic area of historical research.

Women, workplace protest and political identity in England, 1968–85

Manchester University Press

OTHER RECENT BOOKS
IN THE SERIES

The state as master: gender, state formation and commercialisation in urban Sweden, 1650–1780   Maria Ågren

Love, intimacy and power: marriage and patriarchy in Scotland, 1650–1850   Katie Barclay
(Winner of the 2012 Women's History Network Book Prize)

Men on trial: performing emotion, embodiment and identity in Ireland, 1800–45   Katie Barclay

Modern women on trial: sexual transgression in the age of the flapper   Lucy Bland

The Women's Liberation Movement in Scotland   Sarah Browne

Modern motherhood: women and family in England, c. 1945–2000   Angela Davis

Gender, rhetoric and regulation: women's work in the civil service and the London County Council, 1900–55   Helen Glew

Jewish women in Europe in the Middle Ages: a quiet revolution   Simha Goldin

Women of letters: gender, writing and the life of the mind in early modern England   Leonie Hannan

Women and museums 1850–1914: Modernity and the gendering of knowledge   Kate Hill

The shadow of marriage: singleness in England, 1914–60   Katherine Holden

Women, dowries and agency: marriage in fifteenth-century Valencia   Dana Wessell Lightfoot

Women, travel and identity: journeys by rail and sea, 1870–1940   Emma Robinson-Tomsett

Imagining Caribbean womanhood: race, nation and beauty contests, 1929–70   Rochelle Rowe

Infidel feminism: secularism, religion and women's emancipation, England 1830–1914   Laura Schwartz

Women, credit and debt in early modern Scotland   Cathryn Spence

Being boys: youth, leisure and identity in the inter-war years   Melanie Tebbutt

Queen and country: same-sex desire in the British Armed Forces, 1939–45   Emma Vickers

The 'perpetual fair': gender, disorder and urban amusement in eighteenth-century London   Anne Wohlcke

Contents

LIST OF TABLES		*page* vi
ACKNOWLEDGEMENTS		vii
LIST OF ABBREVIATIONS		viii
	Introduction	1
1	Contextualising women's workplace activism in post-war England	26
2	The Ford Sewing machinists' strike, 1968, Dagenham	56
3	The Trico-Folberth equal pay strike, Brentford, 1976	82
4	Sexton's shoe factory occupation and Fakenham Enterprises, Norfolk, 1972–77	111
5	The Ford Sewing machinists' strike, Dagenham, 1984–85	139
	Conclusion	164
	APPENDIX	
	Timeline of Women's Workplace Militancy in Britain, 1968–85	175
	BIBLIOGRAPHY	182
	INDEX	195

Tables

1.1 Proportions of men and women (aged over 16) as a percentage of employees within selected occupations, 1985   *page* 28

1.2 Average gross weekly earnings (in £) of full-time men aged 21 and over and full-time women aged 18 and over in public and private sectors, 1970–81   29

Acknowledgements

I would like to thank the people who gave up their time to share their memories with me and provided a privileged insight into their past. I would also like to thank the staff at the TUC Library Collections, London Metropolitan University; The Women's Library, London; the Modern Records Centre, University of Warwick; and the public libraries in Dagenham and Chiswick. I would especially like to thank Maud Bracke and Lynn Abrams, whose guidance and encouragement has been invaluable since I was an undergraduate student. Thanks also to Selina Todd and Eleanor Gordon for helpful comments on my research. I would also really like to thank Nick Clarke and colleagues at the Universities of Southampton and Sussex for all of their help and for providing a great environment to develop my research and writing.

Finally, thanks to my friends and family for all of their patience, understanding and support. I would not have been able to write this book without the help and advice from my parents Carol, Andy, and Ian, and my grandparents Pat and Steve. I am also forever grateful to Jenny who made the whole process a lot more fun and enjoyable.

Abbreviations

ACAS	Advisory, Conciliation and Arbitration Service
ACTT	Association of Cinematograph, Television and Allied Technicians
AEF	Amalgamated Union of Engineering and Foundry Workers
APEX	Association of Professional, Executive, Clerical and Computer Staff
ASTMS	Association of Scientific, Technical and Managerial Staffs
AUEW	Amalgamated Union of Engineering Workers
COHSE	Confederation of Health Service Employees
CPSA	Civil and Public Services Association
CSU	Civil Service Union
EEC	European Economic Community
GMWU	General and Municipal Workers' Union
IRSF	Inland Revenue Staff Federation
IS	International Socialists
MRC	Modern Records Centre, Warwick
NALGO	National and Local Government Officers' Association
NBPI	National Board for Prices and Incomes
NFWW	National Federation of Women Workers
NJACCWER	National Joint Action Campaign Committee for Women's Equal Rights
NUFLAT	National Union of the Footwear, Leather and Allied Trades
NUGW	National Union of General Workers
NUHKW	National Union of Hosiery and Knitwear Workers
NUPE	National Union of Public Employees
NUT	National Union of Teachers
NUTGW	National Union of Tailors and Garment Workers
NUVB	National Union of Vehicle Builders
PTA	Paint, Trim and Assembly
SWP	Socialist Workers Party
TASS	Technical, Administrative and Supervisory Section
TGWU	Transport and General Workers' Union
TNA	The National Archives
TUC	Trades Union Congress

ABBREVIATIONS

TWL	The Women's Library, London
UCS	Upper Clyde Shipbuilders
USDAW	Union of Shop, Distributive and Allied Workers
WAC	Women's Advisory Committee
WLM	women's liberation movement
WTUL	Women's Trade Union League
WWCC	Working Women's Charter campaign

Introduction

Between 1968 and 1985, thousands of female workers engaged in workplace protest in various public sector and private sector industries across England. This wave of activism occurred in a period often associated with heightened tension in both gender and class relations. The 1970s has been described as the 'zenith' of trade union militancy, when over half the labour force was unionised and working days lost to strikes reached record high levels.[1] The women's liberation movement (WLM) also emerged in this period, which produced a shift in public debates about gender roles and relations in the home and the workplace. Certain industrial disputes involving women – such as the 1968 Ford sewing machinists' strike, the 1976–78 Grunwick dispute or the campaign to unionise night cleaners – are frequently cited as evidence of social, political and cultural change in attitudes towards women's employment.[2] Yet the motivations, experiences and political identities of women who actually engaged in such action have been largely neglected by historians. This book seeks to address this space through an analysis of four industrial disputes that were instigated by, and primarily involved, working-class women. In doing so, it makes several important contributions to labour, women's and working-class history.

The book offers new insights into working-class women's experiences of paid work and workplace protest in post-war England. My investigation focuses on the voices and experiences of women who fought for equal pay, skill recognition and the right to work between 1968 and 1985. Drawing on a combination of oral history and archival research, it explores why working-class women engaged in such action when they did, and it analyses the impact of workplace protest on women's political identity. In doing so, the book contributes a fresh understanding of the relationship between feminism, workplace activism and trade unionism during the years 1968–85.

Industrial action was important during this period because it represented a new assertiveness among female workers who contested unequal gender hierarchies and demanded a greater say in how their work was organised. This is not to suggest that female workers had been unwilling to challenge gender inequality in the workplace until this particular historical moment; case studies of women's workplace militancy from earlier periods illustrate how female workers challenged the social and political roles ascribed to women in English workplaces from the nineteenth century to the interwar period.[3] However, it is significant that the disputes analysed here occurred in a period that coincided with women's increased presence in the labour force, greater access to higher education and professional careers, equality legislation and a surge in feminist activism. This specific context influenced how women's workplace protest was represented at the time. What follows seeks to understand how post-war changes in female employment, trade unionism and feminism were experienced by working-class women who sought to improve their workplace conditions by participating in collective action.

Women and paid work

Women's increased labour force participation was one of the most significant social changes in post-war England. Between 1948 and 1980, the total number of female workers in Britain grew from 6.7 million to 9.2 million. Women as a proportion of the total labour force had only grown from 27 per cent in 1881 to 33 per cent in 1948, before rapidly increasing to 41.7 per cent in the short period between 1948 and 1980.[4] The general trends in post-war female employment have been well established: the growth of the bi-modal work pattern meant that there were more married women who returned to work after having children.[5] Many in this group returned to work in part-time jobs, as part-time female employment increased fivefold from 750,000 to nearly 4.1 million between 1951 and 1981.[6]

The growth of women's part-time work was arguably the most important trend in women's paid work during the post-war period. It was important because the majority of part-time jobs were low paid, low status and perceived to be low skilled. It is commonly argued that married women preferred part-time work because of childcare responsibilities and the potential of part-time work to 'liberate' lives dominated by domestic labour.[7] However, recent research by Laura Paterson suggests that part-time work offered a limited range of jobs and opportunities for career advancement, which meant such jobs are better understood as a temporary expedient during a particular stage in women's lives that enabled them to combine the two roles of mother and worker in a context of extremely limited affordable pre-school childcare.[8] The key point here is that women's propensity to work part-time meant they presented themselves in the labour market on different terms to male workers. The majority of women were still expected to assume responsibility for domestic labour, which reinforced the male breadwinner model and meant work was understood as being less important for women.[9]

Further changes in women's experiences of paid work included the removal of marriage bars in teaching (1944) and the civil service (1946), and greater access to further education after the 1963 Robbins Report meant more women entered the professions and pursued careers that had previously excluded them.[10] The 1970 Equal Pay Act and 1975 Sex Discrimination Act represented a greater commitment of both Labour and Conservative governments to the pursuit of an 'equality agenda', which officially offered individuals a level playing field for equal access to jobs and wages, irrespective of sex.[11] However, inequality between male and female wages represented a significant historical continuity in post-war England. In 1980, five years after the passage of the Equal Pay Act, the average hourly pay of all working women (both full-time and part-time) was less than 66 per cent of the average male wage.[12] Women's low pay was connected to the gendered division of labour and women's propensity to work in part-time jobs that lacked status and career progression opportunities. In 1971, 84 per cent of women worked in occupations dominated by other women, whilst in 1980, 63 per cent of women worked in jobs that were performed only by women.[13]

Whilst these broad trends in female employment patterns have been well documented, historians have only recently started to understand how such changes influenced women's everyday experiences of paid work, as well as their relationships with their families, the state and individual sense of self.[14] This book is the first to explore the relationship between paid work and working-class women's political identities. Arthur McIvor has emphasised the value of personal testimony sources for uncovering the meaning workers ascribed to their employment in the past.[15] Previous oral history projects have suggested that paid work had less meaning for women's identity than men's. Elizabeth Roberts, who carried out oral history interviews in 1970, concluded that although there was greater social approval of women working outside the home after the Second World War, the majority of women continued to be primarily defined by their familial role.[16] This argument was echoed in Angela Davis' study of motherhood in post-war England, and is often accepted in other social and political histories.[17] Davis suggests that whilst women's work was 'reconceptualised' after the Second World War, and paid employment could offer some women an opportunity to gain independence, 'it remained true that only a small minority of educated, professional women considered their role as worker to be as, or more, important than that of mother'.[18] Yet there remains a space here to consider the subtle ways these roles and identities interacted with each other. It seems plausible that women did not consciously privilege one role above the other; their social and political identity was temporally shaped by both at different moments in their lives.

This book argues that paid employment was crucial to shaping working-class women's daily experience and understanding of their position within wider social relations throughout their life course. Selina Todd warns that it is important not to over-emphasise the significance of paid work to working-class identity – pointing out that work was a means to an end, rather than a source of satisfaction, and something that people sought to make the best of.[19] For Todd, the majority of working-class individuals knew they had to work for a living, but frequently imagined escaping from this reality; thus it is more suitable to view class struggle as centring on evading work, rather than identifying with it.[20] The women interviewed in this book had not always enjoyed their work, and drew on many other aspects of their lives to fashion their identity and self-understanding. However, their experiences of paid work were a crucial component to their sense of who they were, and why they engaged in workplace activism in the past. Indeed, it was the fact that they had sacrificed leisure time and other more enjoyable elements of their lives to provide for their families that generated anger when work was taken away from them, or undermined in relation to skill and wages.

A final point to be made here is that it is important to recognise that the workforce was racialised as migration from Asia and the Caribbean changed the character of the female labour force. Black women workers suffered triple oppression through gender, class and racial discrimination. Whilst Chapter 1 considers the experience of black and Asian workers in more detail, a limitation with this study is the attention to race. Race was a key issue I originally wanted to explore in my case studies; however, only white women came forward to be interviewed. As a result, the experiences presented in this book are those of white working-class women, and it has not been possible to explore in detail the experiences of women who faced racial discrimination. This means it has not yet been possible to deploy a fully intersectional approach that explains how these interlocking systems of gender, class and racial oppression worked in practice.

Women and trade unionism

Each chapter also contributes fresh insights into women's experiences of trade unionism between 1968 and 1985 – a period that has been associated with a significant transition in the relationship between women and the labour movement. In 1914, there were 437,000 female trade unionists, a number that rose to 1,342,000 in 1920 following the First World War. Female membership levels declined to 731,000 in 1933, which was symptomatic of high levels of unemployment throughout the 1930s, before increasing to 1,716,000 in 1943 due to the influx of women into the labour market during the Second World War.[21]

Women's lower levels of trade union membership than men's have been explained by the unskilled, part-time and irregular nature of their work and the adversarial attitudes of male trade unionists wanting to maintain their breadwinner wage.[22] Sarah Boston argues that female workers had to fight to become equal members within trade unions before they could fight against their employers.[23] Her authoritative account of women's trade unionism demonstrates how male union officials persistently perceived women workers as inferior throughout the twentieth century. This is supported by Anne Phillips and Barbara Taylor, who argued that skill was an 'ideological category' rather than an economic fact, meaning that women's work was undervalued simply because it was performed by women.[24] Cathy Hunt's history of the National Federation of Women Workers shows how women had to develop their own separate organisations to recruit and organise female workers and raise public awareness of their needs and interests.[25] Whilst these overviews of women's trade unionism emphasise gender antagonism, case studies from earlier periods importantly demonstrate how women organised informally, in spite of the divergence of interests between rank-and-file female workers and male trade union leaders and officials. Studies of female chain-makers in Cradley Heath, the Bryant and May matchstick 'girls', female jute workers in Dundee and food factory workers in Bermondsey, as well as various accounts of women's militancy within interwar 'new' industries, show that gender antagonism within trade unions could inhibit, but did not prevent, women from asserting their rights and seeking to improve their conditions in the past.[26] Female workers were not apathetic, and were more likely to draw on their own cultural resources, without the formal support of trade unions, to influence how their work was organised.

After the Second World War, the number of female trade unionists rose from 1,638,000 in 1945 to 2,743,000 in 1970. The 1970s represented a period of substantial growth as female membership increased to 3,902,000 by 1979. Female union density rose from 32.1 per cent to 39.4 per cent.[27] The growth in women's trade unionism was accompanied by a greater commitment from trade unions to represent the specific interests of female workers. This involved the Trades Union Congress (TUC) and other unions publicly supporting issues like equal pay, maternity protection, childcare provision and better training opportunities. Campaign groups like the Working Women's Charter sought to amplify the female workers' voice within the labour movement, whilst feminist sociologists and economists increasingly drew attention to gender inequality within trade unions. These historical patterns of women's trade unionism have sometimes been understood in terms of the 'feminisation' of British trade unions, yet there is an absence of ordinary female workers' voices from this narrative.[28]

Disputes involving women are often drawn on as examples of female workers becoming more active within trade unions, without a full understanding of what the participants believed they were doing and what they now think they did. A better understanding of women's workplace protest from this period is important because it was perceived to be occurring more frequently than in previous periods, and received wider attention from feminist and trade union activists who claimed it represented a transition in working-class women's political consciousness.[29] In 1981, feminist sociologist Anna Pollert wrote of the 1970s,

> Women began to take on their employers in unexpected areas. ... Most of the new wave of women workers' struggles were not 'spectacular'. Many were small, and because they did not 'grind the country to a halt' could be conveniently ignored by the mass media. Many of the disputes were long drawn out; many ended in defeat because they were isolated and failed to draw support from other trade unionists. ... Yet because they never reached the headlines it should not be assumed they were outside [class] struggle, or that they lived untroubled, uncomplicated lives – content with their lot.... To ignore these would be to take the Hollywood epic view of history, where great battles eclipse the subtle movements behind the scenes: the various shades of consciousness, the motives behind action.[30]

Pollert's concern to understand 'the subtle movements behind the scenes' of women's workplace activism remains unresolved and connects to Josie McLellan's call to move away from Whiggish historical narratives of women progressing towards some endpoint of 'normality' after years of change.[31] Focusing on women's reconstructed experiences of trade unionism through oral history, this book moves beyond accounts that have focused on women's relationship with the labour movement at an institutional level. It aims to draw attention to the values and beliefs of women underlying these broader changes, for whom trade unionism represented a vehicle to try and assert greater control within their workplace.

Workplace protest and second-wave feminism

Each case study also provides new insights into the relationship between women's workplace protest, feminism and the WLM. The first historical accounts of the WLM were written by women who actively engaged with women's liberation and focused on the public face of the movement: the demands, campaigns, national conferences and subsequent fragmentation.[32] Early analyses emphasised the practical effects of women's activism during this period through the development of women's aid and rape crisis centres across Britain, as well as the ideological impact through increased public awareness that 'the personal is political'. Jeffrey Weeks asserted that the WLM 'cast a spell which impacted on the lives of women for over a generation'.[33] More recently, there has been a greater focus on the local and personal impact of the movement on individual participants. Sue Bruley emphasises the novelty of consciousness-raising groups as a process 'by which women sought to understand their oppression, redefine themselves and create new feminist identities'.[34] Sarah Browne has also used oral history to write the first history of the WLM in Scotland from the perspective of grass roots activists. Browne concludes that women's activism in this period, especially around the issues of abortion and violence against women, transformed the way Scottish society both 'discussed and understood the role of women'.[35] The WLM is thus understood to have had a significant effect on women's experience and sense of self.

The WLM was an important part of the story of women's workplace protest in England during the 1970s. Industrial disputes organised by female workers represented sites of convergence between working-class women seeking to alter the relations of power within their workplace and WLM activists hoping to extend the social composition of the movement by raising the consciousness of working-class women. Feminist support was crucial for raising the public profile of women's workplace protest and could provide essential moral and financial backing for women who were not supported by their union. In 1989, Sheila Rowbotham wrote that historians in the future would need to 'explain the experiential encounter between feminism and the labour movement and the transformation in consciousness that has taken place among working-class women'.[36] This claim represented a starting point for my investigation – to examine the nature of the relationship between female strikers and WLM activists from the perspective of female workers.

It must be stressed that by focusing on the relationship between WLM activists and female workers, I do not imply that feminism could only arise, or be pursued, by identifying with the WLM. As Selina Todd points out, the relationship between class and feminism was never without tension, and many working-class women disagreed with some middle-class feminists' belief that male behaviour was the primary cause of women's exploitation.[37] My oral history interviews explore this tension further by asking women to explain in their own words what they felt about feminism, and the extent to which they felt their activism had been influenced by the women's movement, as well as other aspects of their everyday experience. Lynn Abrams has illustrated the value of looking beyond the women's movement and its precursors to take account of the impact of wider cultural and social change on women's sense of self in post-war Britain.[38] The 'sexual revolution', the demise of religion, full employment and greater education and professional opportunities offered women new means of constructing a lifestyle and belief system that was different to that of their mothers.[39] Abrams' oral history respondents often framed their life stories around a liberationist practice, but with little relation to liberationist movements or ideology. The interviews in this book not only provide new insights into the relationship between female workers and WLM activists but offer new understandings of how class affected women's changing sense of self in post-war England.

Research on earlier periods illustrates how women became 'politicised' or practised 'rough forms of feminism', without identifying themselves as feminists.[40] As Annemarie Hughes points out, feminism and women's activism are not coterminous.[41] Focusing on institutions and (in)formal movements can disguise the diversity of ideas, aims and successes of women, and obscure other forms of feminism practised in everyday life by women who did not necessarily identify themselves as feminists. By concentrating on women's workplace protests, the present analysis addresses a form of activism that can be situated in a space between formal and informal politics. The women interviewed in the case studies that follow were all trade union members who interacted with feminist activists who visited their factories, joined them on picket lines and wrote about them. As a result, on the one hand, the book explores what this relationship meant to the women involved. On the other hand, I have also explored the women's broader experiences and everyday responses to unequal gender relations in the workplace. I have made every effort to listen to and respect my respondents' own understanding of feminism. The book thus offers fresh insights into both the relationship between feminist activism and workplace protest during the 1970s and the influence of working-class women's broader everyday experiences of gender antagonism on their sense of self and political identity.

Workplace protest and political identity: remembering the 1970s in post-industrial England

An important aim of the book is to understand why women engaged in workplace activism when they did, and what the impact of this was on their political attitudes, understandings and sense of self in the subsequent period. Glimpses of personal testimony found in letters, strike bulletins and newspaper interviews provide clues to the political identity and subjectivity of women engaged in disputes *at the time*, whilst my own oral history interviews offer an insight into the meaning that participants ascribed to their past experience in relation to their identity and subjectivities *at the time of the interview*.

The disputes considered in this book occurred in a period associated with political crisis and economic decline. Images of strikes, inflation, power cuts, oil price rises, hung parliaments and minority government permeate popular histories of the 1970s. Britain was perceived to have become ungovernable. The period is thus commonly characterised as the moment when the post-war settlement, consensus and economic growth crashed to an end before being rescued by Thatcherism. Historians have increasingly questioned this simplistic narrative and have started to draw greater attention to the range of opportunities and political possibilities that existed during this decade.[42] It is crucial to recognise that the women involved in the disputes considered in this book grew up in a context of growing economic and social security associated with full employment and the development of the welfare state. David Edgerton recently argued that social democracy and the welfare state were at their peak during the 1970s.[43] Income and wealth inequality were at their lowest levels in the twentieth century. Organised labour was stronger by comparison to earlier and later periods. All of this contributed to a sense that a shift in power had occurred between the elite and workers in society. As Robinson *et al.* suggest, 'Two decades of full employment, plus the discourses around the people's war and welfare state had given people a fuller sense of citizenship and entitlement.'[44] Greater security and prosperity accompanied by cultural shifts in education, youth culture and consumerism encouraged the decline of deference and the emergence of new social movements organised around a variety of new 'post-material' values.[45]

Yet it is also crucial to recognise the context in which the women interviewed in this book remembered their workplace activism. Deindustrialisation from the 1950s destroyed large numbers of jobs for both men and women and began to polarise the job market, creating the need for in-work benefits to supplement in-work poverty.[46] Wage inequality and job insecurity accelerated from the 1980s onwards as the Thatcher government sought to reduce inflation by introducing high interest rates, cuts in public spending and higher indirect taxes. High interest rates benefited property owners but exacerbated problems in manufacturing, and mass unemployment followed. High levels of unemployment and the collapse of unionised industries eroded the strength of organised labour, which was further weakened by successive legislation restricting trade unions' ability to organise industrial action.[47] The economic and political context changed considerably from the late 1960s (when this book begins) to the early 1980s (when this book ends). The 2008 financial crisis and politics of austerity that followed further exacerbated economic inequality and political polarisation in twenty-first-century Britain. The context within which the women were interviewed for this book (2012–14) was thus very different to the period when their activism occurred and had significant effects on how women remembered and accounted for the personal effects of their activism.

An approach that privileges the subjective understandings, identities and motivations of workers engaging in industrial conflict is important to challenge popular narratives that characterise the 1970s as a period when unruly unions and working-class greed caused economic decline. As Jack Saunders recently pointed out, historians of the British labour movement have explained rising levels of workplace protest as a direct response to changing economic and political circumstances after the 1950s.[48] Such accounts often take for granted the values, ideas and collective cultures developed by workers themselves, which were also required for workers to unite and engage in collective action.[49] There has been even less consideration given to how these processes were shaped by gender. Strikes did not simply just happen. As industrial relations expert Richard Hyman explained in 1989,

> The very act of striking is a collective act and implies a certain amount of understanding and belief in the efficaciousness of mass action ... strikes are occasionally spontaneous outbursts due to accidental circumstances or long periods of repression – but workers with no feeling of solidarity or common interest would be unlikely to strike.[50]

INTRODUCTION

For Hyman, strikes would not occur were it not for workers behaving as agents with beliefs and values that led them to consciously interpret their employers' behaviour as unjust and perceive collective action as a legitimate and effective response. Therefore, 'only by exploring subjective dimensions – human consciousness and the interrelations of people's definitions and responses – it becomes possible to understand the regularities and patterns that exist within industrial relations'.[51] Hyman's approach to understanding the rationale behind workplace militancy remains valid and can be reconciled with more recent historical approaches to individual subjectivity. For example, after reading British soldiers' letters from the First World War, Michael Roper stressed the importance of focusing on individual subjectivity as a means of investigating the emotional significance of events and practices.[52] James Hinton advocates a similar approach to understanding the past in his analysis of Mass-Observation diaries from the Second World War. For Hinton, the point of examining the motivations, beliefs and values of individuals is not necessarily to offer more 'authentic' accounts of the past, but to 'locate individuals in their social context, and to understand how, in constructing their own selfhoods, they contributed to larger patterns of continuity and change'.[53]

So, it is important to look beyond broad economic change or the actions of large institutions when examining workplace protest during this period and to think about how the political identities and relationships of those who engaged in workplace activism were shaped by their everyday experiences. As Selina Todd argues, workers' growing assertiveness during this period can also be explained by their shared aspiration for greater control over the organisation of their lives, which included the way their work was organised and paid.[54] The following chapters will argue that female workers' demands for equal pay and protests against being treated as a secondary labour force were also shaped by their aspiration to have the value of their work recognised; to have their specific skills and role as economic providers accepted by patronising male employers and trade union officials; to be treated with dignity and respect, which they felt was undermined due to their sex.

Sources and methods

Contemporaneous accounts of women's work and trade unionism during this period suggest that women had a distinct, gendered experience of workplace protest because they were likely to work in different jobs, to be paid less and to have less influence within their trade union than their male workmates (especially if they worked part-time). The period has also been associated with a transition in ideas about women's rights in the workplace evidenced by the passage of equality legislation and greater commitment from trade unions to integrate and represent the specific interests of their increased female membership.[55] Chapter 1 explains how instances of women's workplace protest were situated within these public debates at the time. It provides an overview of representations and public discourses surrounding women's workplace protest found in feminist literature, trade union publications and sociological studies. The rest of the book identifies the personal implications of these broader social and political changes for female workers who engaged in collective action through an analysis of four case studies of workplace disputes organised by women during this period.

The case studies present four different examples of women asserting their rights in the workplace. To start, Chapter 2 provides an original account of the Ford sewing machinists' fight for skill recognition in 1968. The 1968 Ford sewing machinists' strike is widely understood as a crucial turning point that led to the Equal Pay Act in 1970. However, this triumphant narrative of the strike as a victory has served to disguise the fact that the women at Ford perceived the outcome of the 1968 strike as a defeat and continued to fight for skill recognition until 1985, when their work was finally regraded after another nine-week strike. This chapter offers an account of the 1968 strike from the perspective of the women involved. Chapter 3 moves on to examine how the Equal Pay Act was interpreted and challenged by female workers once it was implemented in 1975. It provides a detailed consideration of the longest equal pay strike in British labour history, which took place at the Trico-Folberth windscreen wiper factory in Brentford, west London, during the summer of 1976. Following this, Chapter 4 focuses on the 1972 occupation of Sexton, Son & Everard Shoe Factory organised by female workers fighting to save their jobs in Fakenham, Norfolk. The occupation lasted eighteen weeks before the women involved established their own co-operative that traded with varied levels of success until it entered receivership in 1977. The Fakenham occupation moves the book on to a different track away from the equal pay debates, considered in the previous two chapters, towards working-class women's fight against factory closures and unemployment. Finally, Chapter 5 returns to Ford, in Dagenham, to analyse the 1984–85 sewing machinists' strike for skill recognition and improved grading – the original grievance of the 1968 strike. Ending in the same location where the book begins, the final case study illustrates the centrality and continued salience of the subjective value of women's work that runs throughout the period between 1968 and 1985.

The case studies were chosen for the frequency with which they are cited as examples of women's workplace militancy in histories of women's trade unionism and feminism in post-war England, but without being the subject of a significant investigation from a historical perspective.[56] In terms of representativeness, the aim was not so much to establish broad conclusions about working-class women's behaviour – it could be argued that the women were atypical or extraordinary by engaging in such action in the first place. Instead, it focuses on the meaning of each dispute for the self-selecting sample of women who came forward to tell me stories about their past. Following James Hinton, individual case studies and life histories provide acute insights into more general historical processes because it is the choices made by individuals that drive those processes forward.[57] Similarly, Abrams argues that prioritising women's own voices and interpretations of the past is useful as a means of challenging established historical explanations of women's role in society, but also for offering an 'authentic story with meaning for those who narrated it'.[58] In the context of this book, I have focused on women's voices and local case studies to move beyond existing accounts that situate women's collective action in a general narrative about women's increased presence in the labour force and trade unions, as well as the emergence of second-wave feminism and equality legislation. The case studies and individual stories that follow offer new insights into how female workers interpreted the influence of these wider social and institutional changes on their own personal experience and sense of self.

Each case study draws on a combination of written sources and oral history. Written sources include national and local newspaper coverage of each dispute, WLM pamphlets and articles and trade union publications and correspondence. Written sources were used to establish the context and sequence of events surrounding each dispute. They also indicate how each dispute was publicly perceived, represented and judged at the time, and offer evidence of the social and cultural expectations that surrounded working-class women's behaviour during that period. Finally, the numerous interviews with female workers that appear in these sources, although obviously mediated, provide clues as to women's understandings, motivations and evaluations of their action at the time and are valuable as records of contemporary voices.[59] Oral history was used to reveal what could not be discovered elsewhere: personal experiences of paid work, trade unionism and workplace protest, and the manner in which individuals made sense of these past experiences as they constructed their political identities and sense of self in the present. The book draws on interviews with thirteen women contacted through advertisements in local newspapers, libraries, supermarkets and internet community forums and also by word of mouth.[60]

Oral history provides a useful means of analysing individuals' experiences, motivations and the personal consequences of participating in collective action in the past. Maud Bracke argues that analysis of social and political movements based on the mobilisation of collective identities requires awareness of the individual's sense of self. She shows how feminist groups provoked political and legislative change in Italy, but also draws on oral history effectively to illustrate the movement's 'existential impact' on thousands of women who associated their experiences of feminist activism in the 1970s with a transition in their social attitudes, personal relationships, political outlook and self-understanding.[61] In Scotland, Sarah Browne examines personal testimony with WLM activists to develop a more 'in-depth understanding of who supported the movement and why'. She demonstrates the important effects of the personal experiences of individual members upon the main arguments and campaigns developed by the wider movement in Scotland.[62] Similarly, Celia Hughes uses oral history to illustrate the effects of cultural change in 1960s Britain on political activists' sense of self and identity on the radical left.[63] The point is that oral history represents a useful methodology for examining instances of collective action in the past because it reveals how social and political mobilisation was not just the product (as well as producer) of structural processes, but was also shaped by the personal lives and experiences of active participants and their understanding of the world around them.

Oral history has the capacity to offer similar insights into workers' militancy in the past. For example, Jim Phillips argues in his study of the 1984–85 miners' strike in Scotland that the privileging of high politics has obscured the broader economic, social and cultural dimensions of the strike from a historian's analysis.[64] Using a combination of quantitative data and oral history, Phillips illustrates how the strike was shaped by economic variables, as well as the 'moral economy' of workers involved.[65] Another example of oral history being used effectively to examine workplace militancy from this period is Sundari Anitha *et al.*'s study of the 1976–79 Grunwick dispute, primarily involving South Asian female workers. They argue that celebratory accounts of the strike as a pivotal moment in the labour movement's representation of minority workers often emphasised the 'exoticism' of the 'strikers in saris', without considering the working lives and experiences of the women involved.[66] Drawing on interviews with five participants, they argue that the particular migratory histories and socioeconomic backgrounds of the women were crucial to explaining their decision to engage in collective action. Many of the women came from middle-class backgrounds in East Africa and were indignant at the poor conditions and low pay of factory work. At the same time, some of the women reported feeling ashamed at asking the public for money during the dispute, whilst others felt uncomfortable talking about particular aspects of the strike that violated 'gendered scripts of appropriate behaviour'.[67] Anitha et al. emphasise how these personal, social and cultural factors intersected with women's material experiences of paid work to shape South Asian women's narratives about the dispute.[68] These examples of existing studies illustrate the value of oral history as a methodology for understanding the everyday motivations and personal concerns of workers in a manner that challenges dominant narratives that associate 'unruly unions' with economic decline in postwar Britain.

Joan Sangster's study of a 1937 strike organised by female textile workers in Peterborough, Canada, highlights the value of using oral history to focus on women's subjective accounts of workplace militancy. She argues that oral historians must adopt an approach that reconciles the cultural construction of memory within a framework of social and economic relations and imperatives. She writes,

> Asking why and how women explain, rationalise and make sense of the past offers insight into the social and material framework within which they operated, the perceived choices and cultural patterns they faced, and the complex relationship between individual consciousness and culture.[69]

Sangster suggests that the strength of oral history lies in its ability to interrogate how individuals perceived and understood their past experiences, decisions and behaviour. The interview represents both a linguistic and a social event that elicits a construction of the past rooted in the perspective of the present, yet based on a historical and material reality.[70] The job for the oral historian is to identify how respondents' explanations for their past behaviour are shaped by their personal experiences of social and economic processes, but also the various cultural resources and shared stories they draw on to represent their experience in the interview.

The concept of 'composure' is essential to understanding how individuals narrate their past. It is now widely understood that people relate the stories they tell about themselves to popular and public narratives about particular historical events. In the words of Penny Summerfield, the oral historian must examine not only 'the voice that speaks for itself, but also the voices that speak to it'.[71] Summerfield illustrates how her female respondents drew on popular discourses surrounding the impact of the Second World War (heroic or stoic) on gender roles as they sought to 'compose' coherent memories of their personal experiences of war. Anna Green argued that Summerfield moved too far from interpreting the significance of individual memory by trying to situate women's testimony in pre-existing cultural frameworks. She concluded that oral historians needed to avoid 'culturally deterministic' understandings of individual memories and reassert the 'capacity of the conscious self to contest and critique cultural scripts and discourses'.[72]

Graham Smith advocates a balanced approach to understanding the process of remembering that champions neither the influence of cultural discourses nor the boundless agency of individuals and their memory. Instead, he suggests that oral historians must focus on how memory is the product of both cultural context and individual experience of social processes.[73] Celia Hughes' study of British activists on the radical left provides a good example of this approach. She reflects how her interviewees constructed their identities in relation to the national and international context of expanding social and political boundaries in the 1950s and 1960s, but also emphasises the local and familial context 'which fostered certain ways of seeing, feeling and being' for her interviewees.[74]

In the context of this book, it was not always easy to identify coherent public narratives available to my respondents to draw on when constructing accounts of their collective action. There was no obvious 'third man in the room', an expression coined by Rebecca Clifford that refers to the shared public memories and meta-narratives surrounding 1960s activism that influenced her interviewees' testimony about their experiences of 1968 in Italy.[75] Although each dispute received public attention at the time, and has since been recognised within histories of women, trade unions and feminism, my respondents were often unaware of and detached from these public narratives, with the exception of the Dagenham sewing machinists. Very often the women I interviewed seemed surprised that I had taken an interest in their past. Many expressed views such as 'I haven't thought much about it for a while' or 'I didn't think it was important until this came up'. The public recognition of the oral history interview itself made many women rethink the significance of the dispute within their own lives with comments like 'thinking about it now it was probably quite important' or 'looking back, you realise you have done something with your life'. This was similar to what Anitha et al. found when they interviewed women who participated in the Grunwick dispute.[76] They suggested that their interviews represented the first time their participants had reflected on the historical significance of their agency because they were previously unaware or had not been part of the 'celebratory accounts of Grunwick as a turning point in British labour history subsequently constructed by the trade unions'.[77]

Summerfield's research on women's experiences of the Second World War also showed how composure was difficult for groups who experience 'cultural silences'.[78] She writes,

> Ordinary people who have memories that do not fit publicly available accounts have difficulty finding words and concepts with which to compose their memories whether in anecdotal snapshots or extended narratives. If individuals cannot draw on appropriate public accounts, they must seek to justify their deviation or fit their stories into alternative frameworks, or express memories in fragmentary accounts.[79]

The women interviewed in the following chapters faced some of these challenges as they rethought the significance of their action within the moment of the oral history interview. It was not that there was necessarily a 'cultural silence' surrounding women's workplace activism at the time of the interview – the disputes analysed here have been cited in academic studies, have been memorialised through public events and in the case of Dagenham have been woven into a feature film. Instead, my interviewees' ambivalent relationship with public narratives surrounding their activism recalled Lynn Abrams' reminder that individuals do not always situate their stories in a context that is familiar to historians; whilst I became interested in placing the women's stories in relation to historical narratives about women's employment and trade union trends, my interviewees were more likely to position their experience in relation to their personal, family or local history.[80] Selina Todd has recently emphasised the influence of personal knowledge, constructed from interaction with family, friends, the workplace and state officials, on self-understanding. Todd argues that material circumstances were as influential as public and expert knowledge in shaping individuals' understanding of their place in the world.[81] In what follows, I seek to identify both the wider public narratives and personal contexts that respondents drew on when constructing their testimony.

I aimed to gather life stories from my interviewees to gain an understanding of the personal meaning of each dispute and to examine how each respondent felt it had affected their sense of self. Following Charlotte Linde, people compose their sense of self through the stories they tell about their past: 'In order to exist in the social world with a comfortable sense of being a good, socially proper and stable person, an individual needs to have a coherent, acceptable and constantly revised life story.'[82]

The individual revises their life story to align their past experience with their sense of who they are in the present, and with how they would like to be perceived by other people. The life story can be distinguished from a 'life history' which represents a chronologically told narrative of an individual's past based on transitions between recognisable life stages and events such as childhood, education and marriage.[83] Focusing on a life story is different to a life history because it is less about the details of an individual's life course, and more about how an individual reinterprets their past. The process of retelling and reinterpreting one's life story offers a means of achieving a stable and composed sense of self in the present. Linde suggests that individuals develop coherence systems that emphasise the causality and continuity between their past experiences in a manner that makes sense to themselves, as well as their audience.[84] Lynn Abrams' research on the post-war female self illustrates how some of her respondents framed their life stories around a coherence system that drew on a feminist emancipation narrative that told a continuous story about equality of opportunity, choice and freedom to determine their own lives as individual women, without identifying themselves with feminist politics.[85]

I devised semi-structured schedules to guide life stories from respondents prior to every interview. The aim was to establish where they situated their activism within their wider experiences. Each respondent was asked about their childhood, family and early experiences of work and trade unionism; the details of their practical involvement in the dispute; and the extent to which they felt this had influenced their political attitudes. Whilst I aimed to gain life stories from each respondent, this was sometimes inhibited by two factors. First, all my interviewees knew that I had contacted them because I was researching workplace militancy. The majority of respondents appeared to have prepared themselves prior to the interview to talk about the details and their experience of each dispute specifically – a 'memory frame' that was narrower than the framework I wished to encourage. The implications of this were that respondents were sometimes unprepared, or reluctant to talk about their families or wider experiences of work in other jobs, which were not necessarily seen as relevant or part of the story that they were aiming to tell about themselves. Secondly, the women from Dagenham and some of the Brentford women were only willing to be interviewed together as a group. This possibly demonstrated a lack of confidence in their own stories and may also have prevented individuals from sharing certain information in front of each other, yet also presented its own opportunities.

INTRODUCTION

It would be reasonable to assume that the fact I was a male researcher, born twenty-eight years after my youngest respondent and fifty-eight years after the oldest, will have influenced my interviewees' testimony. It is difficult to judge the precise effects of this without being able to compare my interviews with those of a female researcher. Hilary Young argues that her subject position as a young, educated and liberated woman affected her older male respondents' testimony in her research on Scottish masculinities.[86] She suggests that they perceived her 'as someone who approved of changed gender roles' and composed their testimony accordingly, by either giving examples from their past that conformed with contemporary discourses surrounding the 'new man' or asserting a macho image they felt had been undermined and challenged by women like herself. Young felt that a male interviewee may have elicited a different narrative from the same respondents.[87] In the context of this book, not one respondent commented directly on my gender. Although a female interviewer may have elicited different responses, the key point here is that I have adopted a feminist aim throughout my interviews to recognise and privilege women's own definitions, understandings and interpretations of their experiences.[88]

Although group interviews were not my initial methodological preference, they actually produced an interesting and invaluable opportunity to consider the interaction between individual and collective memory. Graham Smith explains the value of group interviews. First, he suggests they can confer identity and affirm individual competence. Group members cue each other's memories and construct a collective memory that goes beyond the individual recollection of one person.[89] Yet, it is not just the collective accumulation of details about past events that is valuable. Smith also emphasises the value of the interaction between the individual and group memory as individuals construct common identities through talking about lived experience.[90] He points out that remembering represents an everyday pastime that often involves the interchange and comparison of memories between individuals. For Smith, the group interview presents an opportunity to 'chart the terrains of transactive memory', recognise the memories individuals share and take for granted and investigate an individual's capacity to critically engage with inherited ideologies.[91] In the context of this book, three group interviews have been used to examine how participants made sense of their personal experience by collectively reconstructing and interpreting the meaning of each strike. This involved the creation of common accounts, as well as oppositional narratives that challenged pre-existing assumptions about the meaning of each dispute.

A focus on individual case studies – and the accounts of individual women – permits a greater appreciation of the impact of local context and everyday practices on women's subjective motivations to engage in collective action. I have focused on case studies and relied on women's testimony as a primary source to, following the words of Claire Langhamer, 'effect an analysis embedded in everyday practices'.[92] 'Recovering' these women's stories and presenting them together in a collective portrait enables one to identify some shared experiences and understandings, but also allows an appreciation of the differences among individual women's attitudes and the manner in which they made sense of the past.

Notes

1 S. Todd, *The People: The Rise and Fall of the Working Class, 1910-2010* (London: John Murray, 2014), p. 284; For histories of industrial relations in this period, see J. McIlroy, N. Fishman and A. Campbell (eds), *British Trade Unions and Industrial Politics: The High Tide of Trade Unionism, 1945-1979* (Aldershot: Ashgate Publishing, 1999); C. Wrigley, *British Trade Unions Since 1933* (Cambridge: Cambridge University Press, 2001), pp. 40-56; H. Fraser, *A History of British Trade Unionism, 1700-1998* (Basingstoke: Macmillan Press, 1999), pp. 225-229.

2 H. L. Smith, 'The Women's Movement, Politics and Citizenship, 1960s-2000' in I. Z. Bargielowska, *Women in Twentieth Century Britain* (Harlow: Pearson, 2001), p. 283; G. Holloway, *Women and Work in Britain Since 1840* (London: Routledge, 2005), p. 208; D. Bouchier, *The Feminist Challenge: The Movement for Women's Liberation in Britain and the United States* (New York, NY: Schocken Books, 1984), pp. 56-57. A. Coote and B. Campbell, *Sweet Freedom: Struggle for Women's Liberation* (Oxford: Basil Blackwell, 1987), pp. 9-10; S. Rowbotham, *The Past is Before Us* (London: Pandora Press, 1989), pp. 165-166; L. Segal, 'Jam Today: Feminist Impacts and Transformations in the 1970s' and P. Thane, 'Women and the 1970s: Towards Liberation?' in L. Black, H. Pemberton and P. Thane (eds), *Reassessing 1970s Britain* (Manchester: Manchester University Press, 2013), p. 154 and p. 171; S. Boston, *Women Workers and the Trade Unions*, 2nd edn (London: Lawrence and Wishart, 1989), p. 279.

3 For examples see Boston, *Women Workers*; S. Lewenhak, *Women and Trade Unions: An Outline History of Women in the British Trade Union Movement* (London: Benn, 1977); S. Todd, *Young Women, Work and Family, 1918-1950* (Oxford: Oxford University Press, 2005).

4 See J. Lewis, *Women in Britain Since 1945* (Oxford: Wiley Blackwell, 1992), p. 66. The shortcomings with women's employment statistics are well known. Figures for part-time work in Britain have only been available since 1961 and census enumerators often missed casual work, or work performed part-time by married women. Jane Lewis suggests that although the precise degree of growth in married women's employment is unclear, there was an observable shift in the manner with which married women became formally attached to the labour market after the Second World War.

5 Holloway, *Women and Work*, p. 180 and pp. 196–201.
6 A. Myrdal and V. Klein, *Women's Two Roles: Home and Work* (Abingdon: Routledge and Kegan Paul, 1956).
7 A. McIvor, *Working Lives: Work in Britain Since 1945* (London: Palgrave Macmillan, 2014), p. 99.
8 L. Paterson, 'Part-time Work and Working Motherhood, c. 1951–1981', paper presented at the North American Conference of British Studies, November 2017.
9 D. Wilson-Smith, 'A New Look at the Affluent Worker: The Good Working Mother in Post-War Britain', *Twentieth Century British History*, vol. 17, no. 2 (2006), pp. 206–229.
10 Thane, 'Women and the 1970s', p. 179 and P. Summerfield, 'Women in Britain Since 1945: Companionate Marriage and the Double Burden' in P. Catterall and J. Obelkevich (eds), *Understanding Post-War British Society* (London: Routledge, 1994), p. 64.
11 R. Crompton, *Women and Work in Modern Britain* (Oxford: Oxford University Press, 1997), pp. 63–65.
12 Figure from J. West, 'Introduction' in J. West (ed.), *Women, Work and the Labour Market* (Routledge: London, 1982), p. 1; Jane Lewis also argued that the average hourly pay of all women did not improve between 1975 and 1980 in Lewis, *Women in Britain*, pp. 80–81.
13 Lewis, *Women in Britain*, p. 81.
14 C. Langhamer, 'Feelings, Women and Work in the Long 1950s', *Women's History Review* (Published online 18 February 2016), http://dx.doi.org/10.1080/09612025. 2015.1123025; H. McCarthy, 'Women, Marriage and Paid Work in Post-War Britain', *Women's History Review* (published online 17 February 2016), http://dx.doi.org/10. 1080/09612025.2015.1123023.
15 McIvor, *Working Lives*.
16 E. Roberts, *Women and Families: An Oral History 1940–1970* (Oxford: Wiley Blackwell, 1995), Chapter 7 and p. 235.
17 A. Davis, *Modern Motherhood: Women and Family in England, 1945–2000* (Manchester: Manchester University Press, 2012).
18 *Ibid.*, p. 271.
19 S. Todd, 'Class, Experience and Britain's Twentieth Century', *Social History*, vol. 56, no. 4 (2014), pp. 489–508, at p. 506.
20 *Ibid.*, p. 506.
21 Figures from Todd, *Young Women*, p. 171.
22 Lewenhak, *Women and Trade Unions*, pp. 177–270.
23 Boston, *Women Workers*, p. 11.
24 B. Taylor and A. Phillips, 'Sex and Skill: Notes towards a Feminist Economics', *Feminist Review*, no. 6 (1980), pp. 79–88.
25 C. Hunt, *The National Federation of Women Workers, 1906–1921* (London: Palgrave Macmillan, 2014), p. 161.
26 S. Blackburn, 'Working-Class Attitudes to Social Reform: Black Country Chain Makers and Anti-Sweating Legislation, 1880–1930', *International Review of Social History*, vol. 33, no. 1 (1988), pp. 42–69; S. Rose, 'Gender Antagonism and Class

Conflict: Exclusionary Strategies of Male Trade Unionists in Nineteenth-Century Britain', *Social History*, vol. 13, no. 2 (1988), pp. 113–131; E. Gordon, *Women and the Labour Movement in Scotland, 1850–1914* (Oxford: Clarendon Press, 1991); L. Lee Downs, *Manufacturing Inequality: Gender Division in the French and British Metalworking Industries, 1914–1939* (Ithaca, NY: Cornell University Press, 1995); M. Glucksmann, *Women Assemble: Women Workers and New Industries in Interwar Britain* (London: Routledge, 1990); Todd, *Young Women*, Chapter 6; L. Raw, *Striking a Light: The Bryant and May Matchwomen and Their Place in History* (London: Continuum, 2011); U. de la Mare, 'Necessity and Rage: The Factory Women's Strikes in Bermondsey, 1911', *History Workshop Journal*, vol. 66, no. 1 (2008), pp. 62–80.

27 Figures from C. Wrigley, 'Women in the Labour Market and in the Unions' in John McIlroy, Nina Fishman and Alan Campbell (eds), *British Trade Unions and Industrial Politics: The High Tide of Trade Unionism, 1945–1979* (Aldershot: Ashgate Publishing, 1999), Table 2.1, p. 62.

28 S. Cunnison and J. Stageman, *Feminizing the Unions* (Aldershot: Avebury, 1993).

29 For example Rowbotham, *The Past is Before Us*, p. 233.

30 A. Pollert, *Girls, Wives, Factory Lives* (Basingstoke: Macmillan Press, 1981), pp. 13–14.

31 J. McLellan, 'The "Problem of Women" in Post-War Europe', *English Historical Review*, vol. 130, no. 545 (July 2015), pp. 934–944.

32 Rowbotham, *The Past is Before Us*; Coote and Campbell, *Sweet Freedom*; Segal, 'Feminist Impacts and Transformations'.

33 J. Weeks, *The World We Have Won* (Abingdon: Routledge, 2007), pp. 18–19.

34 S. Bruley, 'Consciousness-Raising in Clapham; Women's Liberation as "Lived Experience" in South London in the 1970s', *Women's History Review*, vol. 22, no. 5 (2013), pp. 717–738, at p. 719.

35 S. Browne, *The Women's Liberation Movement in Scotland* (Manchester: Manchester University Press, 2014). For local impact of WLM also see B. Lockyer, 'An Irregular Period: Participation in the Bradford Women's Liberation Movement', *Women's History Review*, vol. 22, no. 4 (2013), pp. 643–657.

36 Rowbotham, *The Past is Before Us*, pp. 166–167.

37 Todd, *The People*, p. 307.

38 L. Abrams, 'Liberating the Female Self: Epiphanies, Conflict and Coherence in the Life Stories of Post-War British Women', *Social History*, vol. 39, no. 1 (2014), pp. 14–35.

39 L. Abrams, 'Mothers and Daughters: Negotiating the Discourse on the "Good Woman" in 1950s and 1960s Britain' in N. Christie and M. Gauvreau (eds), *The Sixties and Beyond: Dechristianisation in North America and Western Europe, 1945–2000* (Toronto: University of Toronto Press, 2013), pp. 60–80.

40 For example, C. Beaumont, *Housewives and Citizens: Domesticity and the Women's Movement in England, 1928–1964* (Manchester: Manchester University Press, 2013); A. Hughes, *Gender and Political Identities in Scotland, 1919–1939* (Edinburgh: Edinburgh University Press, 2010).

41 Hughes, *Gender and Political Identities*, p. 8.

42 Black et al., *Reassessing 1970s Britain*; E. Robinson, C. Schofield, F. Sutcliffe-Braithwaite and N. Thomlinson, 'Telling Stories about Post-War Britain: Popular Individualism and the "Crisis" of the 1970s', *Twentieth Century British History*, vol. 28, no. 2 (2017), pp. 268–304.
43 D. Edgerton, *The Rise and Fall of the British Nation: A Twentieth Century History* (St Ives: Allen Lane, 2018), Chapter 16.
44 Robinson et al., 'Telling Stories', p. 282.
45 F. Sutcliffe-Braithwaite, *Class, Politics, and the Decline of Deference in England, 1968–2000* (Oxford: Oxford University Press, 2018), p. 203.
46 J. Thomlinson, 'De-industrialisation not Decline: A New Meta-narrative for Post-War British History', *Twentieth Century British History*, vol. 27, no. 1 (2016), pp. 76–99.
47 Edgerton, *Rise and Fall*, Chapter 18.
48 J. Saunders, 'The Untraditional Worker: Class Re-Formation in Britain 1945–65', *Twentieth Century British History*, vol. 26, no. 2 (2015), pp. 225–248, at p. 228. For example K. Laybourn, *A History of British Trade Unionism, 1800–1990* (Stroud: Sutton Publishing, 1992); A. Reid, *United We Stand: A History of British Trade Unionism* (London: Penguin, 2005); C. Howell, *Trade Unions and the State: The Construction of Industrial Relations Institutions in Britain* (Princeton, NJ: Princeton University Press, 2005).
49 Saunders, 'The Untraditional Worker', p. 228.
50 R. Hyman, *Strikes* (Basingstoke: Macmillan Press, 1989), p. 37.
51 *Ibid*.
52 M. Roper, 'Slipping Out of View: Subjectivity and Emotion in Gender History', *History Workshop Journal*, vol. 59, no. 1 (2005), pp. 57–72, at pp. 65–66.
53 J. Hinton, *Nine Wartime Lives: Mass Observation and the Making of the Modern Self* (Oxford: Oxford University Press, 2010), p. 18.
54 Todd, *The People*, p. 275 and p. 284.
55 For example Boston, *Women Workers*; Coote and Campbell, *Sweet Freedom*, pp. 9–10; Thane, 'Women and the 1970s', p. 171.
56 For example Boston, *Women Workers* on Ford at pp. 278–280, on Trico at pp. 315–317 and Rowbotham, *The Past is Before Us* on Ford at pp. 165–166, on Trico at p. 227, on Fakenham at p. 200, p. 208, p. 233, and Imperial Typewriters at p. 319.
57 Hinton, *Nine Wartime Lives*.
58 L. Abrams, 'The Unseamed Picture: Conflicting Narratives of Women in the Modern European Past', *Gender and History*, vol. 20, no. 3 (2008), pp. 628–643, at p. 631.
59 For a discussion of revisiting interviews see J. Bornat, 'A Second Take: Revisiting Interviews with a Different Purpose', *Oral History*, vol. 31, no. 1 (2003), pp. 47–53.
60 The interviews were semi-structured, following P. Summerfield, *Reconstructing Women's Wartime Lives, Discourse and Subjectivity in Oral History* (Manchester: Manchester University Press, 1998), pp. 1–42.
61 M. Bracke, *Women and the Reinvention of the Political: Feminism in Italy, 1968–1983* (London: Routledge, 2014), pp. 23–24.
62 Browne, *Women's Liberation Movement in Scotland*.

63 C. Hughes, *Young Lives on the Left: Sixties Activism and the Liberation of the Self* (Manchester: Manchester University Press, 2015).
64 J. Phillips, *Collieries, Communities and the Miners' Strike in Scotland, 1984–85* (Manchester: Manchester University Press, 2012), p. 4.
65 *Ibid.*
66 L. McDowell, S. Anitha and R. Pearson, 'Striking Narratives: Class, Gender and Ethnicity in the "Great Grunwick Strike," London, UK, 1976–1978', *Women's History Review*, vol. 23, no. 4 (2014), pp. 595–619.
67 S. Anitha, Ruth Pearson and L. McDowell, 'Striking Lives: Multiple Narratives of South Asian Women's Employment, Identity and Protest in the UK', *Ethnicities*, vol. 12, no. 6 (2012), pp. 654–775, at p. 763 and 767.
68 *Ibid.*, pp. 769–770.
69 J. Sangster, 'Telling Our Stories: Feminist Debates and the Use of Oral History', *Women's History Review*, vol. 3, no. 1 (1994), pp. 5–28, at p. 6.
70 *Ibid.*, p. 13.
71 Summerfield, *Reconstructing Women's Wartime Lives*, p. 15.
72 A. Green, 'Individual Remembering and "Collective Memory": Theoretical Presuppositions and Contemporary Debates', *Oral History*, vol. 32, no. 2 (2004), pp. 34–44, at p. 42.
73 G. Smith, 'Beyond Individual/Collective Memory: Women's Transactive Memories of Food, Family and Conflict', *Oral History*, vol. 35, no. 2 (2007), pp. 77–90.
74 C. Hughes, 'Negotiating Ungovernable Spaces between the Personal and the Political: Oral History and the British Left in 1960s and 1970s', *Memory Studies*, vol. 6, no. 1 (2013), pp. 70–90, at p. 87.
75 R. Clifford, 'Emotion and Gender in Oral History: Narrating Italy's 1968', *Modern Italy*, vol. 17, no. 2 (2012), pp. 209–221.
76 McDowell *et al.*, 'Striking Narratives', p. 769.
77 *Ibid.*, p. 769.
78 This is also demonstrated by A. Thomson's well know example of Fred Farrell and the Anzac legend, A. Thomson, 'Putting Popular Memory Theory into Practice in Australia' in R. Perks and A. Thomson (eds), *The Oral History Reader* (London: Routledge, 2006), pp. 300–311.
79 P. Summerfield, 'Culture and Composure: Creating Narratives of the Gendered Self in Oral History Interview', *Cultural and Social History*, vol. 1 (2004), pp. 65–93, at p. 93.
80 L. Abrams, *Oral History Theory* (Abingdon: Routledge, 2010), p. 47.
81 Todd, 'Class, Experience and Britain's Twentieth Century', at p. 495.
82 C. Linde, *Life Stories: The Creation of Coherence* (Oxford: Oxford University Press, 1993), pp. 1–3.
83 Abrams, *Oral History Theory*, p. 40.
84 Linde, *Life Stories* in Abrams, 'Liberating the Female Self', at p. 21.
85 *Ibid.*, pp. 29–34.
86 Hilary Young, 'Hard Man, New Man: Re/composing Masculinities in Glasgow, c. 1950–2000', *Oral History*, vol. 35, no. 1 (2007), pp. 78–79.
87 *Ibid.*, pp. 77–78.

88 Kathryn Anderson and Dan Jack, 'Learning to Listen: Interview Techniques and Analysis' in Rob Perks and Alistair Thomson (eds), *Oral History Reader* (London: Routledge, 1998), pp. 155–170, at p. 170.
89 Smith, 'Beyond Individual/Collective Memory', at p. 80.
90 *Ibid.*, p. 80.
91 *Ibid.*, p. 88.
92 C. Langhamer, 'Love and Courtship in Mid-Twentieth-Century England', *The Historical Journal*, vol. 50 (2007), pp. 173–196, at p. 173.

1

Contextualising women's workplace activism in post-war England

The growth of women's employment was one of the most significant social and economic changes in post-war England. But what were the implications of these changes for working-class women's political identities and sense of self? This chapter provides an overview of how women's growing presence in the workforce was understood by contemporaries. It demonstrates that female workers, trade unions, social scientists and WLM activists were increasingly drawing public attention to the poor conditions and inequalities that working-class women were likely to experience in the workplace. At the same time, there was a growing commitment from policy makers and the main political parties to understanding and addressing gender inequality as a political issue. This chapter argues that the growing politicisation of gender inequality in the workplace was part of a broader transition in public understandings of gender roles taking place in post-war Britain. Lynn Abrams shows how women born in the 1940s grew up with different expectations to their mothers, whilst Helen McCarthy argues that parents had higher expectations for their daughters' educational and career prospects in the 1980s than did previous generations.[1] McCarthy argues that such changes were part of 'a very hard to measure' but 'real cultural change towards a greater acceptance of gender equality'.[2]

Women's workplace activism should be understood within this context. On the one hand, women's decisions to engage in collective action in a bid to win equal pay or to save their jobs can be understood as a response to this social and cultural shift. Women's militancy can be conceptualised as an outcome of a transition in how individual women thought about themselves, their individual rights and their political efficacy. On the other hand, workplace activism should be seen as a driver of change in itself. Working-class women went on strike or occupied their workplace to improve their material conditions and in response to the real and perceived injustices they experienced in their everyday lives. In doing so, they drew the attention of trade unions, feminist activists and policy makers; they altered political discourse and created a new set of resources for understanding the impact of these social and economic changes taking place in women's lives.

(Un)equal pay and the sexual division of labour

Women's growing presence in the labour force was a defining feature of twentieth-century Britain. Demographic changes such as smaller families and shorter childbearing periods left women with more time to seek employment outside the home. At the same time, an expanding economy and full employment created more job opportunities for women. As explained in the introduction, the total number of female workers increased by nearly 33 per cent between 1948 and 1980.[3] The proportion of married women in employment and women working in part-time jobs grew substantially.[4] The development of the welfare state and white-collar service industries accounted for the majority of women's employment after the war, yet women often worked in low-paid and low-status jobs with little opportunity for promotion.[5] Jane Lewis pointed out that 84 per cent of women worked in occupations dominated by other women in 1971, whilst 63 per cent of women worked in jobs that were performed only by women in 1980.[6] Table 1.1 demonstrates that the sexual division of labour occurred both in low-paid manufacturing industries that entered decline during the 1960s and in emerging public sector and service industries, either for non-manual clerical work or for manual labour such as cleaning, catering and retail services.

The influx of women into the labour force should not be confused with an amelioration of gender inequality in Britain. Women entered the labour market in a disadvantageous position compared to men. The average differential between male and female wages consistently remained at around 50.4 per cent between 1924 and 1970.[7] In 1980, five years after the passage of the Equal Pay Act, the average hourly pay of all working women (both full-time and part-time) was less than 66 per cent of the average male wage.[8] The lack of state-funded and private nurseries placed constraints on working mothers seeking to combine motherhood and employment, and women could still be sacked on account of pregnancy.[9] Professional job advertisements were directed specifically at men. Many industries' pay scales included a 'women's rate' below the 'unskilled male' rate, whilst men were more likely to boost their wages with overtime opportunities. These historical circumstances contributed to an epistemol-

Table 1.1 Proportions of men and women (aged over 16) as a percentage of employees within selected occupations, 1985

Occupation	Men	Women
Construction, mining and related	99.5	0.5
Professional and related in science, engineering and technology	93.3	6.7
Transport, operation, materials and related	96.4	3.6
Clerical and related	22.8	77.2
Catering, cleaning, hairdressing and other personal services	20.8	79.2

Source: Bradley, *Men's Work, Women's Work*, p. 13.

ogy of skill where work performed by women was conventionally understood as low skilled and low status precisely because it was 'women's work', which was beginning to break down in certain professions where equal pay came earlier.[10] Table 1.2 shows the persistence of wage inequality between men and women in spite of women's growing presence in the labour force.

As Table 1.2 shows, women continued to be paid significantly less than men in both manual and non-manual and private and public sector jobs throughout the 1970s. In spite of an initial narrowing of the differential between total men's and women's wages between 1970 and 1976, this gap began to increase again between 1977 and 1981. One can also see that the largest differentials between male and female wages occurred in the non-manual private sector consistently throughout the period, with women earning 52.9 per cent of men's weekly wage in 1981. However, female workers in the manual private sector remained the lowest paid workers in Britain throughout the period, earning an average weekly wage of £13.30 in 1970 and £72.90 in 1981, £33 less than the average weekly wage for all women, and £75 per week less than the total average male wages during 1981.

Although the majority of women worked in the expanding public sector, white-collar and service industries, a significant amount of women continued to work in manufacturing up until the 1980s – such as the women considered in this book.[11] Women represented 42 per cent of employees in 'new industries' such as electronics, telecommunications and radio during the 1960s; however, the number of women employed in these industries declined from 324,000 in 1961 to 217,000 in 1981.[12] Similar trends occurred in clothing manufacturing, with the overall number

Table 1.2 Average gross weekly earnings (in £) of full-time men aged 21 and over and full-time women aged 18 and over in public and private sectors, 1970–81

	1970	1971	1972	1973	1974	1975	1976	1977	1978	1979	1980	1981
ALL MEN AND WOMEN												
Public sector												
Men	29.7	33	37.6	42.1	48.6	64.3	76.7	82.7	91	102.4	128.7	147.2
Women	19.6	21.6	24.8	27.1	31.8	44.6	55.3	59.6	64	70.5	89.2	105.1
Differential	10.1	11.4	12.8	15	16.8	19.7	21.4	23.1	27	31.9	39.5	42.1
Women's earnings as a % of men's	65.9	65.5	65.9	64.4	65.4	69.4	72.1	72	70.3	68.9	69.3	71.4
Private sector												
Men	29.7	32.9	32.9	36.3	47.3	59	69.4	76.8	88	100.8	122.2	135.8
Women	14.3	16.3	18	20.7	24.3	32.3	39.4	44.4	50.7	57.4	70.7	80.3
Differential	15.4	16.6	18.3	21.1	23	26.7	30	32.4	37.3	43.4	51.5	55.5
Women's earnings as a % of men's	48.1	49.5	49.6	49.5	51.4	54.7	56.8	57.8	57.6	56.9	57.8	59.1
NON-MANUAL MEN AND WOMEN												
Public sector												
Men	35.6	39.4	44.7	48.4	55.7	71.4	87.4	92.9	101.3	112.4	143	168
Women	21.2	23.2	26.6	28.7	33.3	46.5	58.2	62.5	66.8	73.7	92.8	109.9
Differential	14.4	16.2	18.1	19.7	22.4	24.9	29.2	30.4	34.5	38.7	50.2	58.1
Women's earnings as a % of men's	59.5	58.8	58.6	59.3	59.8	65.1	66.6	67.3	65.9	65.6	64.9	65.4

(*cont.*)

(cont.)

Private sector												
Men	34.8	38.9	42.8	48	53.8	66.4	78	86.3	100.3	113.5	140.2	158.1
Women	15.1	17.1	18.7	21.4	25.1	33.1	40	45.2	51.6	58.6	72.8	83.6
Differential	19.7	21.8	24.1	26.6	28.7	33.3	38	41.1	48.7	54.9	67.4	74.5
Women's earnings as a % of men's	43.4	43.9	43.7	44.6	46.6	49.8	51.3	52.4	51.4	51.6	51.9	52.9
MANUAL MEN AND WOMEN												
Public sector												
Men	25.4	28.2	32	37	42.7	58.1	67.2	72.7	81.2	93	114.6	127.3
Women	13.3	15.5	17.8	20.2	25	35.5	42.5	45.9	50.5	55.1	71.4	78.7
Differential	12.1	12.7	14.2	16.8	17.7	22.6	24.7	26.8	30.7	37.9	43.2	48.6
Women's earnings as a % of men's	52.4	55	55.6	54.6	58.5	61.1	63.2	63.1	62.6	59.2	62.3	61.8
Private sector												
Men	27.2	29.9	33.1	38.5	43.9	54.7	64.3	71	80.5	93	110.3	119.2
Women	13.3	15.2	16.9	19.6	23.2	31	38.3	42.9	49	55.2	66.6	72.9
Differential	13.9	14.7	16.2	18.9	20.7	23.7	26	28.1	31.5	37.8	43.7	46.3
Women's earnings as a % of men's	48.9	50.8	51	50.9	52.8	56.7	59.6	60.4	60.9	59.4	60.4	61.1

Sources: Annual Report of the Equal Opportunities Commission (London: HMSO, 1976); Annual Report of the Equal Opportunities Commission (London: HMSO, 1981).

of employees within the industry falling from 629,000 in 1948 to 517,000 in 1968, and to 292,000 by 1981, 85 per cent of whom were women that mostly worked full-time.[13] Women's employment experiences also varied along racial lines. On a national level, 63.5 per cent of Asian and Caribbean women worked in manual occupations in 1972, whilst 45 per cent of white women were similarly employed.[14] Industrial decline and the corresponding expansion of employment in managerial, professional and service sectors is understood to have had an emasculating effect on working-class men; however, less is known about the effects of deindustrialisation on women's attitudes towards paid work.[15]

Women's work in public debates

The implications of women's increased labour force participation for British workplaces and families were frequently debated during the 1950s and 1960s. The growing importance of pronatalism meant that policy makers and social scientists were primarily concerned with the impact of women's work on their role as wives and mothers. Stephen Brooke has shown that married women's employment disrupted 'traditional' working-class identities based on romanticised images of the breadwinner family.[16] Claire Langhamer has suggested that 'the health of children, husbands, nation, and (more rarely) women themselves, was held to rest on the correct deployment of female labour outside the home'.[17] Drawing on sociological studies as evidence of the public meanings ascribed to women's labour, Helen McCarthy argues that women's work became 'normalised' by the end of the 1960s.[18] Social scientists' increased focus on women's dual role as caregivers and wage earners symbolised a shift from earlier understandings of women's employment as a social problem towards a greater acceptance that paid work had positive effects on women's social and psychic needs, as well as economic effects in an increasingly affluent society.[19] As Dolly Smith-Wilson has shown, affluence and the increasing availability of part-time work altered individuals' ideas about acceptable standards of living and the meaning of needing to work. Women believed that they worked out of necessity or to raise their families' living standard, which subsequently removed the stigma surrounding working motherhood and created new ideas about what it meant to be a 'good mother'.[20]

Gender equality and women's rights in the workplace occupied a more prominent position in these debates from the 1970s onwards. Social scientists increasingly sought to explain the causes and effects of wage inequality, occupational segregation and the undervaluing of female labour, as well as the unequal division of domestic labour in the home. Industrial sociologists were conscious of this shift in their collective attention. Richard Brown explained in 1976 that it was still possible to conclude that women were 'sociologically invisible participants in industrial life'.[21] Yet he also observed a noticeable change where recent studies increasingly questioned the inevitability and 'rightness' of women's employment conditions due to the manner in which 'feminists had redefined the issue'.[22] Writing in 1984, Martin and Wallace explained in the introduction to their study of women and redundancy that 'the increase in the number and visibility of women in employment in the 1970s and the growing influence of the feminist movement led to widespread political and academic interest in issues involving women and work'.[23] A range of feminist participant observation studies emerged that provided a new basis for understanding the experience of female workers in factories. Research on women's employment experiences by Judy Wajcman, Anna Pollert, Pauline Hunt and Miriam Glucksmann (as Ruth Cavendish) represented a fresh concern with explaining the relationship between gender, workplace conditions and women's political consciousness, which in the words of Wajcman 'orthodox industrial sociology would find difficult to explain'.[24] In 1980, the Department of Employment conducted the Women and Employment Survey, which aimed to establish the impact of the gender division of labour on women's employment experiences. At the time, it was the most significant and detailed analysis of women's work histories and has been described as 'the cornerstone of a whole raft of studies concerning maternity provision, equal pay ... and the all too glaring inequalities in employment experiences of women and men' taking place at that time.[25]

Economic restructuring from male-dominated heavy industry to a service-based economy and the resulting high levels of unemployment significantly shaped the nature of these debates. Between 1966 and 1979, nearly 3 million jobs were lost in production, 75 per cent of which were male jobs.[26] Over the same period, women's employment in the service sector increased by 33 per cent. Importantly, this increase was largely concentrated among married women working part-time in the service sector. Unemployment also increased among women working in manufacturing by 4 per cent between 1977 and 1979 and a further 14 per cent between 1979 and 1981.[27] Within this context, women's paid employment was recognised as increasingly important to family income and maintaining standards of living. For example, an Equal Opportunities Commission report on women and poverty in 1977 explained,

> Income earned by many women in Britain today is vital, both to their own standard of living, and to the standard of living of their families or dependents. Such evidence strongly suggests that the idea of women being conceptualised as necessarily the dependents of men is outdated. 'Pin money' has become an outmoded concept; if it ever had any validity in reality. Many working women in Britain are now breadwinners in their own right, or provide a necessary addition to the family budget. Single women have always had to take on the responsibility of providing for dependents; and family income is becoming a joint operation between many husband and wives. Because of this process the concept of 'head of the family' is becoming ambiguous and misleading, and social security laws and regulations need to take cognisance of this situation.[28]

These studies provide evidence of a shift from earlier social scientists' concerns with the economic, social and psychic benefits of paid work for women to greater public debates about women's position within the labour force and rights in the workplace. There was greater recognition of the unequal conditions, dissatisfaction and sense of injustice that many women experienced at the time. Underpinning this conceptual shift was the decline of the economic breadwinner family model and its gradual replacement with the adult-worker family model. It has been well established that this ideal seldom met the reality of women's and men's daily lives, as women were more likely to earn less money and assume greater responsibility for unpaid labour. Nevertheless, women were less likely to be seen as economic dependents and more likely to be perceived as economically independent workers.

The growth of studies on women's employment from the late 1960s should be understood in terms of the expansion of social science expertise and evidence of a normative shift in ideas about gender roles taking place in Britain during this period. Identifying the tangible effects of such studies on broader society is difficult, yet Helen McCarthy suggests that social science had a significant 'cultural throw' in terms of its ability to shape both public policy and popular understandings of ordinary people.[29] The fact that the gender division of labour and unequal pay were increasingly problematised and questioned symbolised an increased acceptance of women's role as independent wage earners. This entailed a broader transition in thinking about women's citizenship – in terms of their rights, responsibilities and relationship with the state. Interrogating women's workplace activism provides an opportunity to better understand how this shift was taking place in the minds of working-class women themselves during this period.

Women and the labour movement

One of the reasons that social scientists and policy makers were focusing more on gender inequality was because women themselves were increasingly drawing their attention and protesting against poor wages and conditions. It is difficult to quantify precisely how many women engaged in industrial action during this period, but the timeline in the Appendix demonstrates that women were engaging in various forms of workplace activism in different industries across England.

One of the effects of this wave of militancy was that trade unions began to increasingly recognise the interests of their female members. Sarah Boston clearly demonstrates that male trade unionists and their official bodies remained resistant and unhelpful to women workers throughout the 1960s and 1970s.[30] Yet the growth in women's trade unionism (outlined in the Introduction) was also accompanied by an observably greater commitment from organisations within the labour movement aiming to represent the specific interests of female workers. There was a rise in activism of white-collar women including teachers, nurses and women in the civil service. Militant shop stewards in the Civil Service Union were influential in the Equal Pay Campaign Committee, which pressured the government into introducing equal pay for civil service non-manual grade workers in 1955 (to be phased in over a six-year period), and teachers in 1961.[31] The Labour Party Manifesto for the 1964 General Election included 'the right to equal pay for equal work', and the Trades Union Congress (TUC) adopted a similar resolution at their 1965 Annual Conference.[32] The TUC Women's Advisory Committee (WAC) withdrew its opposition to working mothers and day nurseries in 1957.[33] The National Joint Action Campaign Committee for Women's Equal Rights (NJACCWER) was set up in the aftermath of the 1968 Ford sewing machinists' strike and established an informal network of female trade unionists committed to campaigning for workplace equality. They attracted further public attention by organising an equal pay demonstration attended by 1,000 women in Trafalgar Square in May 1969.[34]

The Working Women's Charter campaign (WWCC) was formed in 1974 by the London Trades Council and drew together women's liberation activists and female trade unionists organised in twenty-seven local groups across Britain. They developed a ten-point charter that included demands for childcare, maternity protection, family allowances and legal equality, as well as equal pay and better training opportunities. They also aimed to get feminist non-unionists co-opted onto women's committees in local trades' councils.[35] Coote and Campbell suggest that the campaign had an unmistakable influence on the TUC, which published *Aims for Women at Work* in 1975 and included the same demands as the charter, with the exception of access to abortion and publicly provided childcare, which were added in 1978.[36] Stephen Brooke describes the charter as 'the most important example of a developing intersection between second-wave feminism and the labour movement'.[37] He argues that by introducing the notion of the double burden and focusing on the division of labour in the family, women in the Labour Party and trade unions became radicalised in this period in a way that signified a break from the past.[38] TUC support for the campaign in 1979 to defeat the John Corrie's Bill, which sought to amend the 1967 Abortion Act, was significant because the TUC General Council had only officially adopted a pro-abortion stance at their 1975 annual conference, having previously claimed it was not a trade union issue.[39]

Further evidence of the evolution in women's relationship with the labour movement can be found in the propagation of campaigns to challenge low pay and 'women's grades' organised by individual trade unions including the Association of Professional, Executive, Clerical and Computer Staff (APEX), the Technical, Administrative and Supervisory Section (TASS), the National Union of Public Employees (NUPE), the General and Municipal Workers' Union (GMWU) and the Association of Cinematograph, Television and Allied Technicians (ACTT).[40] These campaigns were accompanied by a growth in positive action from trade unions on a national level to increase women's representation and activity throughout the 1970s. This included the creation of women's seats on executive councils, separate women's committees, training days and publications for female shop stewards, regional equality committees and some crèche provision at union meetings. There was also an increase in participation rates and the number of motions placed on the agenda for the TUC women's Annual Conference throughout the 1970s.[41] The structure of the WAC was altered in 1978 and extended to eighteen members, eight elected and ten appointed by the General Council, with two seats reserved for women.[42] Esther Breitenbach concluded in 1981 that it offered women a valuable space to build confidence and experience, and to discuss and formulate strategy to combat the various issues they faced, yet remained severely limited in its ability to alter the unequal position of women within the labour movement due to its advisory status.[43]

The wave of women's workplace activism considered in this book occurred at a time when trade unions increasingly committed themselves to improving the conditions of female workers. There was growing recognition that women faced specific problems in the workplace and developed distinct interests from male workers. More people attended the TUC women's conference, and more unions discussed issues surrounding gender equality in the workplace. Indeed, some women began to assume more prominent positions within trade unions and the Labour Party from the 1980s onwards. These trends have sometimes been understood as 'the feminisation of the labour movement'. However, this focus on women's representation within trade unions at an institutional level does not indicate what the effects of such changes were for female workers on the shop floor. Disputes involving women are often drawn upon as examples of female workers becoming more active within trade unions, without a full understanding of what the participants believed they were doing and what they now think they did.

Women's liberation and workplace activism

The rights of female workers were also a key concern for the WLM that emerged at the end of the 1960s. Anna Coote and Beatrix Campbell described trade unions as a central site of struggle around employment, pay and conditions for WLM. They identified industrial disputes as a means of reaching out to women who were not acquainted with feminist politics, an organisational base for feminist campaigns and 'a means of anchoring women's liberation in working-class politics'.[44] In a similar manner, Sheila Rowbotham explained that feminists 'joined picket lines, helped produce strike papers, raised money, monitored civil liberties and organised meetings and conferences', which influenced the development of the WLM by widening its original social base and forming personal links with organised labour.[45] Trade unions were a central concern for socialist feminists in particular, yet there was a lack of agreement about how to negotiate the tension between encouraging women to participate in a movement that had historically excluded them.[46] Some were reluctant to support trade unions, and instead encouraged women to organise autonomously. Selma James offers the best example of this critique; she argued that the WLM had been too quick to equate working-class interests with the Labour Party and trade unions, which she believed had failed to represent women's specific interests and experience of class struggle. James argued that unions were responsible for wage differentials and creating divisions within the working class.[47] As a result, she suggested that women should organise autonomously and demand to have the economic value of their unpaid labour recognised by campaigning for wages for housework.[48] However, other socialist feminists believed that women could only alter the unequal relations within trade unions by joining them. Audrey Wise, who was active in both the WLM and the Union of Shop, Distributive and Allied Workers (USDAW) and went on to become Labour Member of Parliament (MP) for Preston in 1987, described trade unions as 'male-dominated boys clubs', but claimed that it was essential for working-class women to join them in order to improve their workplace rights and establish class solidarity in the future.[49] An article in *Red Rag* provides an insight into how feminists often perceived the role of WLM groups in relation to female trade unionists:

> Trade union women's actions raise possibilities of breaking down divisions between groups of workers, not just men and women, but manual and clerical. Equal pay strikes attempting to force employers to begin to adopt terms of the act show that legislation is the beginning rather than the end of the struggle. Women who have only just joined trade unions are being confronted with the whole repressive paraphernalia of laws and clauses. ... The actions women are taking make our support really urgent. Apart from what we are trying to do in our own unions, there are several things we can do: we can publicise strikes and expose the conditions of women at work. We can help women who are picketing – as we have done already but in a more systematic way. We also need to be more ready to provide help and support if women come to picket in another town where we are. This is a problem of information. We have to know that they are coming for a start. We have still not managed to create any systematic national network to report on and to strengthen women who are involved in industrial conflict.[50]

This quote offers an insight into how WLM activists perceived industrial disputes as sites where they could extend their influence and the social composition of their movement. Equally, it reveals how the movement's informal structure made it difficult to coordinate assistance for female workers' protest. Importantly, it highlights the emergence of a network of women across Britain who aimed to encourage and support female workers in resisting inequality in the workplace. However, Natalie Thomlinson highlights the unequal balance of the relationship between middle-class WLM activists and the working-class women they sought to support. The socialist orientation of many women in the WLM made class a key concern.[51] Thomlinson argues that the struggles of female trade unionists were valorised by middle-class radicals like Sheila Rowbotham and placed in a longer tradition of female left-wing radicalism involving Annie Beasant, Sylvia Pankhurst and Eleanor Marx. At the same time, Thomlinson suggests that WLM attempts to reach out to female trade unionists were discursively framed as what middle-class women could do to help working-class women. Working-class and black and Asian women became 'the subjects of study rather than comrades in arms'. The key problem here was that despite a rhetoric of universality, feminist theory became based on middle-class assumptions about the political capabilities of other women.[52]

WLM activists reflected on the challenge of reaching out to working-class women and negotiating differences in education and social background at the time. The campaign to unionise night cleaners provides a good example of this self-reflection in practice. An activist interviewed in *Shrew* reported, 'At first we were slightly nervous. Most of us felt embarrassingly middle-class. However, we were very encouraged to discover that the majority of the women stopped to speak to us, and several joined within the first month'.[53] Sally Alexander expressed similar concerns at the time:

> It is difficult to raise the subject of women's liberation with the cleaners. Most of the women could only spare a couple of minutes outside of the door before they rushed into work. Those who arrived earlier were obviously more interested in hearing about the union. We were known among the women as the union girls. Whenever women's liberation was raised there was an initial self-consciousness on our part, and probably a joke about bras and man-hating on theirs.[54]

I asked Sheila Rowbotham about the impact of the campaign on her own life, and whether she thought that they had made any difference to the cleaners' lives. She suggested,

> I think we were better at making a noise than at changing the conditions of the cleaners ... I don't think we really influenced their daily lives, I think that was more noticeable in the miners' strike when so many women did take on the personal stuff about lifestyle and feminism but I think the cleaners just thought that ... because we were younger, they saw us as kind of girls. I think probably because the miners' strike disrupted the normal custom of living, because people were doing the picketing as a full-time thing and as a family. I think the cleaners stayed in their own lives and saw us as these girls who were trying to help them.[55]

The emergence of socialist feminist publications like *Women's Voice* as well as *Red Rag* and *Scarlet Women* (published by collectives of Marxist and socialist feminists) are important for understanding the context of women's workplace activism during this period. They provide evidence of how women were increasingly articulating and expressing grievances with their experiences of paid work at a grassroots level, which contributed to this broader shift in thinking about gender equality in the workplace. *Women's Voice* was the women's newspaper, then magazine, of the International Socialists (IS), later the Socialist Workers Party.[56] The paper documented working-class women's workplace activism throughout Britain between 1972 and 1982. In 1978, the paper's editorial team began to establish women-only *Women's Voice* groups across the country that were also open to non-IS members. It raised awareness of the dissatisfaction and the sense of injustice many women felt with their experiences in the workplace and at home. The editorial team encouraged readers to write their own industrial bulletins and send in their stories about various forms of women's activism over issues including housing; food prices; family allowances; immigration policy; childcare; fascism; domestic abuse; maternity leave; and abortion.

A key concern of *Women's Voice* was to make feminism relevant to the 'real lives' of working-class women. The first issue explained,

> Whilst women's liberation has been the subject of hundreds of books, articles, jokes and TV programmes, much of this has made the subject seem a silly and trivial one ... despite this, thousands of women have achieved a new awareness of their position in society and how they would like it to be changed. But in the 'great debate' about women's lib, one thing is hardly ever mentioned – the situation of working-class women. ... Women's Voice is produced to fill this gap. First and foremost it is a magazine for working-class women who want to read something that tries to deal with their real life.[57]

What emerges from the pages of *Women's Voice* is the perception of novelty and the sense that something had shifted within the consciousness of working-class women. The third issue in 1972 explained, 'There is increasing awareness and militancy among women and a rise in female membership of trade unions.'[58] The fourteenth issue declared that 1974 was the year 'women workers fought as never before to gain better wages and conditions. ... Most of them had never done anything like it in their lives before. But they sparked off a new determined mood among women workers – a mood which says women are no longer content to remain the poor relations of the working class.'[59] Similar to the activists involved in the night cleaners campaign, *Women's Voice* were concerned with female workers' views on the WLM. An interview with a shop steward who led a successful equal pay strike at Goodman's electronics factory in Havant was asked if she felt the 'fuss over Women's Liberation' had affected the women at the factory. She responded,

> They read about it in the papers and you hear it discussed in the factory all the time. It boosts their morale to hear that women all over the country are fighting for their rights – especially like the ones at Fakenham. But working-class women are not taken in by gimmicks. ... Women are classed as second-rate citizens all the way down the line. But they're gradually waking up. ... We don't work for pin money any more. With rents and prices rising and all the other things, women today have got to get a decent wage to keep the home running. If women were more interested in unions and fighting for their rights, they'd stand a better chance of getting equal pay. I think women are frightened of unions. ... But once it hits them that the union can really do something for them, women are more militant than anyone.[60]

The quote illustrates how working-class women distinguished themselves from WLM and trade union activists and draws attention to the primacy of their material circumstances leading to their engagement in workplace militancy. A key constraint on working-class women's workplace activism was the limited support that women were likely to receive from their trade union representatives. Although WLM activists often framed working-class women's struggles in a potentially patronising manner about what middle-class women could do to help working-class women, it is also important to recognise that this reflected a pre-existing unequal distribution of power within trade unions that made it more difficult for women to organise. *Women's Voice* explained,

> Again and again what came out of the women's strikes was the need for outside support. For women, who are in a weaker position than men outside support is crucial. Small sections of women cannot win alone no matter how determined they are. Women also need the help of more experienced trade unionists in setting up the running of a strike. Women workers are often without experience of how to run strikes.[61]

Outside the WLM, feminist sociologists were also concerned about the gulf between middle-class feminists and working-class women. In the introduction to her participant observation study of female workers at Smiths Industries in west London between 1977 and 1978, Miriam Glucksmann (as Ruth Cavendish) identified a similar desire as the editorial team of *Women's Voice* to understand the authentic everyday experiences of working-class women:

> I was product of 1960s student movement, formed politically and intellectually by involvement in struggles over education, Vietnam, and other anti-imperialist movements, and by the Women's Liberation movement. ... By the mid-1970s, I felt that sort of politics I had been

involved in was at an impasse. I wanted to put my feet on more solid ground. ... Looking for a new way of being involved politically, where I might have daily contact with working-class women over the long term ... . I worried it would be difficult for me to be accepted by working-class women especially Black and Asian women – who would be suspicious on account of my colour as well as my background, education and speech.[62]

Glucksmann's study was part of a raft of new research into the political consciousness of female workers, which in itself was a response to activists' own disillusionment with their detachment from working-class women's lives. Feminist sociologists increasingly sought to understand why this was the case. Whilst these new studies were a novel historical development in themselves, it is important to recognise how they often judged women's activism and political orientations against their own preconceptions of what this should look like. For example, in her ethnographic study of the Fakenham factory occupation (which is revisited in Chapter 4), Judy Wajcman found that the female workforce's experience of activism had little effect on their attitudes towards trade unionism, their political orientations or the sexually based division of labour in the home. She concluded that their experience did not alter their political consciousness, and the women continued to adopt dominant ideologies as their own.[63] Anna Pollert drew similar conclusions after becoming involved in a strike over wages whilst undertaking an ethnography of Churchman's Imperial Tobacco factory in Bristol in 1972. She described the world of trade unionism as 'hostile to women' and claimed that female workers were demoralised after male union negotiators made a compromise deal on their behalf, which resulted in a 'passive fatalism' among the female workforce. Pollert went on to argue that the women possessed a 'fragmentary consciousness – incoherent ideas, and unresolved common sense ... containing partial acceptance and partial rejections of ruling conceptions of the world.'[64] Both Wajcman and Pollert appear to view the women they studied as 'lacking the tools' to make sense of their private frustration and to 'develop their consciousness' to fight abuses of female wage labour and unequal division of labour in the home.

Such conclusions are problematic because they potentially deny the women's agency and imply that to be political, collective action must be motivated by a coherent view of the world, derived from a socialist or feminist critique of society. In doing so, they fail to account for the political nature of women's everyday concerns and responses to gender and class antagonism. Miriam Glucksmann illustrated this problem in her own study. She pointed out that 'neither the women's movement nor any other political grouping is in a position to affect all the different spheres of [working-class women's] life at present'.[65] She reflected that 'the reason we haven't attracted working-class women to the women's movement is not that they aren't feminist or are unaware. Our discussions are too up in the air for them and reflect a very different way of life.'[66] Glucksmann explained that the women at Smiths Industries 'were more likely to take action on their own behalf at work than outside. Here they were brought together daily under the same conditions, and had a collective awareness of being exploited ... the solidarity that grew out of the shared experience is what gave the women strength and self-confidence'.[67] The point here is that women working in manufacturing industries appeared to be operating with a different set of interpretive devices to articulate their subjective experience and understanding of class and gender relations to the frameworks offered by their unions or the WLM.

These examples offer a broader picture of second-wave feminist approaches to women's workplace rights at this time beyond the WLM. Feminist activists sought to improve the conditions of female workers and support working-class women engaged in workplace disputes. WLM activists often framed this relationship in an unequal manner, but it is important to recognise that activists were often aware of this gap in experience at the time and sought to understand this in greater detail. In doing so, WLM and far-left groups, as well as feminist academics, raised awareness of the unequal conditions many women faced at work. They often did so in a manner that judged women's political orientations against their own preconceptions of what they should look like. But they still raised awareness in a manner that contributed to the shift in public understandings of women's work taking place at the time.

Gender equality legislation

So far, this chapter has argued that women's workplace protest occurred in a context when female workers, trade unions, social scientists and WLM activists were drawing public attention to the poor conditions and inequalities that working-class women were likely to experience in the workplace. At the same time, policy makers and the main political parties increasingly sought to understand and address gender inequality as a political issue. The Equal Pay Act was passed in 1970 and implemented in 1975. The legislation made it illegal for employers to award individuals different wages and benefits as persons of the opposite sex for 'like work', 'work rated as equivalent under an analytical job evaluation survey' or 'work that is proved to be of equal value'. The Sex Discrimination Act was passed in 1975, and the Equal Opportunities Commission was established in the same year, which recognised the necessity to address underlying factors behind pay discrimination. This included the effects of career breaks for caring responsibilities on women's career prospects, men's tendency to work longer hours, and women's over-representation in low-paying and low-status work. Alongside these reforms, both Conservative and Labour governments passed a series of new laws strengthening the rights of married women and introduced statutory paid maternity leave. The Domestic Violence Act was passed in 1976 and Sexual Offences Act in 1977. This series of legislative reforms arguably represented the most significant advance for women's rights in British political history.

The main causes and implications of the legislation have been debated and explained elsewhere.[68] Central to these debates have been questions about the role of the WLM. McCarthy argues these changes would have occurred anyway due to political expediency and impetus from Europe, without second-wave feminism.[69] Others have suggested that the WLM played a more significant role in generating pressure for reform and spreading ideas through feminist networks. Sheila Rowbotham suggested that although the WLM was sceptical towards formal politics and reform, the need for legislation became 'inescapable'.[70] Elizabeth Meehan highlighted the importance of women's informal influence, arguing that many women involved in WLM groups went on to play a more active role within political parties, trade unions and professional associations. In a recent study, Elizabeth Homans suggests that 'references to women's liberation – positive, negative, ambiguous, often garbled – percolated into elite, popular and public culture, helping to create a climate conducive to reform'.[71] Homans argues that the WLM created the space for the greater acceptance of feminist ideas and principles during the 1970s. Although many 'ordinary' people rejected feminism as being too radical, others were able to present similar claims for women's legal and economic rights in a more moderate and publicly acceptable fashion. Alongside the WLM, legislative reform was also dependent on traditional methods of campaigning and lobbying. Groups such as the Fawcett Society and the Six Point Group played a key role in lobbying for the Equal Pay Act and Sex Discrimination Act.

Materially, the impact of legislation was limited due to its inability to alter the pre-existing economic and social conditions that women were entering the labour market. The key impediment to equal pay was the reluctance of employers to pay men and women the same wages. Political parties, governments and trade unions endorsed the principle in public but were reluctant to deliver it in practice. Aversion to equal pay was justified in economic terms as it was often suggested that industries could not afford to offer women wage rises. The passing of the legislation demonstrated the difficulties associated with attempts to articulate and realise equal pay in an unequal labour market. The key problem was that equal pay for equal work meant little in practice because it was rare to find men and women doing the same jobs. It could not be granted in isolation because it undermined assumptions on which social security and various other policies and social and economic arrangements were based. Women worked in low-paid jobs that lacked power and status. Unequal opportunities and training also constrained women, which is what the Sex Discrimination Act sought to address. Rather than satisfying demands for equality, the legislation is better understood as a prompt to further investigation into the causes of and explanations for sex inequalities in the workplace.[72]

South Asian women's workplace activism

As gender inequality occupied a more prominent position in public debates during the 1970s, it is important to recognise there was an increasing awareness of racial discrimination in British workplaces as well. The case studies in the following chapters focus on the experiences of white working-class women. However, it is important to recognise that many black and South Asian migrant women also engaged in workplace protest during this period. The intersections of race, gender and class distinguished these women's militancy from white working-class women's in a manner that cannot be fully addressed in this study. This section identifies some key disputes involving black and Asian women during the 1970s, highlights how they were interpreted at the time and, finally, points towards some of the implications of workplace militancy for black and Asian women's political identities.

Migrant female workers represented the lowest paid and most exploited section of the female labour force. Women of South Asian origin who migrated to Britain in the late 1960s from India, Pakistan, Bangladesh, Sri Lanka and East Africa were likely to find jobs in clerical work, teaching and administration closed to them. Many instead took on low-paid jobs in launderettes, assembly work at factories, sewing garments, food processing and as cleaners. Linda McDowell describes women moving to Britain in the 1970s as 'green labour'.[73] Language barriers limited their choice of jobs, whilst their unawareness of their rights and other workers' pay and conditions left them open to intimidation. South Asian women were popularly perceived to represent a docile, passive and easily exploited workforce. They were less likely than white women to be unionised, and less likely to receive support from their union when they engaged in workplace militancy.[74] As a result, instances of South Asian women's militancy attracted the interest of feminist and far-left activists during the 1970s and have since been identified as transformative moments in the history of the labour movement.

The most obvious example is the famous Grunwick strike by South Asian women in 1976–78.[75] Led by Jayaben Desai, five Asian workers walked out of the photo-processing laboratory in protest against low pay and oppressive conditions. They were followed by 132 workmates the following week, all of whom were sacked when they demanded union recognition. The workers received significant support from APEX, the Brent Trade Council and the TUC who saw it as a crucial battle about workers' rights to join a trade union. Thousands of workers from across Britain joined the predominantly female workforce on the picket line. WLM groups were also involved in the mass picketing that went on throughout 1977. A court of enquiry held in June 1977 recommended that the company recognise the union, but the company ignored the report and the workers were never reinstated. Despite its unsuccessful resolution, the strike occupies a key position in the labour history of the 1970s and is commonly understood as a pivotal moment that brought people of different races and backgrounds together in support of the rights of migrant women workers. Amrit Wilson highlighted the problematic nature of such accounts at the time. She suggested that the workers' dissatisfaction with the strike's outcome 'exposed the myth of the TUC's solidarity with exploited workers' and emphasised the need for black and Asian workers to play a more prominent role within trade unions.[76] More recently, Sundari Anitha and Linda McDowell's work demonstrates how race and ethnicity, as well as gender, divided the experience and interests of the South Asian women on strike at Grunwick from their supporters in 1976–78. They suggest that although the imagery and 'otherness' of South Asian women on strike captured the imagination of the labour movement at the time, the voices of the women were largely ignored by union leaders, and have been absent in the history of the strike since.[77]

The same remains true of the voices of thousands of South Asian women who engaged in less well-known disputes throughout the 1970s. Here, I want to draw attention to three further disputes instigated by predominantly South Asian women in the East Midlands between 1972 and 1974. The first dispute occurred at mill when 400 South Asian workers went on strike demanding a £5 weekly pay increase and access to higher-paid knitting jobs occupied by white workers. Whilst the strike began as a wage dispute, it brought Asian women's concerns about victimisation, bullying and restrictions on wearing saris into sharper focus. A worker named Bhanu Mistry explained at the time: 'The colour bar applies to us all. If our brothers are on strike we have to give them support. They need to feel self-respect when they are treated like dogs. How can we go in, if our brothers are out?'[78] The National Union of Hosiery and Knitwear Workers refused to make the strike official even after it was found guilty alongside management of contravening sections of the Race Relations Act. *Women's Voice* commended those who stood on the picket line, explaining that 'this was particularly hard for Asian women who generally feel shy when dealing with matters outside the home'.[79] They noted that men and women sat separately at union meetings and concluded,

> The women at Mansfield can see the task ahead but most feel it is still beyond them. The women mentioned the confidence they had gained in the strike but one admitted she was still not bold enough to organise women around her in the factory. But they all agreed it would be harder to push them around in future.[80]

Two years later, 500 Asian workers went on strike at the Imperial Typewriter factory in Leicester over unpaid bonuses and a lack of promotion opportunities for Asian workers.[81] The dispute was defined by the lack of support the Asian workers received from their local branch of the Transport and General Workers Union (TGWU). The TGWU district organiser George Bromley told the *Leicester Mercury*, 'The union emphatically repudiates that there is any racial discrimination whatsoever in the union branch.' He later condemned the unofficial action and suggested,

> Now some of these Asian ladies, I feel sorry for them, they are strangers, they don't know much about industrial life, they have led a very sheltered life. ... Because they are semi-skilled they are low rated but they have got to learn to fit in with our ways you know. We haven't got to fit in with theirs. And the way they have been acting, that means they will close factories and people won't employ them – that's all.[82]

The dispute highlighted a gulf between the interests of Asian workers and their white union representatives and evolved into a struggle over the democratic election of shop stewards. A female worker explained to *Race*

Today at the time: 'We are mostly Asians in our section, but our shop steward is a white woman. She doesn't care and the union doesn't care. I pay 11p a week to be a member of the union but I really think it is a waste of hard earned money. Don't get me wrong. I am not against unions but our union is no different from management.'[83] The lack of union support meant that the workers relied on the backing of the Indian Workers' Association and the black and Asian community in Leicester instead.

Although the dispute was unsuccessful, it had a significant local impact as thirty-one Asian female workers went on strike a few weeks later at Kenilworth Components, also in Leicester, demanding the reinstatement of seven sacked workers. The *Leicester Mercury* suggested that the strike illustrated the 'simmering racial hostility in the city' and represented another opportunity for 'Asian militants to demonstrate the raw deal Asians were getting'.[84] The dispute presented an opportunity for both female and male workers to demand pay increases, and the women were joined on the picket line by 150 workmates, which forced the TGWU district organiser and the Department of Employment Conciliation Officer to get involved immediately. However, once again official support from the TGWU was not forthcoming. After seventeen weeks of no strike pay, only £60 was collected from the labour movement and in the face of union hostility, the men yielded to the attempts to split them off from the women and accepted a £5 flat increase and the sacking of seventeen women. *Women's Voice* concluded,

> Unable to split the workers on racial lines the management tried and succeeded in splitting them on sex lines. They succeeded because other workers failed to give moral and financial support and because no pressure was put onto the union to organise effective support. It is a bitter lesson. We should organise to ensure that similar defeats are not possible in 1975.[85]

Focusing on the levels of support these women received and contemporary representations of these disputes illustrates how racism combined with sexism to fragment working-class unity during this period. These disputes were unsuccessful because the unions involved were unwilling to support the workers or even acknowledge how racial discrimination represented a problem within their workplace. The workers faced further hostility from white workers within their local communities. The National Front held regular demonstrations within the area, whilst readers' letters to the *Leicester Mercury* provide further evidence of racist attitudes expressed at an everyday level towards Asian workers seeking better pay and conditions.

> I am sure there is not another country in the world (including their own) where Indians are treated as well as they are here. They ought to be thankful that we are a tolerant race until roused as Hitler discovered.
>
> These immigrants, they were not forced to come and live here and the majority are much better off than back home, but if they don't like the way we run this country why don't they go back home?
>
> A firm that employs over three quarters of Asians on their workforce can hardly be accused of racial discrimination! I would suggest that it is the white people being discriminated against.
>
> From the accusation of racialism made by the Asian strikers against their employer and against their trade union, from their refusal to accept the proposal of a Labour MP, and from the demands of the Indian Workers' Association that the laws of this country be altered in favour of Asians, one feels that they do not want either integration or equality; they want to be an elite.[86]

The prevalence of such attitudes meant that disputes involving Asian workers were understood as protests against racial discrimination in a manner that eclipsed the sexism that Asian women also experienced. WLM publications attempted to draw this out by asking Asian women about their experiences, but there was limited evidence that participation in these disputes led to transitions in their practices or thinking about gender relations. Significantly, the *Leicester Mercury* coverage of the Imperial Typewriters dispute did not once acknowledge the gender pay gap between workers at the factory. Yet it is crucial not to dismiss the importance of these disputes in a manner that perpetuates the myth that migrant women were docile or passive. The fact they took action was important and did raise awareness of the poor conditions and racism that migrant women faced in British workplaces. The decision to strike was driven by the demand to be treated with respect in the workplace; as Pearson *et al.* put it, 'as the result of cumulative experiences of injustice based in large part on the discordance between their perceptions of themselves as women and as workers formed as much by their experiences of migration, and their class dislocation, as by any overt racist and discriminatory practices'.[87] Future research must pay more attention to the economic and cultural constraints on their ability to change how their work was organised. The existence of such constraints, and different migratory histories, clearly distinguished the political identities of black and South Asian female workers' from those of white working-class women during this period in a way that needs to be explored further in the future.

Working-class consciousness and citizenship in 1970s England

Finally, it is important to recognise that women's workplace activism occurred at a time when working-class people were asserting their rights more explicitly in workplaces across Britain. The average number of working days lost to strikes grew from 3.3 million lost on average each year in the 1950s to 3.6 million in the 1960s, before rapidly increasing to 12.9 million annual days lost on average in the 1970s.[88] Todd suggests that the spike in militancy between 1965 and 1975 in particular, which saw an average of 2,885 strikes each year, constituted the most radical wave of industrial unrest Britain had experienced since the 1920s.[89] Understanding the relationship between workers' collective action and their political consciousness was a major concern for labour historians, industrial relations scholars and sociologists during the 1970s.

Whilst some interpreted the wave of militancy as a surge in class consciousness, the general consensus was that militancy was driven by the demand for higher wages. This was in response to wage stagnation in the 1960s, followed by steep price increases during the 1970s after the devaluation of the pound in 1968 and the oil crisis of 1973.[90] The more general histories of the period have attempted to link the widespread industrial action to the developing consumer society, arguing that workers wanted higher wages to purchase colour televisions, foreign holidays and freezers, as opposed to having any political motivation.[91] For example, popular historian Alwyn Turners suggests 'trade unions were not revolutionary institutions but precisely the opposite; despite the rhetoric … the function of trade unions was to achieve an accommodation within a capitalist society to the advantage of its members, and there was little appetite for anything else'.[92] On the left, Eric Hobsbawm at the time warned against confusing militancy with class consciousness and claimed that disputes during this period largely focused around sectional wage demands that divided rather than unified the working class.[93]

There have been more nuanced attempts to understand the motivations behind workplace militancy during this period. In 1984, Richard Hyman concluded that 'strikes bear no necessary relationship to political radicalism; nevertheless they remain of vital importance as expressions of resistance to the dominant repressive trends of our time'.[94] Industrial action may not have radicalised the individuals involved, yet that does not mean it did not alter their perception of the world and their place within it. As Jack Saunders points out, industrial disputes have often been studied in terms of their economic and political effects, whilst workers' values, ideas and collective cultures underlying such action has been taken for granted.[95] Selina Todd's work illustrates that industrial action was orchestrated on the shop floor, rather than by trade union officials, and in many cases was a last resort that spoke of workers' disillusion with their leaders as much as their employers.[96] Florence Sutcliffe-Braithwaite makes a similar point, suggesting militancy is better understood in relation to a decline in deference, rather than a rise in individualism, as workers increasingly refused to subscribe to a moral order legitimating their subordinate position and asserted a basic demand for egalitarianism instead.[97] This is particularly relevant to female workers who were more likely to engage in unofficial action. Existing studies highlight how female workers' trade unionism was inhibited by the unskilled, part-time and irregular nature of their work and the adversarial attitudes of male trade unionists wanting to maintain their breadwinner wage. However, importantly they reveal how women often organised in spite of this and actively resisted exploitation unofficially and informally.

Women's workplace militancy should be understood within this wider context in which working-class people were expressing desires for greater personal autonomy and self-determination – what Robinson et al. describe as a growth in popular individualism.[98] Women were increasingly determined to define and assert their individual rights, identities and outlooks at a time when the state was redefining its relationship with female workers through equality legislation. Examples of women's workplace militancy show female workers understanding and articulating their rights and status as citizens in new ways. Matthew Grant argues that citizenship is a difficult concept to get a handle on because politicians and intellectuals generally rejected the term. In a context of full employment and the expanded welfare state, there was a sense that political rights and social citizenship were secure. He suggests that whilst people were less likely to engage with a formal register of social and political rights, they were more likely to engage with citizenship discourse in their everyday lives – through conversations about education, race, voluntarism and political activism – all of which involved thinking and talking about what it meant to be a citizen.[99] The rest of this book argues that industrial disputes also provide a window on to how experiences at work had a crucial effect on women's ideas about citizenship as a status and practice. Just because strikes might not have radicalised the individuals involved does not mean their concerns should be ignored.

A distinction is often made in studies of women's political citizenship – either implicitly or explicitly – between women's role as wage earners and caregivers. Catriona Beaumont's work on women's activism and associational culture in 1950s shows how middle-class women asserted their rights and pursued equality by adopting the rhetoric of citizenship rights and duties, which often meant emphasising the importance of women's role as mothers and housewives and rejecting a feminist identity.[100] The rest of this book considers how the increasing prevalence and normalisation of working motherhood (which was enabled by the growth in part-time work) from the 1960s influenced this distinction – between the role of mother and worker – in the minds and self-understanding of working-class women themselves.

Conclusion

This chapter has argued that a shift in public debates surrounding women's work was taking place in Britain from the late 1960s to the end of the 1970s. As women's work became 'normalised' by the end of the 1960s, public debate increasingly focused on women's employment experiences and gender inequality in the workplace. Women's workplace participation was less likely to be understood as a social problem. Policy makers, trade unions, social scientists and feminist activists were more concerned with the causes and consequences of women's unequal position in the labour force. These debates did not necessarily result in a coherent or easily identifiable public understanding of women's rights and gender inequality; there existed multiple contested understandings. Yet it is clear that women grew up in this period with different expectations to their mothers. The overarching change was this movement from understanding women as economic dependents to economically independent workers. The rest of this book considers how working-class women contributed to this shift, but also identifies the implications of this shift for working-class women's political identity and sense of self. The key point is that paid work occupied an increasingly important place in women's claims to citizenship. How one interpreted their position in the labour market, their perceived opportunities to sell their labour and their individual experiences in the workplace was crucial in shaping one's broader understanding of the world and their place within it – as well as their capacity to change it.

Notes

1 Abrams, 'Liberating the Female Self'; H. McCarthy, 'Gender Equality' in P. Thane (ed.), *Unequal Britain: Equalities in Britain Since 1945* (London: Continuum UK, 2010).
2 McCarthy, 'Gender Equality', p. 117.
3 These figures are from J. Martin and C. Roberts, *Women and Employment: A Lifetime Perspective* (London: Department of Employment and Office of Population Censuses

and Surveys, HMSO, 1984) quoted in Shirley Dex, *The Sexual Division of Work: Conceptual Revolutions in the Social Sciences* (Brighton: Harvester Press, 1985), p. 3. The shortcomings with women's employment statistics are well known. Figures for part-time work in Britain have only been available since 1961, and census enumerators often missed casual work, or work performed part-time by married women. Jane Lewis suggests that although the precise degree of growth in married women's employment is unclear, there was an observable shift in the manner in which married women became formally attached to the labour market after the Second World War. See Lewis, *Women in Britain*, p. 66 or Dex, *Division of Work*, p. 5.
4 Lewis, *Women in Britain*, p. 65.
5 J. Lewis, 'Women and Social Change in Britain, 1945–1995' in Jonathan Hollowell (ed.), *Britain Since 1945* (Oxford: Blackwell Publishers, 2003), p. 264.
6 Lewis, *Women in Britain*, p. 81.
7 S. Brooke, 'Gender and Working Class Identity in Britain During the 1950s', *Journal of Social History*, vol. 34, no. 4 (2001), pp. 773–795, at p. 774.
8 Figure from West, 'Introduction', p. 1; Jane Lewis also argued that the average hourly pay of all women did not improve between 1975 and 1980 in Lewis, *Women in Britain*, pp. 80–81.
9 See C. Smart, *The Ties that Bind* (London: Routledge, 1984), p. 26.
10 Lee Downs, *Manufacturing Inequality*.
11 S. Bruley, *Women in Britain Since 1900* (Basingstoke: Palgrave Macmillan, 1999), pp. 163–164.
12 Figures from Census, quoted in Bradley, *Men's Work, Women's Work: A Sociological History of the Sexual Division of Labour in Employment* (Cambridge: Polity Press, 1989), p. 169.
13 Figures from Simon Crine and Clive Playford, 'From Rags to Rags: Low Pay in the Clothing Industry' (Report by Low Pay Unit, November 1982), p. 3.
14 T. Martin-Lopez, *The Winter of Discontent: Myth, Memory, and History* (Liverpool: Liverpool University Press, 2014), p. 30; J. Cook and S. Watt, 'Racism, Women and Poverty' in Caroline Glendinning and Jane Millar (eds), *Women and Poverty in Britain* (Brighton: Wheatsheaf, 1987), pp. 53–73.
15 McIvor, *Working Lives*, p. 279.
16 Brooke, 'Gender and Working Class Identity'.
17 C. Langhamer, 'Feelings, Women and Work in the Long 1950s', *Women's History Review*, vol. 26, no. 1 (2017), pp. 77–92, at p. 78.
18 It is important to remember that regional differences meant that certain regions like Lancashire had a stronger tradition of women working alongside men after marriage.
19 H. McCarthy, 'Social Science and Married Women's Employment in Post-War Britain', *Past and Present*, vol. 233, no. 1 (2016), pp. 216–217.
20 Smith-Wilson, 'A New Look at the Affluent Worker', pp. 216–217.
21 R. Brown, 'Women as Employees: Some Comments on Research in Industrial Sociology (and Postscript)' in D. Leonard and S. Allen (eds), *Sexual Divisions Revisited* (London: Macmillan Press, 1991), pp. 153–178.
22 *Ibid.*, p. 172.

23 R. Martin and J. Wallace, *Working Women in Recession: Employment, Redundancy, and Unemployment* (Oxford: Oxford University Press, 1984), p. 2.
24 Pollert, *Girls, Wives, Factory Lives*; P. Hunt, *Gender and Class Consciousness* (London: Macmillan Press, 1980); M. Glucksmann, *Women on the Line* (London: Routledge and Keegan Paul, 1982); J. Wajcman, *Women in Control: Dilemmas of a Workers' Cooperative* (Milton Keynes: Open University Press, 1983), p. x.
25 J. Scott, S. Dex, H. Joshi, K. Purcell and P. Elias, 'Introduction' in J. Scott *et al.*, *Women and Employment: Changing Lives and New Challenges* (Cheltenham: Edward Elgar, 2009), p. 3.
26 J. Cronin, *Labour and Society in Britain, 1918-1979* (London: Batsford Academic, 1984), p. 194.
27 Martin-Lopez, *Winter of Discontent*, pp. 29-30.
28 Equal Opportunities Commission, 'Women and low incomes: a report based on evidence to the Royal Commission on Income Distribution and Wealth' (1977), p. 15.
29 McCarthy, 'Social Science'. See also M. Savage, *Identities and Social Change in Britain Since 1940: The Politics of Method* (Oxford: Oxford University Press, 2010); J. Lawrence, 'Social-Science Encounters and the Negotiation of Difference in Early 1960s England', *History Workshop Journal*, vol. 77, no. 1 (2014), pp. 215-239.
30 Boston, *Women Workers*.
31 Cunnison and Stageman, *Feminizing the Unions*, p. 28.
32 *Ibid.*
33 The TUC's WAC was established in 1930. This was comprised of sixteen members of affiliated unions, five of whom were elected by the unions involved, whilst the remaining eleven members were appointed directly by the TUC General Council. This formal structure remained in place until 1978 and, according to Breitenbach, meant that the WAC was dominated by men. As an advisory body, it had no policy-making power and could only advise the TUC on the interests of female workers. See Boston, *Women Workers*, pp. 149-161 and E. Breitenbach, 'A Comparative Study of the Women's Trade Union Conference and the Scottish Women's Trade Union Conference', *Feminist Review*, vol. 7 (1981), pp. 65-86.
34 S. Rowbotham, 'The Beginnings of Women's Liberation in Britain', in *Dreams and Dilemmas: Collected Writings* (London: Virago, 1983), pp. 32-33.
35 Cunnison and Stageman, *Feminizing the Union*, p. 29.
36 Coote and Campbell, *Sweet Freedom*, p. 156.
37 S. Brooke, *Sexual Politics: Sexuality, Family Planning and the British Left from the 1880s to the Present Day* (Oxford: Oxford University Press, 2011), p. 197.
38 Brooke, *Sexual Politics*, pp. 197-199.
39 Boston, *Women Workers*, p. 334.
40 A full account of the proliferation of positive action from trade unions towards female workers can be found in Coote and Campbell, *Sweet Freedom*, pp. 155-158.
41 There were 166 delegates from 48 unions and 12 trade councils at the 1969 annual women's conference. By 1976, this had increased to 232 delegates from 51 unions and 25 trade councils. See TUC Library Collections, London Metropolitan University, HD 6661: TUC Women's Conference Annual Report, 1969, p. 36 and TUC Women's Conference Annual Report, 1976, p. 37.

42 Breitenbach, 'A Comparative Study', p. 78.
43 The advisory status was eventually dropped in 1986. *Ibid.*, p. 78.
44 Coote and Campbell, *Sweet Freedom*, pp. 144–149.
45 Rowbotham, *The Past is Before Us*, pp. 165–166.
46 See: Rowbotham, *The Past is Before Us*, Chapter 13.
47 S. James, *The Perspective of Winning* (London: London Wages for Housework Committee and Falling Wall Press, 1976), pp. 21–24.
48 S. James, *Women, the Unions and Work ... or What Is Not to be Done* (London: London Wages for Housework Committee and Falling Wall Press, 1972), pp. 1–16.
49 A. Wise, 'Trying to Stay Human', *Red Rag*, no.3, February 1973, pp. 2–5.
50 'Striking Progress 1972–1973', *Red Rag*, no. 5, August 1973, pp. 22–24.
51 N. Thomlinson, *Race, Ethnicity and the Women's Movement in England, 1968–1993* (Basingstoke: Palgrave Macmillan, 2016).
52 *Ibid.*, pp. 49–53.
53 'The Shell Centre ... Waiting for Action', *Shrew*, vol. 3, no. 9, December 1971, p. 6.
54 S. Alexander, 'The Night Cleaners: An Assessment of the Campaign', *Red Rag*, no. 6, - Winter 1973/4, pp. 3–7.
55 Interview with Sheila Rowbotham, 14 June 2013.
56 *Women's Voice* is available online via Marxists' Internet Archive, www.marxists.org/history/etol/newspape/womens-voice-uk/index.htm (accessed 1 March 2018).
57 *Women's Voice*, no. 1, July/August 1972, p. 2.
58 *Women's Voice*, no. 3, November/December 1972, p. 3.
59 *Women's Voice*, no. 14, January 1975, pp. 4–5.
60 *Women's Voice*, no. 2, September/October 1972, p. 11.
61 *Women's Voice*, no. 14, January 1975, p. 4.
62 Glucksmann, *Women on the Line*, pp. 1–2.
63 Wajcman, *Women in Control*.
64 Pollert, *Girls, Wives, Factory Lives*, p. 233.
65 Glucksmannn, *Women on the Line*, p. 163.
66 *Ibid.*, p. 164.
67 *Ibid.*, p. 165.
68 See for example, Thane, 'Women and the 1970s'; E. Meehan, 'British Feminism from the 1960s to the 1980s', in H. Smith (ed.), *British Feminism in the Twentieth Century* (London: Edward Elgar, 1990).
69 McCarthy, 'Gender Equality', p. 113.
70 Rowbotham, *The Past is Before Us*, p. 152.
71 E. Homans, 'Visions of Equality: Women's Rights and Political Change in 1970s Britain' (Unpublished PhD Thesis, University of Bangor, 2014), p. 9.
72 *Ibid.*, p. 102.
73 L. McDowell, *Working Lives: Gender, Migration and Employment in Britain, 1945–2007* (Hoboken: Wiley, 2013), p. 135.
74 *Ibid.*, p. 135.
75 For full accounts of the Grunwick dispute see: J. Dromey and G. Taylor, *Grunwick: The Workers' Story* (London: Lawrence and Wishart Press, 1978); J. Rogaly, *Grunwick* (Harmondsworth: Penguin, 1977); J. McGowan, 'Dispute, Battle, Siege, Farce?

- Grunwick 30 Years On', *Contemporary British History*, vol. 22, no. 3 (2008), pp. 383–404.
76 A. Wilson, *Finding a Voice: Asian Women in Britain* (London: Virago, 1978), p. 70.
77 McDowell *et al.*, 'Striking Narratives', pp. 595–619.
78 *Women's Voice*, no. 4, January/February 1973, p. 11.
79 *Ibid.*, p. 11.
80 *Ibid.*, p. 12.
81 For an accounts of this dispute see Wilson, *Finding a Voice*, pp. 56–59; R. Ramdin, *The Making of the Black Working Class in Britain* (Aldershot: Ashgate Publishing, 1987), pp. 271–280.
82 Cited in Wilson, *Finding a Voice*, p. 58.
83 *Ibid.*, p. 56.
84 'How the Asian Ladies of Leicester Won the Day', *Leicester Mercury*, undated newspaper cutting available online via University of Leicester Special Collections, http://specialcollections.le.ac.uk/cdm/ref/collection/p16445coll2/id/4567 (accessed 3 March 2018).
85 *Women's Voice*, no. 14, January 1975, p. 5.
86 *Leicester Mercury*, undated newspaper cutting available online via University of Leicester Special Collections, http://affectivedigitalhistories.org.uk/files/12702/contentdm-333.pdf (accessed 9 March 2018).
87 R. Pearson, S. Anitha and L. McDowell, 'Striking Issues: From Labour Process to Industrial Dispute at Grunwick and Gate Gourmet', *Industrial Relations Journal*, vol. 41, no. 5 (2010), p. 412.
88 Aldcroft and Oliver, *Trade Unions*, p. 92.
89 Todd, *The People*, p. 275.
90 C. Wrigley, 'Industrial and Labour Relations', in Hollowell, *Britain Since 1945*, pp. 432–438; C. Wrigley, 'Industrial Relations' in N. Crafts, I. Gazeley and A. Newell (eds), *Work and Pay in Twentieth Century Britain* (Oxford: Oxford University Press, 2007), p. 218.
91 See for example D. Sandbrook, *State of Emergency: Britain 1970–1974* (London: Penguin, 2011) or A. Turner, *Crisis? What Crisis? Britain in the 1970s* (London: Aurum Press, 2008), Chapter 4.
92 Turner, *Crisis? What Crisis?* p. 87.
93 E. Hobsbawm, 'The Forward March of Labour Halted', *Marxism Today* (September 1978).
94 Hyman, *Strikes*, p. 238.
95 Saunders, 'The Untraditional Worker'.
96 *Ibid.*, p. 287 and p. 298.
97 Sutcliffe-Braithwaite, *Class, Politics and the Decline of Deference*, pp. 30–32.
98 Robinson *et al.*, 'Telling Stories', pp. 268–304.
99 M. Grant, 'Historicising Citizenship in Post-War Britain', *The Historical Journal*, vol. 59, no. 4 (2016), pp. 1187–1206.
100 Beaumont, *Housewives and Citizens*.

2

The Ford Sewing machinists' strike, 1968, Dagenham

On 7 June 1968, the 187 female sewing machinists at Ford's River Plant in Dagenham, Essex, walked out of their factory and 'into the pages of history' as they went on strike against sex discrimination in their job grading.[1] Ford had introduced a new wage structure in 1967 that separated the workforce into five standard grades, ranging from the least skilled Grade A, which included non-production workers, to Grade E, which comprised the most skilled craft jobs. The sewing machinists, who produced car-seat covers, were placed in the second-lowest, semi-skilled B grade. They believed they were entitled to the higher C grade because of the levels of experience and training required to perform their work. They argued that the company undertaking the job evaluation scheme failed to recognise the skilled nature of their work because it was performed by women, and they voted to strike until Ford regraded them.

The strike lasted for three weeks and brought Ford's entire British production line to a standstill. The women gained official support from the National Union of Vehicle Builders (NUVB) and Amalgamated Union of Engineering and Foundry Workers (AEF). They were joined by the 195 women at Ford's Halewood plant in Merseyside after two weeks. The dispute was resolved when Ford asked Barbara Castle, the Secretary of State for Employment and Productivity, to intervene and 'do whatever it takes' to persuade the women to return to work.[2] Instead of recognising the sewing machinists' demand for skill recognition, they were offered a 7 per cent pay increase, a court of inquiry into their grading grievance and the promise of equal pay legislation in the future. As a result, although the women did not gain the regrading they desired, the strike has been seen as a landmark in British industrial relations, widely associated with prompting the 1970 Equal Pay Act, which made pay discrimination on the basis of gender illegal.

Consequently, the strike occupies a key position in the historiography of feminism and women's trade unionism in Britain.[3] It is generally associated as a turning point in British attitudes towards women's work and gender equality.[4] Feminist activists identified the strike as an important moment in the formation of the WLM.[5] It has also been cited as evidence of the effects of women's growing presence within the labour movement.[6] The strike is an unusual example of an industrial dispute from the post-war period that has publicly been remembered, even celebrated, for its national impact. The idea that the strike was a decisive victory in women's fight for equal pay was popularised by Stephen Wooley and Elizabeth Karlsen's 2010 feature film *Made in Dagenham*, which has been adapted into a West End musical. The film was a box-office hit and has been described as a 'feel-good movie' that portrays the strike as a progressive campaign for women's rights that acted as a direct catalyst for the Equal Pay Act.[7] The subsequent publicity generated by the film has proceeded to weave the place of the dispute firmly within the public history of women and gender equality in Britain. Gregor Gall wrote in the *Guardian* in 2010,

> But make history the Ford women machinists did. Their action was the inspiration for the Equal Pay Act 1970 ... the Dagenham women workers were among those that laid the foundations for something bigger – women starting to play a much fuller part in deciding how their workplace relations were determined.[8]

From the opposite end of the ideological spectrum, the *Daily Mail* claimed the women 'changed the course of British history by going on strike in 1968, demanding the same wages as the men and paving the way for the 1970 Equal Pay Act'.[9]

Such accounts have failed to consider the impact of the strike upon the sewing machinists themselves. Whilst not necessarily denying the wider impact of the strike, by focusing on how it influenced equality legislation, the WLM and the representation of women in the labour movement, the existing literature has centred on its effects on women who worked outside Ford at the expense of the sewing machinists' own interpretation of the strike's outcome. Although former sewing machinists have been interviewed in the press about their experiences of the strike since the production of the film in 2010, the extent to which they felt their militancy allowed them 'to play a fuller part in deciding how their workplace relations were determined' and the position of the dispute within these women's life stories are still to be explored. This is significant considering they interpreted the initial outcome of the strike as a defeat at the time and had to wait until 1985 to have the skilled nature of their work recognised after another seven-week strike (which is analysed in Chapter 5). The sewing machinists' disappointment with the strike's outcome was captured in an interview with shop steward Lil O'Callaghan in 1978 when she reflected,

> We mucked it up. We should have left it open to fight another battle on another day. ... The girls felt they were in B Grade because of sex discrimination. It wasn't the money, it was the principle involved – our skill was not recognised, and we are skilled. Today we still feel it isn't fair.[10]

Looking back on the strike in 2013, a former worker named Gwen expressed a similar view to me:

> I mean really Fords had won, if we're being honest, after we had gone back to work Fords had won because we never got our grading. We hadn't got what we wanted. ... All they had given us was a rise. And not an equal pay rise, not equality.[11]

This failure to analyse the personal meaning of the strike within the participants' life stories raises issues about how class and gender inequality in the past are publicly remembered and interpreted, and whose memory of such inequality is accepted and portrayed in the public sphere. It is a literal example of the 'Hollywood epic view' of history, which emphasises the individual's capacity to produce social change whilst downplaying the fact that they do so within conditions not of their choosing. The women's continued experience of class and gender inequality after their strike spoils the 'feel-good' narrative and is thus ignored.

This chapter offers an original account of the dispute from the perspective of the women involved. It is original because it locates the strike within participants' life stories; it foregrounds their own understanding of why they engaged in the strike and their judgements of its outcome. It accounts for the women's perception of the strike as a defeat and explains how they reconciled this with the public memory of it as a victory for equal pay. For my interviewees, this involved constructing narratives that emphasised their agency but also accounted for the gender and class constraints that characterised their experiences of work and trade unionism, and limited the impact of the strike on their sense of self until the production of the film.

Context

Each dispute examined in this book was shaped by the local context in which it took place. Dagenham was one of the largest housing estates in the world, and Ford represented one of Britain's largest employers with a turbulent history of industrial relations. Ford moved its original factory from Manchester to Dagenham in 1926. The Essex town represented an ideal location due to the ready supply of unskilled and unemployed workers who had moved into the newly built Becontree Housing Estate.[12] The London County Council built 27,000 houses there between 1921 and 1932 in response to the housing shortage in London's East End at the end of the First World War.[13] In 1963, Dagenham's population was 90,000, and Ford employed 35,000 people.[14]

A significant proportion of British people moved from inner-city urban districts to new suburban housing estates during the interwar period.[15] Post-war sociologists were particularly concerned with understanding the effect of this process on working-class people's lives.[16] Some initially felt the transition disrupted family and kinship networks in 'traditional' working-class communities and led to isolation and aloofness in new housing estates. Between 1958 and 1959, Peter Wilmott interviewed almost 900 residents in Dagenham seeking to identify the social patterns that had evolved among the first generation to grow up there.[17] Wilmott found that the town had developed from an isolated 'dormitory' that suffered from a lack of industry, services and transport links into a vibrant community that maintained similar patterns of sociability, kinship networks and political attitudes as 'traditional' working-class communities from where many of Dagenham's first residents had migrated. 'Dagenham is the East End reborn' wrote Wilmott, as he expressed surprise at the levels of affection residents showed for a place he also described as a 'monstrosity in town-planning'.[18] For Wilmott, Dagenham remained a 'one class' town in 1963 and continued to be distinguished by its lack of a civic centre, which he believed inhibited associational culture.[19] However, he concluded that the residents of Dagenham had built a way of life they enjoyed because they had access to local employment and affordable housing that enabled them to spend time with their family and neighbours and pursue leisure activities.[20]

The women I interviewed were part of this first generation to grow up in Dagenham and the surrounding area. The local context was particularly important for understanding the position of the strike in my interviewees' life stories. They all spoke positively about growing up and working in Dagenham at the time of the strike and contrasted this to the sense of insecurity they felt existed in the town at the time of the interview in 2013. Sheila was born in Dagenham in 1936 after her parents had moved from Poplar, East London. Her father worked at Briggs Motor Bodies and Ford. Sheila left school when she was fourteen years old and worked as a sewing machinist producing overalls and jeans at a local factory. She moved to Ford when she was twenty-one and stayed until she retired when she was fifty-five.[21] Vera was born in 1930. She had also left school at the age of fourteen and worked as a sewing machinist in a clothing factory in London. She moved to Ford at the age of thirty-six after the birth of her third child and stayed there until she retired when she was sixty-one. Eileen was born in west London in 1929. She began working as a machinist in a toy factory when she was fourteen years old. She started working at Ford in 1947. She married a fellow worker from Ford in 1950 and had one child in 1954. She returned to Ford when her son went to school and eventually retired in 1985. All three of these women grew up in Dagenham and had lived there for their entire lives. Gwen had a slightly different personal history. She was born in 1931 in Natal, South Africa. She married in 1955 and moved to Dagenham in 1957 with her husband and her mother. Gwen also left school when she was fourteen and worked as a bespoke tailor. She chose to leave Natal and move to Dagenham to be closer to her sister who moved to London in 1955. Gwen emphasised how happy she felt moving to England; she 'fell in love' with it, and spoke about how much she had enjoyed working and living in Dagenham. Between 1957 and 1960, Gwen had three children and her mother moved into her family home, which enabled her to begin working at Ford in 1962 until 1989 when she took early retirement to look after her husband, who was suffering with kidney failure.

It was noticeable that paid work was central to the stories my respondents told, not just about themselves but about Dagenham as a place. I asked the former machinists about their memories of living in Dagenham in the first group interview:

> **SHEILA:** Well in them days you could walk out of one job and into another.
> **VERA:** There were so many jobs about.
> **EILEEN:** No one had to be out of work.
> **GWEN:** There were factories everywhere in Dagenham.
> **EILEEN:** And if you wanted a job, you just walked out and the next day you found another one.
> **VERA:** But I mean every place had machining. I can't believe it now.
> **EILEEN:** There's nothing up there now.[22]

In a second interview, Eileen reflected, 'No it's all closed down now. It's a few warehouses and Tesco's, Sainsbury's, that's all there is isn't it? ... B&Qs. It's all warehouses isn't it?'[23]

Aside from the choice of work, another positive aspect of living in Dagenham that my respondents commented on to contextualise the strike was the availability of affordable housing. In the first group interview, Gwen explained that 'all of us had just started buying our homes when we went to work, didn't we?'[24] Vera was twenty-six and Eileen was thirty-one when they bought their first homes. In the second interview, Gwen remembered, 'We found this house and we have been there ever since so that shows that we are quite happy ... £2,000 we paid for our house. You wouldn't believe it now would you?'[25] My respondents' perception of housing availability illustrated how they believed the strike occurred in a context that was significantly different from the present (prior to the introduction of right-to-buy in the 1980 Housing Act, two-thirds of homes in Barking and Dagenham were owned by the council).[26] For example, in the first group interview Vera talked about how her adult grandchildren could not afford to move from their parents' home but 'did not give any money up'. The women collectively disapproved of this because 'it wasn't teaching them any responsibility', 'did not give them any independence' and meant 'they didn't know anything about money'.[27] Gwen went on in the second interview to point out that this was not the responsibility of the grandchildren themselves:

> [It] was a terrible shame because when they built all those lovely council houses and of course what happened? Thatcher said you could buy them, didn't she? And that was the end of Dagenham really because all the houses were sold, weren't they? I mean when you think, my mother-in-law had a lovely council house ... they'd been there 15 – 20 years and they were offered the house for £11,000. ... Now, those people have sold those houses two or three times and look at the money they have made on it. And they're not building the places for those who can't afford it.[28]

The language the women used to describe how Dagenham had changed is important for understanding where they position the strike in their life story. The strike occurred in a context that appeared to them as significantly different to the present context from which they remember it. They associated the strike with a period when 'no one had to be out of work'; when 'we had a good cinema'; when 'they built all those lovely council houses' and when 'we used to have good times'. By contrast, today's Dagenham from which they remember the strike is 'empty' and 'all closed down'; 'the jobs are not here anymore' and it is 'very hard for young people' because 'there's no work, there's no nothing', which means 'they can't get on'. They thought of 'the thousands that used to work at Ford' and compared them to 'only 2,000 in the engine plant now'; they discussed the long-service men being made redundant at the time of the interview, like Gwen's son, and how 'he has had to accept it'.[29] This narrative of loss the women chose to talk about in the interviews contrasts with the popular narrative of the 1968 sewing machinists' strike as a moment when these women gained something.

The women used this description of local change to make sense of their individual and collective assertiveness during the strike. In a context of full employment, the availability of stable work was central to this story. Wilmott's study in 1963 suggested that Ford was synonymous with Dagenham to outsiders from the town. Twenty per cent of his male interviewees and 6 per cent of his female interviewees worked in the car plant.[30] He believed that 'virtually everybody knows someone, among relatives or neighbours, who works there', which is reflected in my interviewees' testimony.[31] Wilmott also found that nearly two-thirds of his interview sample worked locally, which had a positive effect on community ties; however, he suggested that the lack of a civic centre and long distance between amenities meant 'the people of Dagenham, when they are not at work, opted to stay at home'.[32] Wilmott made this point to illustrate the contrast between inner-city and suburban life, and the increasing 'home centred' nature of working-class life in general. However, this point also emphasises the importance of the workplace as a site of sociability for women and men living in Dagenham. It became clear in my interviews that paid work was crucial to my respondents' stories about Dagenham, but also about themselves – not just in terms of their role as economic providers, but also through the friendships and work culture they established collectively. During both group interviews, the women continued to speak positively about their personal experiences of work as well as their collective work culture to contextualise the strike and explain why it happened and what it meant for them.

Experiences of work

The former sewing machinists I interviewed all emphasised how important their work had been to their sense of self. They considered their militancy in 1968 as a demand to have that personal significance recognised, publicly and materially. Work was central to these women's lives and had been since they left school as young women, as mothers, and when they were older and looked after their own parents. It was the norm. As the women talked about their experiences of working at Ford, three key stories emerged that could be identified with their subjective motivations for going on strike.

The first story was that the women enjoyed their work and had created a strong collective culture, which was important for implementing the strike. For example, Sheila explained that she enjoyed working at Ford because 'I made some really good friends', whilst Vera replied, 'I suppose that's what we went to work for, wasn't it?'[33] For Gwen, 'I enjoyed it. I mean getting out of the house when you had children, you know you'd think oh it's a different sort of life isn't it? You'd meet other people, you'd join in.'[34] It was described as a 'happy shop'; 'We used to go on outings ... and we used to have a real laugh.'[35] Vera summarised, 'I enjoyed it anyway. ... Most of us did. ... It was a happy place wasn't it? I wasn't miserable.'[36]

They enjoyed work because of the social aspects and friendships they made there. But it would be wrong to over-emphasise the satisfying nature of work. For example, Sheila pointed out, 'Some of the supervision was a bit of a pain in the backside, but they always are aren't they?' and 'the conditions we worked in were appalling. How hot it was and the rain used to come in; no joke, it was a couple of old aircraft hangers.'[37] Vera remembered, 'You were tired weren't you?' and you were feeling under pressure because 'you *had* to complete so many an hour' and 'the time and motion man used to stand there and watch you.'[38] There was also antagonism between workers: Vera described the woman who sat in front of her as 'as the worst person you could ever be with' and Eileen 'hated' one of their shop stewards because 'she used to treat you like a little girl'.[39] But it was generally agreed that 'we had a good time' and 'at Fords I can honestly say that they left you alone as long as you were doing your work', which offers a clue towards these women's collective identity and desire for autonomy.[40] Whilst work could be restrictive and conflictual, the women also emphasised their individual agency throughout the interviews, which was epitomised by Eileen's statement: 'It was a job for life for me ... I did enjoy it yeah otherwise I wouldn't have stayed there 31 years!'[41]

Paid work was a central aspect in these women's lives. Work was not a temporary experience between school and marriage and children; rather, work was a continuous feature of the life course. A consequence of this was that the women had cultivated a robust work culture with high levels of solidarity and strong bonds between each other that were necessary for the workers to collectively assert themselves. Again, they contrasted their experience with the present. Sheila said, 'I don't think that [women] have the opportunity that we had. Because the industry, or whatever, the groups of people that used to work together aren't there anymore.'[42] Vera agreed, 'That's it. There's no big place like where we worked.'[43] Sheila came back to this at the end of the interview and said

> people don't sort of gather together and raise these issues anymore as regards to just us women, I don't know about men, but women don't seem to get together any more ... and well there's not the work there for a start there, is there? For women to be together like they were and ... if you can get a big lot, a great number of people to be with you, and shout with you, and make yourself heard, it makes a big lot of difference.[44]

Work was a central site of sociability and a key space where they could 'gather together' and 'stand up for themselves' alongside their friends. It was their work culture and solidarity developed from their shared experiences, in ways that they felt women no longer 'had the opportunity' to do so in the present, that was central to their own understanding of why they went on strike.

The second story my respondents shared about their work experiences emphasised their material interests and role as economic providers across their life course – an aspect of their lives they felt was undermined when Ford regraded them. My interviewees all stressed they had worked from leaving school at the age of fourteen. Vera remembered, 'Yes I needed the money ... but I used to give my mother all my money.'[45] Similarly, Gwen pointed out that 'I came out of school straightaway. I couldn't afford to do anything else, I had to go to work because of circumstances, you know? My mother couldn't afford to keep me at home.'[46] Sheila said, 'I would have liked to have been a hairdresser, but my mum said sorry Sheila, I need your money on the machine, and that was it. I was the eldest one out of my sisters and so she needed my money, even though it was only £2.12s a week.'[47] The sense of 'having' to work, 'needing' to work and being 'unable to afford to do anything else' because of 'circumstances' remained with the women throughout their lives.[48]

An attraction of working at Ford was the higher wages. According to Sheila 'it was pretty well paid, with regards to other work.'[49] The higher wages were an important theme repeated from the group interview with Vera, Sheila and Violet in 2006 as part of the TUC Voices from the Workplace project. Sheila said the wages 'seemed like a lot to me because I had been on piecework prior to moving to Fords. If I didn't work, I didn't earn. When we went to Ford we were on time work, so whatever we done we got a weekly wage. So that was a bonus for us, for me anyway. I could go out and buy a pair of shoes.'[50] The women also spoke about how they needed their wages for informal childcare. A worker named Violet suggested her wages 'went on the oven, the children and I paid my sister because she had my youngest one from Monday morning to Friday night'.[51]

The high wages and material interests of the sewing machinists were reflected on at the time of the dispute. The *Observer* approvingly quoted TGWU research officer Eileen McCullough when she said, 'Most of Ford's strikers are married and the reason for this new found militancy is that increasingly households are budgeted on a double wage packet ... with higher standards of living and large hire-purchase debts, women are finding that they have to work just to keep up.'[52] However, the representation of the sewing machinists as affluent workers was also used to undermine the moral legitimacy of their claim to equal pay. Publicly, the *Barking and Dagenham Post* felt 'it is clear the strike is for *more* rather than *equal* pay'.[53] The *Sunday Telegraph* described the sewing machinists as 'among the highest paid manual women workers' and claimed 'it has long been recognised the most militant agitation comes not from women on the lowest rates of pay from those who receive only a little less than men ... they are demanding 5d. an hour more which is their idea of equality'.[54] Privately, a member of the Court of Inquiry who investigated the women's claim pointed out in a personal letter to the chairman of the investigation that the women had received a 'remarkable' and 'completely unproductive' 35 per cent wage increase that gave them 'considerable monetary gain' as a result of the new grading system.[55] The sewing machinists' comparatively high wages – in relation to other women – were used to suggest that their concept of equality was flawed and to delegitimise their militancy.

By contrast, my respondents did not connect their motivations for working or going on strike with the pursuit of a luxurious lifestyle. Gwen explained,

> My wages just went into the house. ... you never sort of had it for yourself. It was never your money. It was always put together for the family expenses. I mean you didn't go out to work just to clothe yourself. It was to help with the house. And I think most women did didn't they?[56]

Sheila summed up their attitude towards work, pointing out, 'It wasn't pin money; it was for making a better life for yourself and your family'.[57] The strike was partly for recognition of this personal significance. My respondents' experience of 'having' to work from a young age to contribute to their family income represented a source of pride and was crucial to shaping their sense of citizenship. During the first group interview, the women compared their need to work to their perception of people in the present. Gwen pointed that she had never claimed income support from the state and had always had to work to look after her family, which she did not believe was the same today.

> Well in fact, with me being a widow, but having family and having to look after my mum, a few of us went up to social services – I mean today it's so easy to get money isn't it? I mean be honest – but there was a few of us ... we were in the same boat, but nobody got any money from social, but I mean today you can go and then you get hand-outs left, right and centre.[58]

Whilst such stories were clearly influenced by modern discourses surrounding 'benefit cheats' and 'scroungers', the former sewing machinists I interviewed distinguished their own experience from their perception of the present to emphasise the central aspect that work had played in their lives. Their experience of working in a job they enjoyed, learning a skill and earning enough to support themselves and their families was central to how they thought about themselves politically. This was encapsulated most clearly by Sheila, who explained that 'we all vote Labour; we're working-class, so you do don't you? I ain't got anything to conserve, everything I've got I earned! You have to work for it don't you?'[59]

The final theme the women continuously drew on when talking about their work was the skilled nature of their job. They had worked throughout their lives, acquired skills and passed tests. 'Not everyone could machine', as Eileen explained to me.[60] Working at Ford represented a 'proper job', and the women wanted that to be recognised. It is now well established that the strike was originally over grading instead of the issue of equal pay. Some have suggested this meant the strike had little to do with gender because male and female workers had common grading grievances, not just in Ford, but in manufacturing industries across Britain.[61] Yet it was clear, both from contemporary sources and oral history interviews, that the sewing machinists believed gender was the key reason for why their skill had not been recognised. In one of the few instances when the sewing machinists' shop steward Lil O'Callaghan was invited to speak at the court of inquiry, she explained,

> Ford motor company applies for experienced sewing machinists – experienced. You go in and you get a trade test, on three different sewing machines. ... So I feel a machinist should be classed with a skill which would take the women to be in grade C. ... also the females are on the same personal allowances as the males. Where do we stand? One minute we are classed as females, the next minute we are classed as males.[62]

Sex discrimination was central to the sewing machinists' understanding of why they went on strike. In a statement submitted by the AEF as evidence to the Court of Inquiry, a union representative wrote,

> The feeling of women members is that they have not been treated equal to men over a long period of time. ... It was a great disappointment to our sewing machinists when they found that, even under this new wage structure, their skill at the trade did not find the recognition it surely deserved, particularly since the Sewing Machinists were about the only production workers in any trade to have to pass a trade test.[63]

During my own group interviews, the women emphasised the personal implications of having their work devalued. Vera explained, 'I mean I'd had lessons and done machining ever since I had left school. And you had to have that experience before they would even think about employing you, didn't you?'[64] Sheila agreed,

> I mean you had to prove to them that you could machine, didn't you? And so if you have to sit down and show that you can machine and you've had to have experience for two years, it proved that we were skilled at what we were doing ... but they wouldn't accept it.[65]

The regrading and the strike itself made the women acutely aware of not only the training and knowledge required to perform their work but also the significance of their contribution to the company's production process. For example, Gwen said,

> I mean when we were changing seats from a like Cortina to an Anglia, or whatever car they were producing at the time, I mean you were given the new samples, and you had to get on with it and put the new seat together. ... I mean nobody used to sit down and show you how to make all of these seats did they? They didn't know, did they? The designer used to come up from down the road somewhere and speak for a bit and say that goes there, that goes there and then leave.[66]

Looking back on the strike today, the former sewing machinists continuously emphasised how they had brought production at the company to a standstill because it affirmed the indispensable nature of their role.[67] Sheila explained that 'Fords just didn't want to acknowledge us as skilled, just a handful of women – but that handful of women brought Ford motor company to a standstill, you can't sell a car without a seat!'[68] At the time, the strike was born out of the women's desire to assert the value of their work, but looking back on it today, their activism was also an example of their agency.

The distinction between demands for equal pay and skill recognition is not particularly helpful because the two issues are inherently linked. Speaking at the time, shop steward Lil O'Callaghan felt the grading system was unfair because 'we are classed as females'.[69] The AEF pointed out at the time, 'For this union, the question in dispute is that of equal pay and equal grading ... the underlying cause of the dispute is a feeling of sex discrimination amongst all women workers'.[70] A popular trope used by both my interviewees and my respondents in other subsequent interviews was 'there was a man going around with a broom earning more than us. We could get up and use his broom but he couldn't sit down and use our machine.'[71] This simple rhetoric encapsulated the reasons why the women felt they had gone on strike. The point was that the women wanted the value of their work recognised both subjectively and materially on the basis of the nature of the work performed, rather than the gender of who was performing it. However, according to Sheila, 'it was all turned around which was to everybody else's convenience wasn't it?'[72] Sheila's testimony indicates a sense of lost control in relation to the articulation of their demands at the time, but also in terms of how it has been publicly remembered specifically as a victory for equal pay. The following section explores the sewing machinists' experiences of trade unionism, and further considers the influence of their union officials on how the women articulated their demands at the time.

Experiences of trade unionism

Trade unionism and workplace militancy represented a central aspect of working at Ford, Dagenham. Ford refused to recognise trade unions until 1944 and generally avoided major disputes due to relatively high wages and levels of employment.[73] This changed when Ford took over the well-organised workforce from Briggs Bodies in 1952. They developed a strong Joint Shop Stewards Committee with a plant-wide newspaper that sold 50,000 copies in 1960.[74] Graham Turner suggested in 1963 that 'the stewards at Ford are still the most powerful group of their kind in the country'.[75] Ford's grading restructure in 1966 represented an attempt to curtail the high levels of militancy by inviting trade union officials to play an active role in developing a new wage structure based on a nationwide job evaluation scheme.[76] Jack Saunders recently argued that the high level of conflict over factory conditions and management prerogative fostered a collective culture at Ford that shaped workers' expectations and the practices they adopted in response to management failure.[77]

The sewing machinists were also representative of the growing number of women joining trade unions during this period. My respondents had all joined the NUVB as part of a closed-shop agreement before being incorporated into the TGWU. The high frequency of unofficial strikes was a key characteristic of working life at Ford, which they commented on and distinguished as their experience from the women analysed in the other cases considered in this book. It was suggested that 'Fords were known for their strikes ... it would happen so often'.[78] Eileen agreed, 'We had a lot of strikes. We were used to it'.[79] Gwen said, 'I think I was at Fords for 3 months before I went on my first strike', and Sheila remembered returning from holiday to a nine-week strike.[80] Eileen suggested that 'everybody was in a trade union then'; her brother was a shop steward in the engine plant, and she described her husband as 'a union man until the day he died'.[81] Although none of the women I interviewed was active in the union, they wished to emphasise that industrial activism represented an important part of their work culture and everyday lives. They explained that 'there was a group of women who always went to meetings and always kept up with everything, didn't they?'[82] Sheila agreed, 'Yeah your shop steward used to call a meeting in your lunch hour and used to tell you what the situation was.'[83] When it came to their grading grievance in 1968, Sheila explained, 'They were still ignoring our wants, and that was when we said enough is enough. We had a meeting over the canteen didn't we? And we voted that we should stand up and fight, which is what we did.'[84] The narration of the actual decision to go on strike reflects how the sewing machinists solely made the collective decision to 'stand up and fight' from the shop floor, exclusive of their male trade union leaders.

The militant collective culture at Ford and social practices that went with it – electing shop stewards, attending meetings, voting and going on strike – were accepted as a normal part of their work experience, both retrospectively and at the time, and not considered extraordinary. However, the sewing machinists' previous experiences of workplace conflict had ambiguous effects on their attitudes towards trade unionism. On the one hand, they stressed how important it had been (and continued to be) to have a union 'backing us up' and suggested that 'we wouldn't have won anything without them'.[85] Eileen said, 'If you had any trouble, you had the union behind you and they used to fight for you.'[86] On the other hand, they felt that the high frequency of strikes limited the impact of their dispute. Sheila said, 'Let's be honest, at Fords we went on strike so many times even though ours was just for us, it didn't meant a thing to the local people.'[87]

The women differentiated between their own interests and those of their union. This became clear from the way they assumed ownership of the strike in the oral history interview. Sheila said,

> The difference in this strike really for us was that it was *for us*. We were always in and out on some strike or other, but not for ourselves. The men came out for different things and laid us off without even thinking about it, so it didn't mean a thing to us except that when we done it, it was for us.[88]

They felt they lacked control in the past when they had been on strike over wage issues that they regarded as unrelated to their own situation. 'We didn't have a choice whether we wanted to or not; we had to go', explained Gwen.[89] To my respondents, their strike represented the first time that they assumed their own voice within the factory, which was evidenced by the way they referred to it as 'our' strike throughout the interviews. It was a moment in their memory when the unequal nature of the bargain between male and female union members was brought into sharper focus.

The women's relative autonomy from the wider activities of their union officials was evident in contemporary accounts of the strike. The NUVB reported, 'The strike which took place on the 7 June was not called by the union but having regard to the frustration experienced by our members and our conviction in the justice of their claim the union recognised the dispute at a meeting held on 13 June.'[90] The AEF described the strike as 'a spontaneous reaction', which reflects a longer trend of women's workplace resistance being represented as the product of short-term self-interest or irrational behaviour.[91] The Dagenham sewing machinists illustrate the continuation of this historical trend of women organising autonomously within the formal labour movement. On 17 June, the union officials representing the women agreed on the women's behalf that they would return to work the next day in exchange for an investigation into their grading by a 'fact-finding committee'. The following morning, eighteen women picketed the factory with posters supporting their strike. Ford's personnel manager suggested that this 'extraordinary refusal to get this situation back on the rails' demonstrated the union's lack of authority over its members.[92] In a letter signed by the 'Women workers at Fords of Dagenham' to Harold Wilson, they wrote,

> You can call all the enquiries you wish, the women at Fords have the backing of a great number of MPs. We will not go back to work. We are fighting a great fight for Equal Pay for women. We at Fords have

started the ball rolling. Our unions are backing us, funds are coming in, we're all out for battle. Fords is the beginning, soon it will be every industry in Britain out because of us women at Fords. We will force you to give us all equal pay, or strike with our unions' blessings. We're sorry for Fords, we're sorry for the men out of work, but more sorry for ourselves. It's all for us now. Some women may be hard up. We'll help them from our growing funds.[93]

The women believed their union's support was important and necessary for sustaining their action. Yet the women made the decision to strike independently of their union, and understood their struggle, both at the time and retrospectively, as being for 'us' and 'ourselves', as well as other women in industry.

The sewing machinists I interviewed had quite ambiguous judgements about their experiences of trade unionism. Although they did not criticise the NUVB, they talked about conflict with their union officials. Gwen acknowledged that 'not all the union members were keen on us'.[94] Bernard Passingham felt the women 'got totally ignored' and 'that some of our national officials, they didn't agree with what we were doing, they didn't think it was right. And so we, particularly myself, had to push them aside'.[95] The sewing machinists differentiated between their own interests, represented by their shop stewards, and those of their union officials who they held responsible for sacrificing their grading concern in favour of the issue of equal pay. Sheila pointed out in the first group interview, 'The union's officials got it changed, they must have changed it because we never had any say so in it did we?'[96] There was evidence of this at the time. Charles Gallagher, the NUVB National Official, wrote to the company on two occasions suggesting that equal pay might be a 'compromise solution'.[97] Passingham explained, 'Women's rate of pay was abolished. To be quite honest, I thought we'd done a good job but the girls didn't think so. As a union, we thought we'd done a great job because we'd got equal pay.'[98]

The result was that the sewing machinists saw their strike as a defeat at the time, and doubted their political efficacy until they saw the film. Eileen pointed out, 'Nothing changed for us. Being honest, nothing changed.'[99] Sheila said, 'I think we could have stayed out longer. I put my hand up to stay out, we had a vote in the morning and some others did as well, but ... I didn't want to go back but it was only a handful of us that put up our hands.'[100] Eileen suggested that 'when we went back to work, everything was forgotten, we carried on working and ... it's only since the film that all this stuff has come up.'[101] The union were held partly responsible for this failure. In 2006, Sheila said,

The union worked it ... I was just really really annoyed that what we eventually came out for was just swept under the carpet you might say ... I suppose in a way we did start off the equal pay for women, but it wasn't even equal pay then, men were still getting more than us. When equal pay come round again, then that's when you realise that maybe you started something quite big. But not at the time, no.[102]

The sewing machinists' memories of the strike reveal the uneven balance of power in the relationship between the women and their male trade union officials. On the one hand, the women stressed their agency: 'we decided that we had to do something', 'we were tired of it being turned down all the time', 'we stood up and fought'. They were aware that it was their own action, their own decision to stand up and strike which had forced their union officials to act and negotiate the equal pay deal on their behalf. On the other hand, the way they spoke about their experiences of trade unionism also revealed the lack of control they felt they had over their experiences of work: 'they turned it around' and 'they worked it', but also 'without them we couldn't have got it' and 'we definitely wouldn't have got it without the union'.

Writing in 1978, Henry Freidman, the union convenor who represented the sewing machinists, dismissed their criticism of the strike's outcome and labelled their concerns about skill recognition as 'local', 'transient' and 'craft consciousness', suggesting that they lacked the 'high degree of political and social awareness required to appreciate the wider concept of equal pay'.[103] Such a dismissive and patronising attitude towards the women's grievance reflects the relationship between the sewing machinists and their union during this strike, and perhaps explains why the women I interviewed felt less inclined to play a greater role within the NUVB after the strike was over, or to identify the union as a meaningful influence on the way that they thought about themselves politically. Interviews with the shop stewards involved in the strike may have offered a different perspective on the extent to which it influenced their experience of trade unionism. However, the sewing machinists I interviewed perceived the strike as a women's fight, organised by women, for women, and did not think that it changed their own relationship with the trade union movement.

Feminism and gender relations

Contemporary debate centred on the strike as an industrial relations issue, rather than as part of a progressive campaign for equal pay. Equal pay was described as a 'smokescreen' to disguise the unions' disregard for the company's grievance procedure.[104] Ford suggested the strike was unconstitutional and represented a 'critical problem for the British economy'.[105] Much of the national and local press focused on the implications of the disruption for male workers and the national economy. Nevertheless, the sewing machinists' collective action was widely understood as being novel because it involved female workers.

In the meeting of the National Joint Negotiation Committee (NJNC) to discuss the dispute, personnel manager Leslie Blakeman said, 'We appreciate the peculiar circumstances of the case.'[106] He also described the situation as 'both disturbing and confusing'.[107] When the NUVB district official first raised the sewing machinists' complaint with management in August 1967, he apologetically acknowledged, 'We appreciate that generally this type of work is carried out by female operators.'[108] As the dispute unfolded, the emotional state of the workers was frequently referred to: The *Ford Bulletin* suggested that 'there has been lots of emotional talk about equal pay for women';[109] a union official said in a meeting with the company, 'our view is that there is a great deal of emotion in this dispute' and another explained 'you are dealing with women who are emotionally involved'.[110] It was suggested that the Court of Inquiry must account for the 'present emotional atmosphere'.[111] The management and unions responded to the strike differently because it involved female workers. They saw it as 'emotional' because of the personal sense of injustice and moral justification for their demands; the women were perceived to misunderstand the 'logic of equal pay'.[112]

There was also a sense from contemporary representations that the strike represented a wider shift in the way that female workers thought about themselves as women. The AEF justified their breach of the company's grievance procedure because they suggested that the existing machinery for dealing with grading disputes was unable to deal with 'such a radical change, required by our women members brought with radical action'.[113] *The Times* claimed the strike indicated a 'new and distinctly more militant stage' in the battle for equal pay. It went on to suggest that 'the biggest barrier left may be the attitude of women themselves ... If only more felt like the Ford ladies ... most of the obstacles would vanish.'[114] The *Observer* declared, 'Not since the match girls' strike of 1888 has a group of women pressed strike action as militantly as Mrs Lil O'Callaghan and her sister Ford machinists'.[115] It went on to identify 'a distinct change of mood' as a result of the example set by the 'Dagenham girls' and a 'sharpened awareness by women of the injustice of their position'.[116] Shirley Summerskill, Labour MP for Halifax, hailed the sewing machinists' action in Parliament on the day the Equal Pay Act was passed in 1970, saying

> I do not like strikes any more than anyone else, but those women had to take really forceful action to achieve this principle. Like the early pioneers for women's suffrage, they faced abuse, misrepresentation and ridicule, but they demonstrated their great industrial power and their vital role in the export drive, so that politicians and public alike were made to realise that working women are indispensable to the economy.[117]

The sewing machinists also felt their strike defied expected norms at the time. In the 2006 interview, Violet pointed out, 'Rosie Boland was the shop steward at the time; she got a lot of bad letters from men, from farmers, firemen, from women who didn't work.' She also mentioned that her husband opposed her personal involvement in the strike.[118] The *Barking and Dagenham Post* claimed that male workers were angry, and the *Romford Times* suggested they had caused inconvenience by defying the NJNC's recommendation to return to work.[119] Sheila explained, 'Because we were women, it wasn't the done thing at the time. We really frightened them.'[120]

Although the sewing machinists' action was perceived to be unusual, it was less unexpected for the women themselves. The shop steward Lil O'Callaghan identified herself as a feminist and said 'I have been fighting for the cause of women for as long as I can remember.'[121] As can be seen from the previous section, the women had been involved in numerous workplace disputes in the past. They were well organised and not afraid to stand up for themselves. Although the actual processes and practices involved in organising the strike were not particularly new, the difference was that this time 'it was for us'. 'It was 'a women's strike over a women's issue', and they were 'fighting for themselves' and speaking with their own voice. The women believed they had their own distinct interests shaped by the gendered devaluation of their labour. Yet it was clear from the interviews that they did not perceive the strike as part of a wider rupture in their experience and perception of gender relations.

The strike has often been considered a formative moment within the WLM. The formation of the NJACCWER at a meeting organised by the machinists' NUVB district official Fred Blake on 28 June 1968 is the main evidence to support the notion that the dispute 'reignited' the women's movement.[122] The group was described as 'a minority affair ... several shades paler than revolutionary red' by the *Guardian*.[123] It called on all trade unions and the government to promote equal pay as a statutory right. On 18 May 1969, the NJACCWER organised a 1,000-strong rally in Trafalgar Square calling on the government to pass equal pay legislation. The press commented on the diversity of the group's membership, pointing out that there were women from the Labour Party and the Conservatives, as well as organisations as different as the International Marxist Group and the Status of Women Committee.[124] Writing in 1972, Sheila Rowbotham suggested that the group had an 'impressive existence on paper' but did little campaigning in practice.[125]

Whilst the group has been cited as a meeting place that provided a starting point for the development of a network of WLM groups in the following period, my respondents did not feel that this was something they were a part of. Gwen told me:

> The trouble is that all these groups never bothered with us did they? Cos we were asked this a little while ago … if we had been fighting with the feminists, and really to tell the truth, I know they had a lot of walks and they got together in London at one time but they never ever thought to invite us did they? I mean once our strike was over I think we were just forgotten about until the film come out.[126]

Eileen agreed that it was not until recently that she became aware of the wider movement fighting explicitly for women's rights during the 1970s. She spoke about a meeting she attended in London after the film with 'all kinds of groups that had been fighting for equal rights', but pointed out '[I] had never heard of them until we all got together … it seems as though women are always fighting on their own all the time'.[127]

To the Ford women, although they felt that they had been fighting for women's rights and equality by demanding to have the skill of their job recognised, they felt that they were doing so on a personal level. Sheila said, 'I've got a bit more militant now, rather than then' and Eileen exclaimed 'We were stupid weren't we? We didn't take no notice did we?'[128] During my second interview, Gwen explained,

> Everybody said: 'feminists', you know? And I said: 'well, I didn't even think of myself as one until we realised what we had done.' I was just a working mother and working wife fighting for her rights [laughs].[129]

There was a divergence between the public memory of the strike as a milestone event in the evolution of the women's movement, and the sewing machinists' self-understanding over 'what we had done' and how it affected their political subjectivity. In 1972, Sheila Rowbotham suggested the sewing machinists had provoked women on the left to 'feel that they could do something' and made it easier for women within trade unions to discuss women's specific oppression.[130] By contrast, Eileen said to me, 'speaking honestly, it was just like another day's work and then we just carried on. ... Nothing changed for us. Being honest ... I didn't think that we achieved all that much until everything that's happened.'[131] Sheila said, 'You know, you want equal rights and things like that, and that was the time to do it', but as Vera suggested, 'it didn't happen did it? It didn't happen.'[132] Gwen said, 'Really we hadn't got what we had wanted. ... Fords just didn't want to acknowledge that we were skilled.' The important point here is that 'equal rights' did not materialise for these women. Their experiences of work and trade unionism continued to be characterised by unequal gender relations in ways that made them doubt their political efficacy, and reluctant to associate their militancy with feminism.

This raises a significant tension with the historical meaning of the dispute. On the one hand, it is a great example of people making change from below: the strike stimulated a significant debate about equal pay in the labour movement, and its impact on equality legislation and early members of the WLM is undeniable. On the other hand, the former sewing machinists' interpretation of the strike as a defeat illustrates the ineffectiveness of the strike's resolution and how the government, company and unions involved militated against them to preserve the interests of capital and of male workers in the factory. The value of their work was not recognised until 1985.

Conclusion

The Ford sewing machinists' strike is a useful starting point for this book. The strike was optimistically hailed as a turning point symbolising a new era of equality for the growing number of female workers and trade unionists in Britain. However, the extent to which the strike represented a wider change in the experiences of female workers becomes less clear after interrogating the impact of the strike on the sewing machinists themselves. The women's demand to have the value of their specific 'female' skills recognised and appropriately remunerated represented an active attempt to alter their position within the power relations of the factory. However, their voice was heavily diluted by their trade union officials and employers, as well as the government and lawyers, who continued to rely on legal and managerial definitions of the sewing machinists' work and preserved the gendered hierarchy of labour by offering them equal pay on a formal basis, instead of recognising their specific skills as women. The women had to 'fight' for the next seventeen years before their skill was recognised. The consequence of this was that my respondents felt the strike had very little impact on their subsequent experiences of work, which made it difficult for them to reconcile their personal memories with their newfound role as history makers. This tension between women asserting their autonomy and agency during workplace disputes and the material reality of their unequal power relationship with employers and trade union officials, which characterised their subsequent experiences of work, was a key theme that was to influence respondents' testimony in the case studies that follow.

It is important not to downplay the importance of the sewing machinists' activism and its impact on forcing the government to address the issue of equal pay, yet to celebrate it as a victory of and for 'all' women and 'all' workers sidelines the protagonists' own reading of events and continues to deny their specific agency in the present. The government's failure to recognise 'work of equal value' in the Equal Pay Act meant that many women continued to fight for their own right to be paid an equal wage with men by going on strike in the following decade, as the next chapter will demonstrate.

Notes

1 J. Friedman and S. Meredeen, *The Dynamics of Industrial Conflict: Lessons from Ford* (London: Croom Helm, 1980), p. 1.
2 *Ibid.*, p. 96.
3 Rowbotham, *The Past is Before Us*, pp. 165–166; Segal, 'Feminist Impacts and Transformations', p. 171; Smith, 'The Women's Movement, Politics and Citizenship', p. 283; Bouchier, *The Feminist Challenge*, pp. 56–57.
4 Thane, 'Women and the 1970s', p. 154; Holloway, *Women and Work*, p. 208; McCarthy, 'Gender Equality', p. 111.
5 S. Rowbotham and B. Campbell, 'Class Struggle in Britain', *Radical America*, vol. 8, no. 5 (1974), p. 66; Coote and Campbell, *Sweet Freedom*, pp. 9–10; Pollert, *Girls, Wives, Factory Lives*, pp. 12–13.
6 Boston, *Women Workers*, p. 279; Wrigley, 'Women', p. 55; Todd, *The People*, pp. 288–289.
7 T. Brown and B. Vidal (eds), *The Biopic in Contemporary Film Culture* (London: Routledge, 2014), pp. 11–13.
8 G. Gall, 'Women didn't just Strike in Dagenham', *Guardian*, 4 October 2010.
9 M. Paton, 'The Dagenham Girls: Meet Four Friends whose Crusading Work Inspired a New Film', *Daily Mail*, 11 September 2010.
10 Interview with Lil O'Callaghan and Rose Boland in Friedman and Meredeen, *Dynamics*, p. 176.
11 Interview with Gwen, Eileen, Sheila and Vera, 21 June 2013.
12 Friedman and Meredeen, *Dynamics*, p. 54.

13 P. Willmott, *The Evolution of a Community: A Study of Dagenham After Forty Years* (London: Routledge and Kegan Paul, 1963), p. 6.
14 *Ibid.*, p. 13.
15 Mark Clapson, 'Cities, Suburbs, Countryside' in Paul Addison and Harriet Jones (eds), *A Companion to Britain: 1939-2000* (Oxford: Blackwell, 2005), pp. 60-61.
16 *Ibid.*, p. vii. See also S. Todd, 'Affluence, Class and Crown Street: Reinvestigating the Post-War Working Class', *Contemporary British History*, vol. 22, no. 4 (2008), pp. 501-518.
17 Willmott, *Evolution of a Community*, p. ix.
18 *Ibid.*, at p. 9, at p. 110 and at p. x.
19 *Ibid.*, Chapter 2, Chapter 7 and Chapter 9.
20 *Ibid.*, Chapter 8.
21 Interview with Gwen, Eileen, Sheila and Vera, 21 June 2013.
22 *Ibid.*
23 Interview with Eileen and Gwen, 11 August 2015.
24 Interview with Gwen, Eileen, Sheila and Vera, 21 June 2013.
25 Interview with Eileen and Gwen, 11 August 2015.
26 'Safe as Houses', *Guardian*, 30 September 2008.
27 Interview with Gwen, Eileen, Sheila and Vera, 21 June 2013.
28 Interview with Eileen and Gwen, 11 August 2015.
29 Interview with Gwen, Eileen, Sheila and Vera, 21 June 2013.
30 Willmott, *Evolution of a Community*, pp. 16-17.
31 *Ibid.*, p. 17.
32 *Ibid.*, p. 89.
33 Interview with Gwen, Eileen, Sheila and Vera, 21 June 2013.
34 *Ibid.*
35 *Ibid.*
36 *Ibid.*
37 *Ibid.*
38 *Ibid.*
39 *Ibid.*
40 *Ibid.*
41 *Ibid.*
42 *Ibid.*
43 *Ibid.*
44 *Ibid.*
45 *Ibid.*
46 Interview with Eileen and Gwen, 11 August 2015.
47 Interview with Gwen, Eileen, Sheila and Vera, 21 June 2013.
48 Interview with Eileen and Gwen, 11 August 2015.
49 Interview with Gwen, Eileen, Sheila and Vera, 21 June 2013.
50 Interview with Violet Dawson, Sheila Douglas and Vera Sime for film produced by Sarah Boston for TUC in 2006. Film available at TUC Archives, London Metropolitan University.

51 *Ibid.*
52 'The Logic of Equal Pay', *Observer*, 30 June 1968.
53 *Barking and Dagenham Post*, 3 July 1968.
54 'Government Anxiety over Ford Women's Dispute', *Sunday Telegraph*, 16 June 1968.
55 Modern Records Centre (MRC), MSS.178/17, Ford Motor Company Limited: dispute with the National Union of Vehicle Builders about the grading of women sewing machinists (inquiry held in June and July 1968), 1965-1968, Letter from J. Grange Moore to Jack Scamp, 9 July 1968.
56 Interview with Eileen and Gwen, 11 August 2015.
57 Interview with Gwen, Eileen, Sheila and Vera, 21 June 2013.
58 *Ibid.*
59 *Ibid.*
60 Interview with Eileen and Gwen, 11 August 2015.
61 S. Cohen, 'Equal Pay – or What? Economics, Politics and the 1968 Ford Sewing-Machinists' Strike', *Labor History*, vol. 53, no. 1 (2012), pp. 51-68, at p. 57.
62 TNA: LAB 10/3312, Court of Inquiry into Strike of Sewing-Machinists Employed at Dagenham Plant of Ford Motor Co Ltd: Transcripts of Evidence (London: HMSO, 1968), pp. 60-61.
63 MRC, MSS.178/17, Statement on Behalf of The Amalgamated Union of Engineering and Foundry Workers Concerning the Present Situation of Women Sewing Machinists Employed by the Ford Motor Company, Gt Britain.
64 Interview with Eileen, Gwen, Sheila and Vera, Rainham, Essex, 21 June 2013.
65 *Ibid.*
66 *Ibid.*
67 *Ibid.*
68 *Ibid.*
69 TNA: LAB 10/3312, Court of Inquiry, pp. 60-61
70 MRC, MSS.178/17, Statement on Behalf of the Amalgamated Union of Engineering and Foundry Workers Concerning the Present Situation of Women Sewing Machinists Employed by the Ford Motor Company, Gt Britain.
71 Interview with Eileen, Gwen, Sheila and Vera, Rainham, Essex, 21 June 2013; Interview with Violet Dawson, Sheila Douglas and Vera Sime for film produced by Sarah Boston for TUC in 2006.
72 *Ibid.*
73 Friedman and Meredeen, *Dynamics*, pp. 54-57.
74 H. Beynon, *Working for Ford* (London: Penguin, 1973), p. 51.
75 Graham Turner, *The Car Workers* (London: Pelican, 1963), p. 139.
76 Henry Friedman interviewed by Kay Fraser, 14 June 1994 in Kay Fraser, *Same or Different: Gender Politics in the Workplace* (Aldershot: Ashgate, 1999), p. 186.
77 Saunders, 'The Untraditional Worker', pp. 239-242.
78 Interview with Eileen, Gwen, Sheila and Vera, Rainham, Essex, 21 June 2013.
79 *Ibid.*
80 *Ibid.*
81 Interview with Eileen and Gwen, 11 August 2015.

82 Interview with Eileen, Gwen, Sheila and Vera, Rainham, Essex, 21 June 2013.
83 *Ibid.*
84 *Ibid.*
85 *Ibid.*
86 *Ibid.*
87 *Ibid.*
88 *Ibid.*
89 *Ibid.*
90 MRC, MSS.178/17, NUVB Vs. Ford Motor Company, Submissions to the Court of Inquiry, Dispute Regarding the Grading of the Sewing Machinists.
91 MRC, MSS.178/17, Statement on Behalf of the Amalgamated Union of Engineering and Foundry Workers Concerning the Present Situation of Women Sewing Machinists Employed by the Ford Motor Company, Gt Britain.
92 MRC, MSS.178/17, Court of Inquiry Company Submissions, 'Detailed History of the Dispute'.
93 TNA, PREM 13/2412, Letter to Harold Wilson from 'Women workers at Fords of Dagenham' (undated).
94 Interview with Eileen, Gwen, Sheila and Vera, Rainham, Essex, 21 June 2013.
95 TUC Interview with Bernard Passingham, 2006.
96 *Ibid.*
97 MRC, MSS.178.17, Company Submissions to Court of Inquiry.
98 TUC Interview with Bernard Passingham, 2006.
99 Interview with Eileen and Gwen, 11 August 2015.
100 Interview with Eileen, Gwen, Sheila and Vera, Rainham, Essex, 21 June 2013.
101 *Ibid.*
102 TUC Interview with Sheila, Violet and Vera in 2006.
103 Friedman and Meredeen, *Dynamics*, p. 181.
104 'The Real Issue', *Ford Bulletin*, 21 June 1968.
105 TNA, PREM 13/2412, Telegram from Bill Batty to Harold Wilson, dated 26 June 1968.
106 RC, MSS.178/17, Notes of Proceedings at a meeting of Ford National Joint Negotiating Committee, Monday 17 June 1968.
107 MRC, MSS.178/17, Company Submissions to Court of Inquiry, 'A Detailed History of the Dispute'.
108 MRC, MSS.178/17, Letter from Charles Gallagher to Leslie Blakeman, dated 4 August 1967.
109 'The Real Issue', *Ford Bulletin*, 21 June 1968.
110 MRC, MSS.178/17, Notes of Proceedings at a meeting of Ford National Joint Negotiating Committee, Monday 17 June 1968.
111 MRC, MSS.178/17, Letter from J. Grange Moore to Jack Scamp, 9 July 1968.
112 'The Logic of Equal Pay', *Observer*, 30 June 1968.
113 MRC, MSS.178/17, Statement on behalf of the AEF workers concerning the present situation of women sewing machinists employed by the Ford Motor Company, Gt Britain.
114 *The Times*, 6 November 1968.

115 'The Logic of Equal Pay', *Observer*, 30 June 1968.
116 *Ibid.*
117 House of Commons Debate, 9 February 1970, vol. 795, col. 976.
118 *Ibid.*
119 'Ford's Lay off 400 Men', *Barking and Dagenham Post*, 19 June 1968; 'Girls Defy Fords', *Romford Times*, 19 June 1968.
120 Interview with Eileen, Gwen, Sheila and Vera, Rainham, Essex, 21 June 2013.
121 'Ford's Lay off 400 Men', *Barking and Dagenham Post*, 19 June 1968.
122 Coote and Campbell, *Sweet Freedom*, pp. 9–10; McCarthy, 'Gender Equality', p. 112.
123 'Mao Mascot at Women's Pay Rally', *Guardian*, 19 May 1969, p. 18; 'Meeting Votes to Keep the Sex War Going', *Guardian*, 29 June 1968, p. 3.
124 'Feminist Ranks Unite to March for Equality', *Guardian*, 18 January 1969, p. 3; Sally White, 'Feminists Meet to Talk Equality', *The Times*, 29 June 1968, p. 10.
125 Rowbotham, 'Beginnings of Women's Liberation in Britain'.
126 Interview with Eileen, Gwen, Sheila and Vera, Rainham, Essex, 21 June 2013.
127 *Ibid.*
128 *Ibid.*
129 Interview with Eileen and Gwen, 11 August 2015.
130 Rowbotham, 'Beginnings of Women's Liberation in Britain', pp. 33–34.
131 Interview with Eileen and Gwen, 11 August 2015.
132 Interview with Eileen, Gwen, Sheila and Vera, Rainham, Essex, 21 June 2013.

3

The Trico-Folberth equal pay strike, Brentford, 1976

The longest equal pay strike in British labour history took place at the Trico-Folberth windscreen wiper factory in Brentford, west London, during the summer of 1976. It began on 28 May when 400 female production workers voted to go on strike to eliminate a £6.64 weekly wage differential between male and female assembly line workers. The assembly line had traditionally been split between an all-female day shift and an all-male night shift. Workers on the night shift had earned an overtime premium on top of a higher 'male' piecework rate. In June 1975, the night shift was eradicated as part of a company's cost-cutting exercise, and male workers were offered the choice between joining the female day shift or taking redundancy. Most of the men took redundancy or moved to a new intermediary shift, with the exception of five men who decided to join the women on the day shift. Those men lost their overtime premium but continued to earn a higher piecework rate than the women who were performing the exact same work alongside them. Such a differential became illegal in 1975 after the implementation of the Equal Pay and Sex Discrimination Acts, and the female assembly line workers demanded to be paid equally.[1]

After six months of failed negotiations, 400 female workers at Trico were led out of the factory by their shop stewards to the neighbouring Boston Manor Park, where they voted unanimously to begin an all-out strike until they received equal pay. They received support from 150 male workers in the factory and the Southall District Committee of the Amalgamated Union of Engineering Workers (AUEW). The strike was made official by the AUEW National Executive after one month, and the women organised an official strike committee, which coordinated strike pay and hardship money and produced a weekly bulletin to inform workers of their progress and dismiss company propaganda. They organised a twenty-four-hour picket of the factory, which attracted widespread support from the labour movement, the radical left and women's liberation groups. It also provided the setting for some intense clashes with strike breakers and the police in what was to be a record breaking hot summer.

Trico argued that the five men working alongside the women represented a 'historical anomaly' and claimed that their differential would eventually be phased out.[2] The management requested an industrial tribunal to justify their case, which was boycotted by the workers on the grounds that only 31 of 110 previous cases had found in favour of women seeking equal pay since the implementation of the act in 1975.[3] The women's rejection of the tribunal sent a message of their intent to the company, who began to dismiss male workers as production was brought to a halt in the strike's third month. The Trico management entered negotiations with the union and on 18 October reached an agreement with the union to implement a common payment-by-results operational rate of pay, irrespective of sex.[4] After twenty-one weeks, the women had defeated the company and won equal pay.

The dispute did not attract as much media coverage as the Dagenham strike, due to the smaller size of the company and the lack of government intervention. Whilst the Ford sewing machinists were heralded for initiating the Equal Pay Act, the Trico workers were regarded as having highlighted the legislation's failure to secure equal pay for working-class women. The *Guardian* claimed that the strike exemplified how 'working women have not benefited fully from the Equal Pay Act because of its loopholes and the way in which it is being interpreted by industrial tribunals'.[5] The AUEW proclaimed,

> The Trico workers were thrown into the forefront of the struggle for equal pay. From the word go, they were determined to end this exploitation of women. They have never shirked the fight, and the part played by the women here will go down in history like the match girls strike.[6]

This chapter will be the first detailed consideration of this strike from a historical perspective.[7] Having discussed the Equal Pay Act's failure to achieve a meaningful reduction in the differential between male and female wages in Chapter 1 and considered the key role that the Ford sewing machinists played in the origins of equal pay legislation in the previous chapter, this case study provides an opportunity to examine how the Equal Pay Act was interpreted and challenged by female workers once it was implemented in 1975. The chapter considers the Trico women's experiences of work and trade unionism. It considers the women's subjective motivations for going on strike, and examines the extent to which they associated the dispute with a shift in their expectations of paid work.

The strike also received a large amount of support from community organisations and political groups, such as the Labour Party Young Socialists, as well as the WLM. The support the Trico workers received from local feminist groups distinguished their experiences from the women at Ford, who went on strike prior to the formation of WLM groups across Britain. The final part of this chapter examines how the WLM attempted to engage with the Trico strikers during this period; crucially, it considers how the women perceived their encounter with feminists, socialists and fellow workers on the picket line and what it meant for their own political identity in the subsequent period. In particular, it considers the extent to which they felt their protest influenced the way they thought about their rights as women.

Context

The strike took place in Brentford, which was heavily industrialised but without the same reputation for worker militancy as areas like Dagenham. Brentford is a town in west London that became incorporated into the Greater London borough of Hounslow in 1965. The Great West Road opened in 1925, forming the main artery linking London with the west of England. The section of road around Brentford was soon known as the 'Golden Mile' because a large number of factories, such as Firestone and Gillette, relocated there due to the good communication links, which provided employment and stimulus to the local economy. There was a ready supply of labour from the London docks and gasworks that entered decline in the interwar period, as well as the large amount of white, rural migrant labour attracted to the area due to the demise of agriculture in the neighbouring countryside and post-war development in cheap housing.[8]

Trico opened in 1927 and was the largest supplier of wiper blades and electronic accessories to the British car industry. The factory eventually relocated to Wales in 1982 after entering a state of decline due to foreign competition.[9] According to my respondents, the company was renowned for paying low wages, and it was common knowledge that it was the only factory on the 'Golden Mile' not to have negotiated equal pay after the implementation of the Equal Pay Act in 1975.[10] There had been no industrial disputes of any note in the factory before the equal pay strike, and the shop stewards frequently commented upon a lack of militancy among the workforce during the strike. A worker named Lisa Parrish said at the time, 'We're not a bunch of militants. Some of the women were definitely anti-union before this started.'[11]

Two of the women involved in the strike expressed similar views in their interviews with me. Sally said, 'Before the strike, Trico didn't have much of a reputation for supporting causes outside of the factory ... no we didn't really support much.' Peggy, who was a shop steward, agreed, 'Well before the strike, if somebody came into Trico's collecting for a strike nobody would be interested, but afterwards it was different.'[12] The Trico workforce had less experience of industrial action compared to the Ford sewing machinists considered in the previous chapter. A consequence of this was that the equal pay strike was perceived as novel at the time and represented a break from the past in the stories told by my interviewees.

Although industrial relations at Trico had been non-conflictual, the surrounding area covered by the Brent and Southall district trades councils had experienced some distinct political battles in the period leading up to the strike. A large number of south Indian and Afro-Caribbean emigrants had settled in the area during the 1950s, attracted by the employment opportunities in the factories and cheap housing. Barbara, who had grown up in the area and chaired the Southall District Committee of the Labour Party Young Socialists at the time of the strike, discussed the mounting tension between white racists and the growing number of migrants moving their families into the area.

> You had the National Front who had organised a march and there were continued attacks on Asian workers in the area around Southall as the area became more Asian ... but in the summer of 76 a couple of thugs stabbed an Asian student in the town and he died. This led to enormous protests against the police and authorities, as people didn't feel protected ... and the Labour party and district trade councils got together and organised a unity march through Southall under the banner of one race – a unity march. This all happened at same time of Trico – so it was an interesting time.[13]

Barbara remembered the growing activism of local groups and progressive trade unionists in the community surrounding the factory.[14] At the time, the *Spectator* described the area as 'fertile soil' for 'communists, socialists and revolutionaries' and predicted a 'long summer of protest' the week before the Trico strike became official.[15]

So whilst the Trico factory had a tranquil history of industrial relations, the area surrounding the factory was heavily politicised at that time. These high levels of local activism were important to the context of this strike in terms of the support that the women received. My interviewee, Sally, explained that the AUEW Southall District Committee had 'a progressive left-wing leadership there at that time, and the whole of that district committee, which wasn't a very big committee, were all progressive and prepared to fight for us'.[16] There were a large number of IS and Labour Party supporters, as well as feminist activists in the area who were keen to offer their support to female workers in a fight for equal pay. This was to have a key effect, not just on sustaining the strike, but also on a personal level for the women involved, as many of the strikers told stories, at the time and in my oral history interviews, about coming into contact with groups of people and ideas on the picket line they had not encountered before. In this manner, the context in which the Trico strike took place was quite different to the Ford sewing machinists' dispute, where the workforce was well organised, but the women felt there was little interest from within the town.

Experiences of work

Similar to Ford, the 400 female assembly line workers at Trico worked in a segregated, all-female section of a manual manufacturing industry, whose work was deemed to be of lesser value than work performed by men. I interviewed Sally, Peggy and Phyllis in a group interview at Sally's home in Ealing in April 2013. Sally was interviewed on a second occasion in June 2013. My respondents told stories that emphasised the importance of their wages as well as the subjective value of their work. Peggy was born in Brentford in 1941 and had lived there her entire life. She explained at the start of the interview

> [I started work] when I was 15, I had several jobs ... I worked at BHS [British Home Stores] when I left school, till I was 19 and then I went to an engineering factory in Brentford, where I met my husband, he started on the same day as me and we got married in 1960, and I started work at Trico the following year.[17]

Paid work was central to her narrative. She went on to say

> I just worked in engineering factories ... and then when I did leave Trico ... in 1982 because I was made redundant ... and went and worked in an office as a administrator and then from there I went to look after people with learning difficulties and I retired from there ... And that's my life really ... [laughs].[18]

Similar to the Dagenham women, Peggy emphasised the importance of her wages. She claimed that the £6.64 differential between male and female wages represented a lot of money to her at the time and said, 'work definitely became more important to me in the 60s because I bought my house in 1965, until then I had lived with my mum, but in 1965 I bought my house and I needed my wages to pay the mortgage'.[19] Phyllis also emphasised the necessity of paid work. She emigrated from Ireland, and claimed to have 'no education', which meant she felt she had worked all her life in order to 'get by and support her family'. She said,

> Where I came from, we used to live on the border in Ireland and I didn't have an education. So [after Trico] I worked in garages, I worked in chip shops, I worked in a launderette, I worked in the trade union club in Acton for a while ... bits and bobs ... I worked as a cleaner as well ... because my husband died very young and I then had to support my daughter so I did everything I could to put her through university. But to do that I had to take anything ... I didn't mind it, but I'm glad to have retired now![20]

Leaving school at the first opportunity and working in a low-paid, segregated labour force in a factory was a common experience shared between the majority of women I interviewed, and stood in contrast to popular conceptions of the post-war period offering new career and education opportunities to middle-class women. For my respondents, paid work was central to their sense of independence, whether that was expressed through buying their own home or providing for themselves and their families. They connected this broader narrative to their motivation for going on strike and to explain the sense of injustice they felt when male workers received higher wages for performing the same work.

Sally had a slightly different trajectory to my other respondents. She was born in Hertfordshire and had lived in Lewisham, Surrey and Norwich before she was fifteen years old. She had what she described as a 'Tory upbringing from Tory parents', before she moved to London in 1969, where she married and became a social worker until 1975, when she decided to go back to college to study for a degree in sociology. During that time, she left her husband and moved into a bed-sit in Ealing. She found work at Trico through the job centre and joined the AUEW immediately. Sally explained the importance of work to her livelihood:

> I needed to get a job ... it was quite a stressful time because of splitting up, and it would have taken ages to get another social work job – you can't just walk into them, it can take a few months, and so at the time there was lots of industry, because this was pre-Thatcher, and they paid much better in the factories, and so I went down the job centre and that day there were two jobs they offered me in local factories. ... So I turned up at Trico and I stayed. Then, six months later, we were all out on strike for equal pay![21]

Sally spoke about the unsatisfying nature of assembly line work, and re-emphasised the material value of women's wages at the time of the dispute. She explained that she chose to work at Trico because 'you could earn a bit more if you worked the hours' by comparison to office and shop work. She also pointed out,

> It wasn't a nice job. It was just people in a factory you make the time go by having a laugh together and the friendships you have and some of the fun you, you *make*. But the actual work is hard and pretty awful.[22]

Similar to the Ford sewing machinists, Sally talked about the collective culture and friendships established by the women themselves that made work worthwhile. She felt this was particularly important for women in the face of patronising attitudes of male managers and co-workers.

> I wouldn't say I really enjoyed it. ... There were some terrible attitudes. There still are for women, but that pin money thing is not now quite the same is it? ... Pin money was not true for the vast majority of women at Trico. You wouldn't do an awful job like that ... there might be one or two whose husbands were working and they didn't have too many outgoings – their rent and stuff – maybe some of that money would go towards holidays – that woman having a holiday and stuff. But no one had a really cushy life.[23]

The Trico workers believed their strike was about having the economic and subjective value of their work publicly recognised. At the time, one worker told *Women's Voice*, 'I've worked here for eleven years altogether. That means that I've made a lot of money for this firm, but I have no security!'[24] Looking back on the strike, my interviewees also emphasised the uneven balance between women's wages and their contribution to the production process. The introduction of five men to the assembly line earning higher wages than the women brought into sharper focus the sex-based devaluation of assembly line work. Sally pointed out in the first interview,

> The management at the plant really did treat the women with contempt, but the women at Trico were all the production workers. All the other workers were just supporting the production. ... But they did treat the women with contempt even though without us there was no production ... having those guys, on the same assembly line, doing identical work, assembling the same thing, and then at the end of the week, if you had worked at the same rate, the same performance they were coming away with approximately £6.50 more than the women in their pay packet. ... and that was incendiary![25]

Sally went on in the second interview to describe this sense of injustice and gradual realisation among the female workforce of their unequal status in the factory:

> I think most of the women realised, particularly the ones who had been there a long while that they worked probably the hardest, some of the hardest of any of the workers in the factory and were very good at their job because sometimes it was noted that women worked faster than machines could do the job and they realised that they were being underpaid for it. So there was quite a lot of resentment towards men in the factory because most of the men – like in the tool room and in the press shop, setters, tool setters – half the time could sit around; they weren't working constantly. On the lines you were working constantly unless it broke down. ... And the men, most men, in return, really the attitude was very contemptuous, towards women.[26]

Collectively, my interviewees constructed a narrative that emphasised how they felt patronised and undervalued as female workers in the build up to the strike. The introduction of five men to the assembly line represented the turning point that brought clarity to a vague sense of injustice they felt before. Sally explained this transition in awareness: 'Once they were working beside you, yeah they had all that additional money, oh that was dynamite, that really was dynamite because ... you have to see an injustice in your face really, don't you? If it's still theoretical or it's somewhere out there ... [it's not the same]'.[27]

The idea that gender equality was 'theoretical' or 'somewhere out there' encapsulated the notion that a broader shift was taking place in the way they thought about themselves as women as political subjects. Ideas about paid work were central to this process; for example, my respondents identified the sewing machinists' strike and the Equal Pay Act as key moments that altered the way they felt about their own experiences of work. But they also situated the strike in a context where they felt their attitudes towards equality outside the workplace were changing as well. Peggy said,

> To be honest ... when I got married in 1960 ... you weren't man and wife in the way you are now ... there wasn't that independence, until the sort of thing that came up in the 1970s with the Equal Pay Act ... I don't think [equal pay] was ever discussed to be honest in the 60s. I think women just went to work and did their job and then went home again. I'd never ever heard it until it was brought into law really. ... In the 70s when it first came out, when the unions said, 'well we're

working at getting equal pay', then it was planted and you realised! But before in the 60s I don't think anybody really used that term. ... And then of course there were Ford's and there were lots of other little equal pay strikes around the country wasn't there?[28]

Sally agreed with Peggy's assertion that she had never really thought about equal pay and women's rights until the passing of the Equal Pay Act and the Ford strike. She said,

> It [equal pay] wasn't on the agenda in the 60s. ... Yes and so it [Equal Pay Act] did help, didn't it? Because the Ford's women if I'm right, when they came out, they were looking to get the rate for the job to do with their grades weren't they? ... And then it focused our minds, even though it didn't help us, it focused our minds on what we needed to fight for.[29]

Phyllis, on the other hand, suggested that society in general was changing during this period in a way that made her feel differently about her rights as a woman.

> I don't think it [equal pay] was ever discussed [during the 1960s], the woman would stay at home whilst the man would go out to the pub and the woman would be minding the kids and doing the housework, but once the 70s came in then maybe ... women got a little bit more of an independence? In the 70s things were changing, times were changing, people were more liberated. ... But maybe it was always the same in London, but it wasn't like that in Ireland so that's how I felt. And women were getting their own little bit of independence and things like that.[30]

The Trico workers I interviewed contextualised their motivations for going on strike by suggesting that the years surrounding the dispute represented a break from the past and a moment of realisation about their experiences as women. They constructed a narrative where the Equal Pay Act represented a key moment that inaugurated an idea about equality that had hitherto not existed in their minds.

Although the women interpreted the period around the strike as a time when attitudes towards women's role as workers were changing, the press coverage and union publications surrounding the strike indicate that public attitudes were less clear. On the one hand, women's increased presence in the labour force, the passage of the Equal Pay Act and increased male unemployment in the early 1970s meant that the importance of female wages to the household economy was increasingly recognised during the Trico strike.[31] For example, an article written for the International Marxist Group's paper claimed,

For a large majority of women at Trico, the strike has highlighted the importance of their earnings – Women don't work for pin money these days, they work to keep their homes together. ... They have sent a message to employers that you can't treat women as cheap labour anymore.[32]

An article in the *TASS News and Journal* suggested that 'the idea that women work for pin money is a myth. Two incomes are now needed to support a family.'[33] The *Guardian* commented that the strike had placed family budgets under strain, saying 'if women did work for pin money there would be little problem, but myths do not pay the rent.'[34]

The press suggested that the strike revealed problems with equal pay legislation. The Equal Opportunities Commission had been established in 1976, but only 31 of 110 industrial tribunals had found in favour of women seeking equal pay, whilst a further 335 had been thrown out of court in the first six months after the Equal Pay Act was implemented.[35] *Time Out* described the strike as the 'most significant happening to highlight the problems with the Equal Pay Act'.[36] The *Sunday Times* observed that the Trico women were 'pushing an open door as dissatisfaction at Barbara Castle's act grew amongst female workers'.[37] The *Guardian* suggested that the women had demonstrated the need to change the wording of the act to recognise women performing 'similar work' to 'work of equal value'.[38] In this sense, the strike gained public recognition of the importance of female wages to household economies and exposed the wider issues surrounding the failure to recognise the specific skills involved in work performed by women in a labour market still segregated by sex.

On the other hand, some accounts of the strike patronised the women and undermined their cause on the basis that their work was secondary to their familial role. The inflationary effects of the £6.50 weekly pay rise required for equal pay were also discussed within the context of the Labour government's incomes policy, largely at the expense of the women's demand to have the value of their work recognised. For example, the *Brentford and Chiswick Times* wrote,

> Superficially it appears to be a straightforward case of a wicked management exploiting cheap female labour, contrary to contemporary thinking and legislation. But if the Trico management is guilty of anything, it is of short sighted humanity ... men made redundant took on new jobs on the production shift with a considerable drop in wages ... the management agreed to allow them to keep their higher piecework rates as a reward. ... It so happened that the 400 other production workers on the day shift were women. It is easy to interpret

men on this line – on a higher rate – as sexual discrimination. It is very obvious that this is not the case ... this is not a chauvinistic defiance, but a fair minded assessment of the issues ... they will not strike a blow for sexual equality, but throw a below the belt punch at the government's fight against inflation.[39]

The local papers continued to support the company, with reports of European rivals taking advantage of the factory's halt in production, the inflationary nature of their equal pay demand and criticism of the women when male workers were laid off in August, suggesting that their irrational protest had 'prevented married men from running their families'.[40] The economic context meant that the women's demand to have the value of their work recognised was sometimes overlooked; instead, they were publicly understood as irrational and connected to some abstract notion of 'contemporary thinking' about equality.

The tabloids also discussed the levels of disruption the strike caused to household relations as much as it affected production at Trico. The *Mirror* reported that 'a bitter equal pay strike by women has threatened to split families', whilst the *Sun* claimed, 'Angry factory girls are on a kitchen sink strike in an attempt to force husbands to support their battle for equal pay. The Men are grumbling about wives refusing to cook dinners or even doing their normal wifely duties'.[41] This quote was repeated frequently in the local press, and the women were continually harassed about whether they were on a 'sex strike' as well.[42] The press continued to trivialise the strike by focusing on the physical appearance of the women on the picket line or discussing it in relation to their sexuality and domestic life.[43] *Time Out* magazine summarised the situation at the time, claiming that the newspaper coverage had 'exploited the "sex" angle while the more mundane reality is that the strikers are expected to go home after a hard day's picketing and cook the family's evening meal'.[44]

The Trico women connected their motivations for going on strike to the personal importance of paid work in their daily lives. They retrospectively associated the strike with a growing awareness among female workers of their unequal status in the workplace and in wider society. Their experience of workplace militancy was distinguished from male workers because they had to contend with public assumptions about their domestic role and levels of skill, which undermined their right to equality. The disapproval in the press also suggested that the women were defying cultural norms, despite the fact that women had fought to improve their conditions in the workplace since the nineteenth century.

Experiences of trade unionism

The official backing and large amount of support the Trico women received directly from their union distinguished my interviewees' experience from the women involved in the case study discussed in Chapter 4 on the Fakenham factory occupation. The AUEW provided strike pay of £9 a week for every striker. It organised delegations of workers to visit factories across Britain and raised £34,644 from its own members, which was used to pay hardship money to women who were struggling financially.[45] The union raised the strike's profile by publishing a weekly bulletin and urged its own members and other unions to support the women on the picket line in its monthly journal.[46] The district official, Roger Butler, and factory convenor, John Inwood, advised the women's strike committee on how to coordinate their action and led the negotiations with the company.[47]

The high levels of support the women received locally and from the wider labour movement were crucial to the strike's success. The solidarity and organisation necessary to sustain the twenty-four-hour picket line for twenty-one weeks should not be taken for granted. The AUEW Southall District Committee printed notices that they issued around British car manufacturers urging workers to blacklist Trico products, and followed this up with letters to branches in Essex and Bedfordshire to investigate workplaces that did not comply.[48] They organised mass meetings throughout the duration of the strike to keep the workforce up to date with negotiation procedures.[49] The Greater London Association of Trade Union Councils (GLATC) organised fundraising events and asked each of its affiliated trades councils to join the women on the picket line to ensure victory in what they perceived as a 'crucial and historic dispute'.[50]

The high levels of organisation and widespread appeals for public support were necessary to combat the opposition from male workers and AUEW members within the factory. The Southall District Committee explained in an appeal for support that Trico was 'only able to maintain a small amount of production through the use of non-union labour and scabs' who 'resorted to breaking our picket line at 3am in the morning with convoys of non-union lorries and with the assistance of the police'.[51] The shop stewards representing the labourers, setters and tool-room workers were reported to the AUEW Executive Committee because they had 'actively worked with the management of Trico to break the official dispute ... and had at many times abused our women on the picket lines and had at least on one occasion caused an injury to a woman shop steward'.[52]

The shop stewards representing the labourers, setters and tool-room workers wrote to Hugh Scanlon, the AUEW General Secretary, voicing their shared objections to the strike:

> It has been requested by many employees at Trico (AUEW members), that the present dispute and the serious consequences that have resulted are not in the best interest of full employment, nor a state of solidarity among our members ... no useful purpose can be served by closing down our place of employment resulting in some 1600 people being out of a job. All this strike has achieved is to split the membership of what was largely a loyal group of trade unionists who can see that this non-issue ... can result only in loss of jobs if the strike continues.[53]

The letter included a petition with 232 signatures of workers who opposed the women's demand for equal pay.[54] In a letter to the AUEW Southall District Committee, the tool-room shop steward described the strike as 'mindless action' that would 'cause endless troubles' and 'does not benefit our real members one iota'.[55] He concluded,

> All this can achieve is to lose members, and I mean long-term members, as against the in and out membership of the women, our hold on them was always tenuous, most of them never see their cards ... I have in past year strived to keep a union shop, even stubborn people who held out for forty years. I got them round to joining by patient pressure, explaining how they would benefit in various ways, and finally achieved a 99 per cent membership. This of course has now been destroyed by this strike action which so many of them could see no clear justification, years of work down the drain![56]

The women did not receive full support from male workers, who perceived equal pay as a 'non-issue', women's union membership as temporary and the strike as a threat to their livelihoods. Peggy mentioned her brother was a 'scab' (but had little else to say about this), whilst Sally described how they also faced opposition from male workers:

> We were still far outnumbered by men, some of them were supportive ... but there were some very reactionary guys working in the factory, some of which were in the tool room and in the press shop and other places. There were some very unpleasant characters. There were some men actually in the National Front. ... I remember on one occasion we were meeting in the park and some of the men who were scabbing on us climbed over the fence and were very threatening towards us.[57]

At the time, the strike committee explained that the opposition and company tactics 'though prolonging the strike and causing terrible hardship to those involved, also had the effect of strengthening the bonds of comradeship of both the strikers and their many supporters'.[58]

The conflict between male and female workers at Trico meant that the women's collective action was distinguished from an 'ordinary' strike and was conceptualised as novel by the unions involved. Female workers were perceived to face unique difficulties; the AUEW Southall District Committee reported that 'many of the women are single, widowed, and unsupported parents. You will understand the urgent need for finance in this dispute.'[59] The GLATC suggested, 'It is very difficult for the women in the dispute to picket at night time and at weekends.'[60] The women's lack of union or 'political' expertise was continually stressed; the chairman of the Brent Trades Council wrote a poem that emphasised the women's lack of experience and the important role of the union in supporting the women:

> The strikers had courage and guts galore but never were in a strike before.
> Courage and guts needs something more to put Trico bosses on the floor
> But the Union Southall Districts a tremendous role did play
> To weld and lead this fighting role as day succeeded day[61]

At the end of the strike, the women's convenor John Inwood suggested the women

> had entered a new world to them and in the early stages were somewhat bemused, apprehensive and not particularly organised. However by sheer courage and endurance they gradually formed themselves into such an impregnable unit that they succeeded in changing the course of society in this country as far as its attitudes towards equality for women was concerned.[62]

The women's lack of organisation prior to the dispute shaped the women's political subjectivity at the time. Shop steward Betty Aitson said in an interview, 'I must admit that we were a very, very inexperienced union. Although I have been a shop steward for 9 years, I've learned more since I came out on strike in 14 weeks I think than I would have learnt in the 15 years I've been in the factory. It's been thoroughly educational to me.'[63] The sense of novelty was reflected in the words of a worker appearing in a contemporary strike bulletin: 'At first there was a kind of disbelief about it all – that we'd need to collect money, to organise. We had to take it into our own hands … at first we suffered from a lack of confidence.'[64]

In the oral history interviews, Peggy discussed her inexperience despite being in the union since 1960 and a shop steward: 'To be honest when I first went out on strike ... I was green. ... But once we got organised, it went so smoothly after that ... but the atmosphere was ... at the beginning, in the first three or four weeks, we didn't really know what we were doing.' Sally agreed pointing out, 'We didn't even get the strike committee together for a while, or there was one but it didn't really function at the very beginning.'[65]

The women's prior lack of union experience contributed to the notion that the strike was 'historic'. It was frequently described as 'an historic struggle for equal pay' or 'the most important going on in the country'.[66] The union assumed responsibility for the strike and almost presented itself as the vanguard of women's rights. For example, one bulletin proclaimed,

> We [AUEW] are leading a strike, which is now recognised as the most major battle for equal pay since the coming into effect of the act – and we have shown what solidarity and a united trade union movement can achieve.[67]

Another bulletin said,

> Our main strength lies in our organisation and collective action. We have justice on our side and when we win we will tell the world: OUR MOVEMENT WON FOR US THESE RIGHTS AND NOBODY WILL TAKE THEM AWAY FROM US.[68]

The opportunity to highlight the failure of equal pay legislation provided the union with a chance to attack the Labour government's incomes policy and assert their right to determine wages through collective bargaining. For example, the AUEW Southall district secretary Roger Butler declared after their victory,

> This is a lesson to the movement on how equal pay can be achieved. It will not be brought about by tribunals. It is only through trade union unity and working-class struggle that justice for women workers will be won.[69]

The AUEW's support for the Trico women indicated the type of success female workers could achieve when they received official backing from their union. It also illustrated how British industrial relations continued to be dominated by men. Similar to the Ford sewing machinists' strike, whilst the original decision to strike was taken by female workers on the shop floor, the dispute was similarly resolved by all-male union officials negotiating equal pay on behalf of female workers. In both cases, the unions involved claimed to have won justice for their members.

The high levels of support and solidarity influenced the Trico women's political subjectivity at the time, as well as my interviewees' retrospective explanations of their motivations, and the effects of the strike on their self-understanding. The women I interviewed had joined the AUEW when they began working at Trico. There was no closed-shop agreement, and Sally suggested that, in total, the factory was 70 per cent unionised, with 93 of the 400 female workers non-members before the strike.[70] Peggy explained that she joined the AUEW in 1960, even though none of her family was a member, because it represented something that she 'believed in', and was proud that she had been voted shop steward in 1971.[71] Sally remembered joining as soon as she arrived at Trico in 1975 and pointed out that it represented the first opportunity for her to become involved in the labour movement:

> I arrived at Trico and obviously joined the union ... because I was already [pause] I would actually have said I had become, I would say socialist from when I was doing my social work training, and part of the influence was a great guy who taught us sociology, he was Marxist, but he was a real character, and he was terrific and he really made me begin to see the difference between the haves and have nots, and it did start me thinking much more about that sort of thing because my parents were both Tory, so it wasn't like I was getting any of this from home.[72]

Sally played an active role in the strike committee as the press relations officer. She was voted in as a shop steward after the strike and operated as women's delegate for the AUEW Southall District Committee until she left Trico in 1982. She participated in the anti-poll tax protests in 1989 and remained active in local campaigns against hospital closures and government cuts to public services at the time of the interview. Subsequently, the strike marked a pivotal moment in Sally's narrative that portrayed a politically inexperienced pre-strike self, transformed by the strike into an active, politically engaged trade unionist post-strike self.[73] Sally's experiences of trade unionism formed a crucial aspect of this narrative. During the second interview, she explained,

> Well it changed my life but eh. [pause] I suppose it made me realise the importance of ... you know this thing that was said about a woman's place is in her union? We used to always say that, and that you need your organisation and women need it as much as men.[74]

Sally and Peggy both emphasised the importance of the solidarity they experienced on the picket line and further afield. Similar to the Dagenham sewing machinists, they contrasted their experiences to their perception of organised labour at the time of the interview. Peggy remembered: 'One of the things that surprised me was how generous people were. People giving all their hard earned cash. ... A lot of young people now haven't had that experience where people actually support you!'[75] Sally believed that the new alliances forged with fellow workers represented an eye-opening moment for her workmates, as well as herself, pointing out, 'I mean locally we met trade unionists and the working women's charter, but also up and down the country, Scotland, Wales, England and even people sent letters and unions wrote letters from France and Switzerland ... it completely changed people's attitude towards the trade union movement.'[76] Phyllis felt 'there were a lot of women in the factory for which it opened their minds'.[77] Whilst their account was obviously shaped by memory, in the words of Selina Todd, this 'does not mean the incident did not loom large at the time'.[78]

The women's experience of trade unionism was shaped by how their union was organised locally, rather than the attitudes of their national leadership. They emphasised the personal relationships they established in their local branch and suggested they were fortunate to have sympathetic officials. Sally said, 'We were very lucky politically having the Southall district committee and not ... some AUEW district committees, which were quite right wing ... in which case we would have almost certainly lost.'[79] She went on to explain how female workers had demanded equal pay at the Electrolux factory thirty miles away in Luton only six months earlier, but had difficulty sustaining their strike, even though they won their employment tribunal, because their AUEW district committee were unwilling to support them.[80]

Whilst the union's support for the strike was important, it is crucial that its significance does not disguise the agency of the individual women who actually organised it. Phyllis explained that she had 'always belonged to the union' because she 'had a socialist background' and 'was always on the left'. However, she had been less involved in the AUEW than Peggy and Sally and was slightly more critical of its treatment of female members. She pointed out that the union had five years to sort out equal pay before the Equal Pay Act was implemented and suggested, 'But then after the women at Ford went on strike, wouldn't you think all of the trade unions would have been talking about giving all the women in factories ... you know ... equal rights?'[81] Phyllis's alternative perspective on the AUEW's influence on the women's strike importantly highlighted how the decision to organise and fight for equal pay was made by the women themselves, and was not part of a wider campaign initiated by the AUEW. Peggy and Sally discussed the organic nature of the way the women originally decided to go on strike. Peggy remembered ordering all the women into the park for a mass meeting after the union's equal pay negotiations had broken down:

> There were about 400 women in the park and they said they wanted some action there and then ... the women who had been directly working alongside these five guys were so angry! There was actually three proposals put to the meeting; one was for lightning strikes, one for one or two days a week strikes and then the last proposal was for all out strike action. Well, the last proposal was put first and it was overwhelmingly supported. So suddenly everyone realised that we were now on strike. Our District Secretary, Roger Butler, said it was obviously up to the shop stewards and the members to decide what they were going to do, not necessarily thinking that that it would be there and then ... it was incredible. I mean there were feelings of excitement, confusion, anger about the whole issue, about how management was treating people, especially as there now was an Equal Pay Act actually on statute since the end of the previous year.[82]

The Trico strike demonstrates the essential role that trade unions could play in supporting women's fight for equal pay. The women interviewed here all agreed that they would not have won equal pay without the financial backing and guidance of the AUEW. In this sense, the Trico strike also revealed the unequal power relationship that continued to exist between male trade union officials and female workers in Britain during the 1970s. Whilst the AUEW claimed to have won equal pay for its members, this was not part of some 'top-down' campaign that sought a re-evaluation of their female members' labour across Britain. Instead, it was the self-organisation and desire of the women themselves who had raised the issue in the first place and sacrificed twenty-one weeks of their time and wages to obtain a victory. My interviewees felt 'lucky' to have progressive union officials who were willing to support them. The following chapter on Fakenham will show that not all trade union officials were interested in listening to women's voices.

Feminism and equal pay

A significant distinction between the Trico strike and the Ford sewing machinists' dispute was the presence of the WLM. In the eight years between the two strikes, the first UK women's liberation conference had taken place at Ruskin College, Oxford, in 1970, consciousness-raising groups had spread across the country and numerous feminist publications emerged that demanded equality and recognition of women's specific skills in the workplace. Feminist groups recognised the Trico strike as a valuable opportunity to engage with the growing number of working-class women who were joining trade unions in this period. *Shrew* described the strike as the 'first major strike by women for equal pay since the passing of the act' and pointed out,

> Equal pay is one of the demands of the WLM, and the movement has taken a great deal of interest in the Trico women's strike. Individual women from within the movement, who have become involved in the strike, have found it a valuable experience because they have had firsthand contact with one kind of action that is necessary if the demands of the movement are to become a reality.[83]

Spare Rib reported the strike's progress, and *Women's Voice* interviewed workers involved in the strike and urged 'women and readers to help the Trico women in their fight for equal pay by organising a collection at their work, coordinating a delegation or a public/street meeting or by asking repair shops, and garages to boycott Trico windscreen wiper blades'.[84] The Women's Theatre group, which was a feminist ensemble that performed agit prop in factories, clubs, women's groups, women's prisons, hospitals, schools and theatres to raise public awareness of gender inequality, produced a play about the women called *Out on the Costa Del Trico*.[85] Sally told me,

> The Working Women's Charter came down to the picket. They were very active at the time and they came down to the picket line a lot and gave support, and they gave money too. In fact, we did have some money from groups, for example, north London Women's Liberation group; they raised quite a lot for us.[86]

The Working Women's Charter group was a collective of feminists and female trade unionists organised in twenty-seven local groups across Britain, which encouraged female workers to join trade unions and pressured trade union officials to support the concerns of their female members. Cunnison and Stageman explain that they aimed to enable female trade unionists to campaign alongside WLM members, who were not necessarily union members, by organising their own committees within district trades councils.[87] Member Pat Longman explained that they aimed to extend networks of support in their local branches by supporting women involved in industrial disputes, such as Trico. They assisted the strikers on the picket line, raised money and promoted the strike by producing badges and pamphlets.[88]

The promotion of the Trico women's cause by WLM groups shows feminists attempting to reach out and support working-class women at an everyday, grassroots level. The Trico workers' perception of feminism was also a key concern for contemporary feminist journals, which nearly always asked the workers for their views on the WLM. For example, shop steward Betty Aitson told *Shrew*,

> I've watched them [WLM groups] but I've never taken part because of work and union activities from 8–5pm. I have a family as well; husband, daughter and granddaughter, and they take preference. So as far as women's organisations are concerned, no, I haven't really participated in any of these things, though I read about them and I watch with interest, and they have given us tremendous support.[89]

Another worker named Peggy Long told *Women's Voice*,

> I also didn't realise that there were so many organisations supporting women's equality till I was on strike and I've seen all of you down here. But I've also learnt a lot, noticed a lot of things since I have been on strike. Like this morning I heard on the radio about how women get less benefits than men, even when they pay the same stamp. I never realised such things before. Normally you don't even have time to think about things, you take them for granted.[90]

Spare Rib suggested that 'women's lib was not left on the picket line' as one of the women 'horrified' her manager by applying to become a forklift truck driver when she returned to work.[91] There was also evidence that the strike influenced how the women thought about the relationship between their exploitation in the workplace and the home. For example, their strike bulletins discussed the double burden:

> Women on strike are faced with having to overcome particular difficulties. We have two jobs. One running the strike, and the other at home, where we are still expected to care for the children, cook, wash and clean. But our strike has proved that women can unite and fight for their rights and that we can overcome the tradition of women accepting an inferior role.[92]

Another Trico worker wrote about how the strike highlighted women's specific interests and experiences as political subjects in an article for the *TASS News and Journal*:

> We have come up against many obstacles associated with being women – total lack of union experience and confidence, having to bear the burden of looking after homes, families, picketing then returning home to cook dinner and housework. Our dependence as women was brought home to us when we found that only two of us had cars for the purposes of visiting other factories to enlist supporters. Attitudes are deeply ingrained ... loyal trade unionists find it difficult to consider the issue of equal pay with the same seriousness as other kinds of disputes. References to 'the girls on the picket lines' reflect well-meaning but patronising attitudes.[93]

My respondents retrospectively associated the strike with a broader transition in how they thought about themselves as women, but they did not feel this was because of any direct engagement with WLM groups. Peggy said,

> They didn't influence me at all ... I mean I never spoke to them in *that* way, you know? They only spoke to me about the actual strike, and I didn't get involved with them but they were there and I remember them being there.[94]

Phyllis thought 'they didn't have too much to do with the Trico strike' yet at the same time connected the strike to a shift in attitudes towards gender relations within the factory:

> But you'd think that people got more interested though, I mean when you think about people who didn't know anything about trade unions and then became interested in trade unions. I think I used to look at it [feminism] as quite important ... you would have been reading about these women's meetings ... it probably influenced teenagers, you know 16–18 year olds who wanted to change from the old way of life to the new way of life. I'd say it probably influenced a lot of us.[95]

For Sally, 'I did not see it as a feminist issue because I mean sometimes it's been posed as a strike of men versus women, but of course it wasn't like that.'[96] However, she clearly felt the strike had an important influence on her own and other workers' attitudes towards gendered privilege within the factory. She said,

> At the time we did realise that although we'd got equal pay, there was still a whole battle of equal opportunities, because when we went back in, someone put themselves forward to be a forklift truck driver and later on I put in to be a trainee setter and got the job, and so we began challenging all of these things that I don't think we'd have had the confidence to before, or the awareness. And then the whole thing

about crèches for women in workplaces and elsewhere, that was quite a big agenda. I think the strike and the experience of the strike for those who were most involved gave us as women much more confidence in ourselves for fighting for not only what's your right, equal rights, but also that you can do it and you can succeed.[97]

Sally's testimony provoked Peggy to think about how her own views about women had changed during this period. Although she did not feel as if she had been guided by the WLM, she said,

> I think that the generation of women from the 70s influenced all women didn't you … I think because the 70s began to change people and their outlook, I think we got liberated in our own way, you know what I mean? We never sort of joined any group. … But I think even talking to other people on the picket line made you realise that we were in that category, really you know, we were doing something not all other women would do. Pushing it over the line you know … I suppose you might call that women's lib if you like?[98]

Although the women did not identify themselves, or their militancy, with the WLM, they did associate their encounter with feminists and other activist groups on the picket line with a transition in terms of how they thought about themselves as women. However, rather than associating this with a shift in political outlook, or even behaviour, they retrospectively associated it with having increased confidence as individuals and awareness of unequal gender hierarchies, which was clearly linked to the aims of WLM. The women I interviewed reconstructed the strike, and the picket line in particular, as a unique space where they encountered different people and various political ideas that opened their minds and enabled them to imagine themselves, and the organisation of the factory, in a different way.

The strike was framed as a turning point and crucial learning experience where the women refused to accept unequal pay, or to be 'treated with contempt' by their employers and male co-workers. However, the legacy of the strike for their sense of self was not explicitly related to any 'political' or 'feminist' framework. Barbara did not work at the factory but spent a lot of time on the picket line supporting the women with the Labour Party Young Socialists. She observed,

> A lot of groups like us went down to try and talk to them, but you had to be quite careful, because sometimes they didn't want to talk about politics, you know? They didn't see things from the same point of view. They really just wanted the strike to be over. For instance, somebody

once said to them: 'oh isn't this good?' And they said, 'well no it isn't good because we're still out here!' To be involved in a strike of that length ... I had no idea because at that time I had never been involved in a strike myself.[99]

My respondents did not relate the dispute or themselves to any ideology or formal political party. Instead, they were more likely to offer anecdotes about individual acts of defiance or informal solidarity that they remembered from the picket line. For example, at one stage Peggy said, 'I don't know how many times I was called a communist? They would walk by and say you're all communists you know ... but that wasn't what it was about'.[100] At the time, the women's convenor John Inwood commented on 'mass propaganda portraying the women as "reds under the bed"' and explained that 'the ladies themselves had made the original decision to strike and there was no indication that many of them were red or indeed pink' but were 'responsible caring human beings just like the rest of us'.[101] This emphasis on the everyday nature of the women's concerns was used to justify and legitimise their demand for equal pay. They were 'responsible caring human beings' with a genuine grievance generated from their personal experience of inequality on the assembly line, rather than derived from an external set of 'red' or 'feminist' political beliefs.

Similar to the Dagenham sewing machinists interviewed in the previous chapter, my respondents associated the Trico equal pay strike with a change in how they thought about themselves as women. It represented a moment when the 'injustice' of the Trico pay structure became visible, but also occurred at the same time as a wider societal transition was taking place to 'a new way of life' where they felt 'liberated in our own way'. After the strike, fifteen female workers were elected to the Trico shop stewards committee.[102] The women were invited by various organisations and union branches to give presentations and encourage female members to play an active role within their union.[103] The AUEW Southall District Committee organised a 'Women's Shop Stewards School' the following year, which was another example of how the strike stimulated greater commitment from local unions to integrate their female members. Sally reflected, 'The strike gave women terrific confidence. And to value themselves and what they could do. It changed people enormously.'[104]

Yet, Sally was different in that she had gone on to play an active role as the Women's Delegate on the AUEW Southall District Committee. She later became involved in the anti-poll tax protests when she worked as a mental health social worker. For Peggy and Phyllis, the strike had a different impact. Whilst they both identified it as a key moment in their narratives where they gained greater independence and confidence in standing up for themselves, they had less evidence to draw on to demonstrate how it affected them 'politically' and appeared more reluctant to talk about their lives after the strike. Phyllis had left Trico the year after the strike when her husband died and had gone on to work in a range of low-paid jobs with little opportunity to join a union. Peggy was made redundant in 1982 and had gone on to work as an office administrator and a care assistant. Changing jobs brought their AUEW membership to an end, and the strike seemed to occupy a distinct phase in their working lives that was remembered differently thirty years after leaving Trico. As a result, Peggy remembered the dispute in a similar manner to the Dagenham sewing machinists, who suggested that their strike had been forgotten about until its significance had been publicly recognised in the nation's collective memory via the feature film:

> In all honesty I'd not thought about it for a while until recently ... but all these things come back to you after all these years ... I mean you sort of close your mind to it, but I was fascinated by Sally's scrapbooks ... and then people like yourself come and ask you questions about it ... and although it was hard work at the time, you feel as though you have done something with your life.[105]

Peggy's and Phyllis's narratives of life after the strike were imbued with a sense of decline. Trico closed in 1982, as did many of Brentford and Britain's manufacturing industries, and the power of the labour movement went into decline. The result was that, with the exception of Sally, these women's union activities were brought to a halt shortly after they had begun, and the history of workers' struggles such as this has been publicly remembered less fondly then the women may have anticipated at the time of their victory in 1976. This did not reduce the significance of the strike in their own understanding of how it influenced their political views and perspective today; however, it limited the material effects of the dispute on their subsequent experiences of work and meant that it occupied a distinct phase of their lives, as well as England's history of industrial relations.

Conclusion

Taken together, the Dagenham and Trico strikes show that equal pay was not given to women by an increasingly liberal, meritocratic society; women had to go out and win these rights for themselves and continue to fight for them by taking direct action against employers, politicians, lawyers and trade union officials, who were unwilling to recognise the value of women's work in a manner that would alter the gender hierarchy of labour. As a result, the majority of women continued to receive lower wages than men after the Equal Pay Act was implemented in 1975. The strikes analysed here show that these workers' militancy was born out of transitions in their own attitudes to work and forged in their own direct experiences of unequal gender relations within their factory. Whilst these disputes occurred in different contexts, work increasingly occupied a central role in these women's lives and affected how they thought about themselves in relation to wider gender relations outside the factory. They became increasingly aware of their own importance to their employers and were unwilling to have their work devalued on the sole basis that they were women.

The strikes also demonstrate the importance of trade unions in representing women's voices in battles for equal pay. Unions were the main vehicle through which female workers could pursue their demands for equal pay and generate change. Whilst the NUVB and AUEW supported the workers at Ford and Trico, such support was not uniform across Britain, and was largely the result of the attitude and interests of their local officials and district committees at a grassroots level. Both strikes show how women were treated differently by unions, employers and the press to male workers. This was highlighted at the time by the growing WLM, which provided an extra form of support to women at Trico and influenced the way the workers thought about themselves as women, without necessarily identifying themselves with the movement.

Notes

1 Details from TUC Library, London Metropolitan University, HD. 6061: AUEW Official Trico Equal Pay Strike Bulletins, sixteen produced from Wednesday 29 June to Monday 18 October 1976.
2 'Trico Waits for Ruling', *Brentford and Chiswick Times*, 19 August 1976, p. 1.
3 M. Rabstein, 'Equal Pay Battle at Trico', *Morning Star*, 23 August 1976, pp. 2–3; J. Fryer, 'Vive La Material Difference', *Sunday Times*, 5 September 1976.
4 MRC, MSS.259/AEU/6/3/SL/3/43, AEEU Southall District Branch Papers, Trico-Folberth Ltd, 1970–78, Letter to All Branches in Southall District from R. C. Butler, 18 October 1976.
5 'Women Find Pay Fight Too Tough', *Guardian*, 8 September 1976, p. 6.
6 D. Turner and H. Hewland, 'They've Won!', *Morning Star*, 16 October 1976, p. 1; 'No Cash for You', *Brentford and Chiswick Times*, 16 September 1976.
7 S. Boston and S. Rowbotham give short accounts of the strike in Boston, *Women Workers*, pp. 314–317; Rowbotham, *The Past is Before Us*, p. 227. A celebratory account of the dispute was also published in 2018: S. Groves and V. Merritt, *Trico: A*

Victory to Remember: *The 1976 Equal Pay Strike at Trico Folberth, Brentford* (London: Lawrence and Wishart, 2018).
8 J. Grigg and B. Humphries, 'Labour Heritage in West London', *Labour Heritage Bulletin* (Spring 2010), www.labour-heritage.com/spring-2010.php (accessed 21 May 2013).
9 *Ibid.*
10 Interview with Peggy, Phyllis and Sally in London, 10 April 2013.
11 MRC, MSS.539/4/17, Papers of Alan Clinton, Julia Langdon, 'Where Women are Wiping the Smiles off the Bosses' Faces' (untitled and undated newspaper cutting).
12 Interview with Peggy, Phyllis and Sally in London, 10 April 2013.
13 Interview with Barbara, London, 16 April 2013.
14 *Ibid.*
15 A. Roy, 'Summer in Southall', *Spectator*, 19 June 1976, p. 11.
16 Interview with Peggy, Phyllis and Sally in London, 10 April 2013.
17 *Ibid.*
18 *Ibid.*
19 *Ibid.*
20 *Ibid.*
21 *Ibid.*
22 Interview with Sally in London, 19 June 2013.
23 *Ibid.*
24 'Trico Women Keep Fighting', *Women's Voice*, no. 3, September 1976.
25 Interview with Sally in London, 19 June 2013.
26 Interview with Peggy, Phyllis and Sally in London, 10 April 2013.
27 Interview with Sally in London, 19 June 2013.
28 Interview with Peggy, Phyllis and Sally in London, 10 April 2013.
29 *Ibid.*
30 *Ibid.*
31 The number of registered unemployed increased by 50 per cent between 1970 and 1975. James E. Alt, 'The Politics of Economic Decline in the 1970s' in L. Black, H. Pemberton and P. Thane (eds), *Reassessing 1970s Britain* (Manchester: Manchester University Press, 2013), p. 33.
32 MRC, Papers of Alan Clinton, MSS.539/4/17: Gary Gurmeet, 'Just One Small Step for Women – A Minor Victory as Equal Pay Strike Enters 9th Week', *International Socialists Newspaper*, September 1976.
33 TUC Library, HD. 6061: *TASS News and Journal*, August 1976, pp. 9–10.
34 'More Equal Pay: Geoffrey Sherdian Looks at the Trico Dispute, where Men May have to Wait for Women to Catch Up', *Guardian*, 14 July 1976, p. 9.
35 J. Fryer, 'Vive La Material Difference', *Sunday Times*, 5 September 1976; only 22 per cent of industrial tribunals involved trade unions and their long-term ineffectiveness was illustrated by fact the number of tribunals fell from 1,742 in 1976 to 91 in 1980 in Boston, *Women Workers*, p. 314.
36 'MRC, Papers of Alan Clinton, MSS.539/4/17', A Long Haul to Equal Treatment for Women' (untitled and undated newspaper article); 'Hot for Equality', *Time Out*, 2–8 July 1976.

37 J. Fryer, 'Vive La Material Difference', *Sunday Times*, 5 September 1976.
38 'Women Find Pay Fight Too Tough', *Guardian*, 8 September 1976, p. 6.
39 'Below the Pay Belt', *Brentford and Chiswick Times*, 24 June 1976, p. 1.
40 *Ibid.*
41 T. Pattinson, 'Husbands v. Wives in Equal Pay Battle', *Daily Mirror* (undated); Keith Deves, 'Wives in a Kitchen Sink Pay Strike', *Sun* (undated).
42 'Factory Girls Deny "Sex Strike"', *Evening Mail*; K. Deves, 'We're on Sex Strike Say Wives in Equal Pay Strike', *Sun*, 1 June 1976.
43 See T. Pattinson, 'Standing Put ... The Petticoat Pickets', *Daily Mirror* (undated).
44 'Hot for Equality', *Time Out*, 2–8 July 1976.
45 MRC, MSS.259/AEU/6/3/SL/3/43, Final Statement and Balance Sheet from the Trico-Folberth Strike Committee (undated) pays tribute to 150 male workers who supported the strike.
46 *AUEW Engineering Section Journal*, vol. 43, no. 9, September 1976.
47 See TUC Library, HD. 6061: AUEW Trico Strike Bulletins, sixteen produced from Wednesday 29 June to Monday 18 October.
48 MRC, MSS.259/AEU/6/3/SL/3/43, Letter to South Essex District Secretary of AUEW from Roger Butler, 8 October 1976; Letter from Bedfordshire County Association of Trades Councils to Roger Butler, 13 October 1976.
49 MRC, MSS.259/AEU/6/3/SL/3/43, Report of William McLoughlin, London Divisional Organiser FAO Southall District Committee, 21 September, 1976; Reports of Brother W. McLoughlin, Divisional Organiser FAO Southall District Committee, 13 October 1976.
50 The women were joined on the picket line by representatives from the Acton Rails AUEW; Brent Trades Council; Barnet Trades Council; Enfield and Edmonton Trades Council; Hammersmith Trades Council; Westminster Trades Council; Battersea and Wandsworth Trades Council and Working Women's Charter, according to rota in MRC, MSS.259/AEU/6/3/SL/3/43, Letters from Frank Stiller, Secretary of the Greater London Association of Trades Councils to his members, 6 September 1976.
51 AUEW Southall District Committee Circular, 2 August 1976.
52 MRC, MSS.259/AEU/6/3/SL/3/43, Letter from Roger Butler to John Boyd AUEW General Secretary, 28 September 1976.
53 MRC, MSS.259/AEU/6/3/SL/3/43, Letter from 'AUEW Shop Stewards and Members' (Setters; Labourers; Tool Room) to Hugh Scanlon 27 August 1976.
54 MRC, MSS.259/AEU/6/3/SL/3/43, Signed Petition.
55 MRC, MSS.259/AEU/6/3/SL/3/43, Letter from R. Brown, Shop Steward, Tool Inspection, to Roger Butler 21 September 1976.
56 *Ibid.*
57 Interview with Peggy, Phyllis and Sally in London, 10 April 2013.
58 MRC, MSS.259/AEU/6/3/SL/3/43, Final Statement and Balance Sheet from the Trico-Folberth Strike Committee (undated).
59 AUEW Southall District Committee Circular, 2 August 1976.
60 MRC, MSS.259/AEU/6/3/SL/3/43, A letter from Frank Stiller, Secretary of the Greater London Association of Trades Councils to his members dated 6 September 1976.

61 MRC, MSS.259/AEU/6/3/SL/3/43, 'Tribute to the Trico Strikers', poem by Tom Durkin, member of Union of Construction, Allied Trades and Technicians (UCATT) and chairman of Brent Trades Council.
62 MRC, MSS.259/AEU/6/3/SL/3/43, Final Statement and Balance Sheet from the Trico-Folberth Strike Committee (undated).
63 'Trico Women Strike', *Shrew*, Autumn 1976.
64 TUC Library, HD. 6061: AUEW Trico Strike Bulletin no. 3, 15 July 1976.
65 Interview with Peggy, Phyllis and Sally in London, 10 April 2013.
66 MRC, MSS.259/AEU/6/3/SL/3/43, Letter from Frank Stiller, Secretary of the Greater London Association of Trades Councils to his members dated 31 August 1976.
67 TUC Library, HD. 6061: AUEW Trico Strike Bulletin no. 4, Thursday 22 July.
68 TUC Library, HD. 6061: AUEW Trico Strike Bulletin no. 8, Thursday 12 August.
69 TUC Library, HD. 6061: AUEW Strike Bulletin no. 16, Monday 18 October.
70 Interview with Peggy, Phyllis and Sally in London, 10 April 2013.
71 *Ibid.*
72 *Ibid.*
73 *Ibid.*
74 Interview with Sally in London, 19 June 2013.
75 Interview with Peggy, Phyllis and Sally in London, 10 April 2013.
76 *Ibid.*
77 *Ibid.*
78 Todd, 'Experience, Class and Britain's Twentieth Century', p. 498.
79 *Ibid.*
80 *Ibid*; Electrolux dispute also mentioned in Boston, *Women Workers*, p. 317.
81 *Ibid.*
82 Interview with Peggy, Phyllis and Sally in London, 10 April 2013.
83 'Trico Women Strike', *Shrew*, Autumn 1976.
84 'News', *Spare Rib*, no. 49, July 1976, p. 20; 'News', *Spare Rib*, no. 51, September 1976, p. 19; 'Trico Women Keep Fighting', *Women's Voice*, no. 3, September 1976.
85 'Out on the Costa Del Trico', *Spare Rib*, no. 56, March 1977, p. 41.
86 Interview with Peggy, Phyllis and Sally in London, 10 April 2013.
87 Cunnison and Stageman, *Feminizing the Unions*, p. 29.
88 Pat Longman, 'Restarting Our Women's Work', Alliance of Worker's Liberty, www.workersliberty.org/node/8199 (accessed 12 December 2013).
89 'Trico Women Strike', *Shrew*, Autumn 1976.
90 'Trico Women Keep Fighting', *Women's Voice*, no. 3, September 1976.
91 'Work News: Trico Women Win', *Spare Rib*, no. 53, December 1976.
92 TUC Library, HD. 6061: AUEW Trico Strike Bulletin no. 4, 19 July 1976.
93 TUC Library, HD. 6061: *TASS News and Journal*, August 1976, pp. 9–10.
94 Interview with Peggy, Phyllis and Sally in London, 10 April 2013.
95 *Ibid.*
96 *Ibid.*
97 *Ibid.*
98 *Ibid.*

99   Interview with Barbara, 16 April 2013.
100 Interview with Peggy, Phyllis and Sally in London, 10 April 2013.
101 MRC, MSS.259/AEU/6/3/SL/3/43, Final Statement and Balance Sheet from the Trico-Folberth Strike Committee (undated).
102 GLATC Circular 2 November 1976.
103 MRC, MSS.259/AEU/6/3/SL/3/43, Letter to R Butler from AUEW Croydon District Secretary 6 January 1977; Request to talk at Oxford Trades Council Meeting on Women's Rights, March 1977; Letter from Chair of Britain's GDR Society 17 January 1977; Letter from History Workshop Collective, 12 January 1977.
104 MRC, MSS.259/AEU/6/3/SL/3/43, Interview with Sally in London, 19 June 2013.
105 Interview with Peggy, Phyllis and Sally in London, 10 April 2013.

4

Sexton's shoe factory occupation and Fakenham Enterprises, Norfolk, 1972–77

In the spring of 1972, forty-five female workers organised an eighteen-week occupation of Sexton's shoe factory in the small market town of Fakenham, Norfolk. The manufacturers entered receivership at the end of February and announced that 800 jobs would be lost across their two factories in Norwich and Fakenham. The unions representing the workforce, National Union of the Footwear, Leather and Allied Trades (NUFLAT) and Association of Scientific Technical and Managerial Staffs (ASTMS), arranged a public meeting where it was agreed that workers would occupy the main factory.[1] Within days, NUFLAT negotiated a deal with a local property developer that saved 500 of the 800 jobs in the Norwich factory, but excluded the satellite factory in Fakenham.[2] This sparked outrage among the all-female workforce who complained that both unions had failed to consult them throughout the negotiation process.[3] Led by their supervisor Nancy McGrath, on 17 March 1972 the women implemented the unions' original plan and barricaded themselves inside the factory, where they were to remain for the following eighteen weeks.[4]

During the occupation, the women reorganised themselves on a new collective basis. They participated equally in decision making, and all information about the factory was shared between the workers. They held demonstrations at the NUFLAT and Department of Social Security (DSS) offices, which gained them publicity and attracted both moral and financial support from feminist campaign groups.[5] Using scraps of suede and leather that remained in the factory, the women began to produce skirts, bags and belts that were sold to markets in Fakenham and Norwich. They received numerous orders for leather products from feminist and trade unionist activists as news about their operation travelled across the country. The income generated from these sales was reinvested in further materials to produce more goods, whilst any surplus was used to pay the workers a wage allocated equally or according to need.[6]

The workforce planned to set up a co-operative, where they could continue the practices they had developed during their occupation. They also wanted to re-employ their former workmates who had been forced to leave the factory. Following the advice of their prospective Labour Party candidate, the women sought assistance from the International Common Ownership Movement. They received a £2,500 loan from chemical company Scott Bader that allowed them to rent a new factory, purchase their old equipment and pay themselves the minimum union wage of £15.63 for a forty-hour week.[7] Scott Bader became the majority shareholder of the company, but the twelve women who agreed to the terms each received their own shareholding and ability to elect three board members and a chairperson of the company from among themselves. The co-operative was fully established and declared open on 17 July 1972 under the name Fakenham Enterprises.[8]

The following five years were characterised by a continuous struggle for survival. The co-operative was undercapitalised from the outset and was unable to develop its own products.[9] Throughout its existence, Fakenham Enterprises relied on low-paid, unstable sub-contract work – precisely the type of work the women had sought to avoid. They manufactured a variety of products, including suede jackets, plastic postal bags, chastity belts and golf club covers. It is worth noting that the co-operative reached a peak in 1974, when it employed thirty women and made a small profit due to a steady shoe contract. However, economic recession and a slump in the shoe industry led to a decline in contracts from 1975. Scott Bader returned their shares and withdrew from the board of directors. Threatened with collapse, Fakenham Enterprises operated for a further two years essentially as a collective of 'home-workers under one roof', completing sub-contract work for a local clothing firm.[10] The women had to accept the external company's wage and productivity agreements and no longer operated under the principles of self-management on which the factory was founded.

This remarkable story received considerable attention from political activists and the press at the time. The occupation occurred at the beginning of a wave of 260 factory occupations across Britain, inspired by the 1971–72 'work-in' of the Upper Clyde Shipbuilders (UCS). The Fakenham women were one of the first groups of workers to try and establish workers' control, and were followed by some more high profile co-operatives at Fisher Bendix, Merseyside, Triumph, Meriden and the *Scottish Daily News*.[11] During the occupation, the women received visits and thousands of letters of support from workers engaged in similar occupations, as well as WLM groups, trade unionists and Labour politicians

Tony Benn and Michael Foot.[12] The occupation's progress was reported regularly in the local press; it was commented on in national newspapers; it was publicised by feminist and political activists; and it was the subject of three political films and an episode of BBC's *Women's Hour*.

The Fakenham occupation has since been cited by historians as an example of working-class women's protest that symbolised changing ideas about gender and paid work in the 1970s.[13] According to Marie Cerna *et al.*, it 'focussed attention both as labour and women's issues and broadened the appeal of feminism from university educated to working-class women'.[14] The most detailed study of the Fakenham women exists in the form of Judy Wajcman's book, *Women in Control*. This was developed from her doctoral thesis, an ethnographic study documenting Wajcman's experience of working in the factory for three months in 1975 as a WLM activist from Cambridge University. For Wajcman, Fakenham Enterprises was unsuccessful for two reasons. First, it failed to alter the factory's relationship to the market. The women were unable to operate on labour-only contracts because of their irregularity and low profit margin, whilst they lacked the capital and managerial expertise to develop their own product. The co-operative only survived due to the 'self-sacrifice' of the women involved. Second, it failed to alter the women's political consciousness. Wajcman described the women as 'apolitical'. They voted Conservative; they were apathetic towards trade unionism; they expressed views that accepted and justified gender inequality, including the belief the co-operative would have been more successful had it been run by men. As a result, Wajcman concluded,

> Whatever the potential for political radicalisation in a worker-controlled enterprise, a failed attempt of this kind may actually increase workers' sense of powerlessness. Having fought to take control over their workplace, and having seen that attempt fail, the Fakenham women experienced more intensely the apparent inevitability of the capitalist system. ... Co-operatives are not a panacea. Naively embarked upon, they cannot provide more than a temporary alternative and are as likely to inhibit as to develop consciousness.[15]

Whilst the economic problems with Fakenham Enterprises are self-evident, Wajcman's second conclusion about disempowerment and depoliticisation is more problematic because she appears to equate political consciousness with 'radicalisation'. Political consciousness could only arise if the women developed an explicitly socialist or feminist critique of society, whilst the effect of working in a co-operative on the actors' everyday experiences of paid work and sense of self is left unexplored.

This chapter revisits Fakenham Enterprises from the perspective of women who were involved at the time. The Fakenham occupation moves this book on to a different track away from the debates about skill recognition and equal pay considered in the previous two chapters, towards working-class women's fight against factory closures and unemployment. Whilst these women were fighting for different ends, their narratives of work and industrial struggle continue to offer insights into the themes discussed in the previous chapters: working-class women's experiences of manual labour; the relationship between female workers and their trade union; the interaction between working-class women and the WLM; and working-class women's political identity.

Context

Fakenham is a small market town in Norfolk, which had a population of fewer than 5,000 people in 1972. Like most of East Anglia, the economic structure of the area was dominated by agriculture and low rates of pay, with typical earnings almost 8.5 per cent below the national average in 1975.[16] With no train station and poor bus links to the largest neighbouring towns of Norwich and King's Lynn, it was difficult for residents to seek work elsewhere. As a result, a small number of manufacturing firms had been attracted to Fakenham due to the ready availability of cheap female labour and the town's close proximity to natural materials. This included a print works, a construction company and three food-processing plants, which, alongside the shoe factory, provided the only alternative source of employment to agricultural work in the area.[17] The women who carried out the occupation characterised Fakenham as a 'conservative little town' in their interviews with Judy Wajcman; a NUFLAT shop steward named Edna described it as a 'backward area, purposefully kept so' to maintain the interests of the local landowners.[18]

Shoe manufacturer Sexton, Son and Everard was a family firm based in Norwich that had produced shoes since the nineteenth century. They set up a satellite factory in Fakenham in 1964 after a peak of prosperity in the 1950s. The firm employed sixty women for the sole purpose of closing shoe uppers with custom built sewing machines. In February 1972, forty-five machinists worked at the factory under the supervision of Nancy McGrath, who represented the only form of contact between the workforce and management at the main factory in Norwich, and became a key figure in organising the occupation.[19] At the end of the 1960s, the British shoe manufacturing industry entered a state of decline due to competition from cheap foreign imports. Between 1960 and 1970, the number of people employed in the shoe industry in Norfolk alone had fallen from 8,500 to 6,000.[20] With falling profits, Sexton's entered receivership on 29 February 1972.

The factory's closure was symptomatic of a national economic slump that led to a decline in manufacturing and an increase in unemployment to more than 1 million by 1972. Female unemployment increased three times as fast as male unemployment between 1972 and 1978.[21] Unemployment rates in Fakenham averaged between 1 per cent and 2 per cent higher than the rest of East Anglia as a whole, due to a weakening in agriculture and limited opportunity for the development of new forms of manufacturing, services and facilities.[22] The town's distinct sense of decline was investigated as a matter of urgency by the East Anglia Economic Planning Council in 1972, which emphasised the importance of women's labour due to low wages and high male unemployment in the area.[23]

The Norfolk shoe industry did not have a culture of industrial struggle, and there had not been a dispute at Sexton's since 1926.[24] Whilst the factory was unionised as part of a closed-shop agreement, NUFLAT was a conservative trade union that aimed to attract contracts and preserve employment in a faltering industry. Their policy was characterised by the pursuit of peaceful coexistence with employers, which generally meant low wages and poor conditions for workers.[25] The ASTMS District Official for Norwich explained in an interview at the time that he became involved in the dispute because 'it became clear very early on that the experience of the shop-floor trade union (NUFLAT) was limited, being limited to the footwear industry and had not dealt with this problem in this way before and not really experienced it'.[26]

Despite the lack of conflict within the factory, the occupation occurred against a backdrop of turbulent industrial relations in the national context. The 1972 miners' strike caused national power cuts and led the government to declare a state of emergency, three weeks before the women were made redundant.[27] There had been a swelling of industrial action and protest during the previous year against the 1971 Industrial Relations Act, whilst the UCS's successful 'work-in' in 1971-72 inspired workers across Britain to adopt the occupation as a new defensive tactic against wage cuts and the growing threat of unemployment. Labour historian Ken Coates argues that 'prior to 1971 the vocabulary of sit-ins was hardly ever used', but after the success of the UCS work-in 260 factory occupations were recorded to have taken place across Britain between 1971 and 1976.[28] Nancy McGrath reflected at the time that the UCS work-in provided a source of inspiration for their action: 'It was reckless to do it, to really defy the law and everything ... I think possibly the fact that the Clydeside workers had done it before us ... meant I thought there's somebody making a stand against these redundancies. Why don't we?'[29] One of my interviewees described their decision to form a co-operative as 'automatic', which suggests the powerful influence of the work-in and growing prevalence of occupation as a legitimate tactic used by workers during this period. Yet it must be stressed that the women also understood their action as novel because of the local context in which it occurred. A worker explained in 1976:

> Nothing like that had ever happened before in nice conservative little Fakenham. You walked down the street and somebody said, 'oh go home you old bag or something like that'. ... You didn't expect them to because you thought that they should have understood. But then it wasn't Clydeside and Jimmy Reid, it was Fakenham and that sort of thing was illegal. It had never happened here before.[30]

The women were aware of industrial disputes on a national level, and placed their own action within that context at the time. However, with the exception of struggles between labourers and landowners, Fakenham did not have a history of industrial militancy, and the surrounding constituency of North Norfolk continually elected Conservative MPs throughout the 1970s. So the occupation took place in a very different context to the Ford sewing machinists' strike, which was a very militant workforce with a culture of unofficial rank-and-file activism; there was considerably less racial and ethnic diversity in the area and far less opportunity to engage with progressive social movements and trade unionists locally than was available to the women considered in the other case studies in this book. Yet in spite of these differences, the Fakenham women shared similar experiences of work and expressed similar attitudes towards trade unions and feminism. Whilst their personal circumstances and local contexts were considerably different, it is significant that these women took similar decisions to engage in industrial struggle.

Experiences of work

Working-class women's jobs in Fakenham, like much of the rest of England, were concentrated in the lowest paid, least skilled sectors of the labour market. At the time of Judy Wajcman's study in 1975, Fakenham Enterprises employed twenty-two women, all of whom had worked on production lines in food-processing or clothing factories, or in the service sector as shop assistants and waitresses before working in the co-operative.³¹ My respondents for this case study shared similar experiences of work to the women in Brentford and Dagenham. The typical trajectory was to leave school at the age of fifteen to work in low-paid manual labour; many women remained in these types of jobs until being made redundant in the late 1970s, when they moved in to services, retail or care work. Like the women in the other case studies, the Fakenham respondents felt they had worked from an early age due to economic necessity and believed they had no alternative. For example, Margaret discussed how she was from a poor family, which meant that she had worked on the land as a child before getting her first 'proper job' at Sexton's in 1966, when she left school at the age of fifteen:

> My father worked on the farm and he never claimed benefits or anything, even though he had eight children. And even though he didn't earn very much, he gave all his wages to my mum, he never took any of them. … My mum worked on the land, and in the school holidays I went to work on the land, even when I was five or six. And I remember that when I was about 11, this man used to come and pick us up in a gang and we used to go potato picking … I went to the shoe factory when I was 15. So that was my first proper job. But it sounds bad when you say it, but we never starved and we never went without anything. We always had cooked meals and everything.³²

Margaret did not explicitly identify herself as working-class, but explained that her parents had struggled financially when she was growing up, which meant she had worked since she was a child. Although this might 'sound bad', she felt this information was significant because it suggested that the work they performed, although low paid, had guaranteed her family's independence from 'claiming benefits', and as a result was something she was proud of. Whilst this use of modern language was clearly influenced by contemporary debates about welfare at the time of the interview, Margaret understood her early experiences of working out of economic necessity as sign of her independence and personal resilience.

Marees left school at the age of fifteen to work as a shop assistant at the Co-op, before moving to the shoe factory when she married a farmer in 1970. She was twenty-two years old and pregnant with her first child at the time of the occupation and accepted her early experiences of work as natural.

> My parents were just ordinary people … you know they weren't any different, they were just ordinary people. Well ordinary working-class people; they went to work, scraped a living; which is what I am.³³

For Marees, being an 'ordinary working-class person' meant going to work and scraping a living. The inevitable acceptance of low-paid work among the Fakenham workforce was also evident in Wajcman's study. It showed that of the seventeen married women who worked at Fakenham Enterprises in 1975, fifteen were married to manual labourers who earned between £27 and £42 per week at a time when low pay was defined by the Low Pay Unit as £40 a week.[34] One worker discussed the importance of her wage to her family's income in an interview at the time: 'Men's wages are so low in Fakenham it barely covers the housekeeping. We are not working for luxuries but essentials.'[35] Materially, the Fakenham women emphasised the need to work to raise their families above the poverty line; redundancy represented a serious threat to their family income and a source of personal anxiety.

Yet, the decision to occupy the factory was not simply contingent on the lack of alternative sources of employment in the area; it was also understood as an assertion of the subjective value of women's work. A worker explained in 1976:

> We said why we sat-in, or worked-in to be correct, is to keep a job. But the reason we wanted to keep a job was because it was something more: we felt that we shouldn't be ditched ... I mean a job wasn't the only thing ... we felt that we'd been badly treated. ... And we were against being badly treated, being treated more or less like dirt, for want of a better word.[36]

The women resented the way they had been treated by the previous management, and the dehumanising nature of the labour process. During the occupation, the leader Nancy McGrath explained that they sought to form a co-operative because after eighteen weeks of struggle, the last thing she wanted was to be taken over by another firm 'and have some other board of management or whatever they call themselves stepping in and using our skills, our brains and our labour to swell their profits'.[37] Another worker named Edna said, 'When you work in a factory and you don't make your own decisions ... you just get rusty and don't care. Once you've had your eyes opened, you'd never accept it again.'[38]

Running their own co-operative meant they reinterpreted their previous experience of employment as unfair. Nancy claimed, 'We don't want to revert back to being creatures behind a machine with all the decisions being made by remote control.'[39] By occupying the factory and developing a worker co-operative, the women took control of the factory's orders, produced what they wanted for who they wanted and paid everybody an equal wage. A company director from Scott Bader reported to the International Common Ownership Movement, 'Through the solidarity developed by their sit-in, the group works very well together and some of the group approaches to problem solving they have evolved are surprisingly sophisticated.'[40] This democratisation of the shop floor tells a story about working-class women challenging the drudgery and dehumanising aspects of manual labour, and attempting to establish control of the decision-making process in their workplace, and in doing so taking control of their own lives. Marees explained, 'I definitely enjoyed it and we had laughs whilst we stayed there, trying to persuade somebody to help us. Yeah we did have a lot of fun and we were a very close knit, friendly lot. And em … I think I have grown up thinking that I should stick up for myself as well.'[41]

My interviewees remembered working at Fakenham Enterprises as an enjoyable experience where they appreciated their friendships and ability to make their own decisions. It was clearly a unique work environment that was unlike anywhere else they ever worked before or since, in terms of being a company director or having free childcare (which is discussed later in the chapter). Marees had spent most of the rest of her life working for Sainsbury's supermarket, Margaret had worked in pubs and hotels and Patricia had spent the rest of her life working in the care sector, working with children and the elderly.[42] Like the women interviewed in the previous chapters, the work they performed, despite its low pay and value, was essential to their income and personal identity. Whilst the Sexton's management were willing to treat them like a disposable form of labour, they certainly did not consider their work as temporary and fought not only to preserve their jobs, but to recreate a working environment that would suit their needs as women. However, the initial anger and desire to alter the system of production expressed at the time was difficult to trace in the interviews today, in the context of their post-industrial experiences of work. Instead it had been remembered in terms of the personal impact, teaching them to stand up for themselves as individuals.

Experiences of trade unionism

Like the women in the previous case studies, the Fakenham workforce became unionised during the 1960s and were representative of the growing number of female workers joining trade unions in post-war England. In 1972, all forty-five female production workers were members of NUFLAT, with the exception of supervisor Nancy McGrath who was a member of ASTMS. The women were outraged that NUFLAT had been willing to save the jobs of male workers in the Norwich factory, without even consulting them.[43] NUFLAT refused to make the action official and offer strike pay, and later seized money raised unofficially by workers in the local district council to support the occupation.[44] The Norwich Branch secretary explained in an interview at the time: 'I think the girls over at Fakenham were annoyed because ... when the parent factory closed down we were so busy here dealing with it that for a few days we'd forgotten Fakenham. And they were rather angry.'[45] The behaviour of NUFLAT was a far cry from the unions considered in the previous case studies, and demonstrates how male union officials ignored the interests of their rank-and-file female members.

The women's anger and determination was directed against the union as much as it was against the company. The union's dismissal of their demands and subsequent action only compounded the sense of alienation and exploitation they had experienced after being casually discarded by the company. A banner appeared outside the factory proclaiming, 'FORGOTTEN FACTORY SOLD OUT BY THE UNIONS', which was to remain there for the full eighteen weeks of the occupation, in spite of the union leaders' attempts to remove it during the early stages of the protest.[46] The women who were interviewed at the time resented the way NUFLAT had treated them, and clearly felt that they had been ignored due to the fact that they were women. A female shop steward reported, 'The union called us "a silly bunch of girls" and told us to "go back to the kitchen sink". ... They didn't know what to do with us and were embarrassed.'[47] Later on, she pointed out,

> Men expect women to back them up and women do; look at the Miners' Strike and the Post Office strike. I'm afraid that they will have to learn that women are to be heard as well as seen. They're not just something trotting down the high street in a mini skirt to be whistled at. Women are human beings and to be treated as equals, not something to be locked in four walls in a house.[48]

Forewoman Nancy McGrath said, 'They should declare immediately that our action is official and pay us strike pay. ... We are fighting for the right to work and will not give in. We will not be bought off, and with the support of other workers we will win.'[49] Another worker pointed out how the unions' rejection had spurred them on: 'We know damn well that if we make this work then we will put ourselves on the map, because we're unique and women have never done this sort of thing. That's why the union officials told us to go home and stop being a silly bunch of girls.'[50]

The women organised a demonstration against their treatment by NUFLAT outside the union's office in Norwich, where members of the

Norwich women's liberation group joined them. They picketed an official meeting and distributed leaflets that declared, 'We are not a group of silly women. We have acted as trade unionists. Now the union should make our action official and give us full strike pay. Union officials should declare publically that they support us.'[51] A worker named Edna commented at the time:

> They weren't going to pay us our out-of-work money ... we went up to the union meeting and took it over and that's the only time the union doors have ever had to be locked, because we had loads of the women's liberation movement outside and they wouldn't let them in. They were dead scared of them getting in.[52]

The important point here is that the workers felt patronised and undermined by their male trade union officials on the basis of their sex. One can see that this moment of genuine radicalism was organised entirely on a shop-floor level by the workers themselves, and was a reaction to what they perceived as sexist treatment by their union, as much as their employers. To this extent, the Fakenham occupation offers an insight into the continuation of sexist attitudes within trade unions during this period of increased female membership. It also demonstrates the frustrating everyday effects this had for female members attempting to organise at the time and assert their identity as both workers and trade unionists. Without the official support of their union, the women were forced to develop alternative methods of resistance by occupying their factory, which was a practice adopted by other female workers involved in disputes at Plessey Electronics in west London in October 1972, Lucas Industries in Birmingham in March 1974 and Lee Jeans in Greenock in 1981.[53] The effects of independently developing alternative methods of resistance on women's political identity can be seen from considering the workers' memory of the occupation today. They viewed it as a unique moment when they assumed their own voice and emphasised the informal nature of their collective organisation, as well as their personal resilience and individual autonomy.

The Fakenham women were unionised as part of a closed-shop agreement, and my respondents were not particularly active within their union. Patricia explained, 'Well I suppose we paid the union, but the union didn't really sort of want to know.'[54] Margaret had a similar sense of ambivalence towards the union and her membership. She said,

> It's difficult to remember but I should imagine we were members [of NUFLAT], but no, I didn't want to do anything like that. I was just a

worker really. ... No, well I wasn't political really. I did go on the march once for the farmers when they wanted the 39 hour week at Norwich and I had a banner, because my dad worked on the farm all his life you see ... but apart from that no, I wasn't political, and the occupation was not really, because it meant another place was closing. ... It was just about that we want to prove a point.⁵⁵

Patricia understood the occupation in a similar fashion. She said, 'No [the occupation didn't affect me politically], no – I just carried on with life, you've got to haven't you? Just deal with what life throws at you.' Neither Margaret nor Patricia played an active role in the union, and distinguished its activities and politics from what represented the norm to them. This is unsurprising, as Karen Sayer claims that female workers in rural England historically organised and protested outside the labour movement from the nineteenth century onwards. She argues that there were heightened expectations for rural women to conform to idealised notions of respectability and femininity compared to urban women, which meant that agricultural women's involvement in political activity was often condemned both by unions and the middle class, and largely isolated from wider political movements taking place locally and nationally. Sayer suggests this left a legacy for the way that rural women negotiated their identities throughout the twentieth century.⁵⁶

Although the women at Fakenham did not work in the fields, one can see how this moment of genuine radicalism was similarly isolated from a wider political movement locally. The owner of Sexton's commented in 1976,

> I honestly feel that this was entirely a self-generated thing at Fakenham. The people at Norwich, I don't think had any influence on them at all ... people in Fakenham I think they just thought it was a bit of a curiosity. I don't think there was much reaction outside because I've spoken to other Fakenham people and, as I said before, it was rather a curiosity and like something at the zoo as far as the other Fakenham people went ... some weird plant that flowered in their midst and they wondered what it was.⁵⁷

However, at the national level the women received letters of support and solidarity from numerous other trades councils. For example, fellow NU-FLAT members from the Bally shoe factory in Lowestoft, Suffolk, organised a collection for the women and wrote 'We are sorry that our union officials did not give you immediate recognition and financial help, but knowing how difficult they are sometimes through our own experience we are hardly surprised.'⁵⁸ Their action was also perceived as novel and historic. The Wycombe Trades Union Council wrote to the women 'sending you our best wishes, and our admiration for what you are trying to do, in some sections of the industries women do not seem to realise what "it is all about" and it is a shot in the arm, as it were to learn of the determination and sheer guts that your ladies have'.[59] The Ealing branch of the AUEW offered the women free advertising space in their journal and said 'the value of such work by you girls cannot be measured and a place of honour in the workers' history of its struggles will most certainly be recorded for you by the historians'.[60]

For my interviewee Marees, it did not feel like she had been involved in a 'historic struggle'. The lack of support she received from NUFLAT during the occupation had changed her attitude towards trade unions. She said, 'I was in a union before I went there. I was in the union at my previous job at the Co-op. So it was automatic for me ... for some reason back then I believed that you needed to be in a union, to stick together!' However, her attitude towards trade unions changed considerably after the experience of the occupation. She said,

> No the union did not support us, that was a waste of money, a complete waste of money ... they just sold us down the river, they just decided to look after the big factory and they forgot about us, they just left us. They wouldn't even pay us unemployment money, which only used to be a few pence ... I'd been paying my union dues and I didn't get anything back.[61]

Marees did not 'believe' in unions after the occupation. Rather than valuing an organised workforce, she described how the occupation had taught her that she could stand up for herself as an individual and did not need to rely on the support of other people.

> I think it [the occupation] probably did affect me because I always sort of ... especially in recent years and I know because people have said to me, that I do stick up for myself now. I did join the union again when I went to Sainsbury's but I left after 3 months because I thought why am I paying to the union when I don't have to? So I didn't bother because I thought 'I can stick up for myself – I don't need other people' you know so yeah I think I am quite independent, and possibly that is from going back to then, which was quite important really.[62]

Marees identified the occupation as an education about herself, rather than 'politics' and collective action. Remembering it in a post-industrial context, where she felt isolated from other workers, it represented a learning curve where she gained her own personal independence and autonomy.

Marees also suggested that there was a gulf in understanding of the occupation between the workforce and the groups that supported them at the time. She did not see their action within a 'political' context, but understood that journalists, political activists and probably people like me (who have asked her questions about it since) do view it that way. The extent to which the women's action was driven by a deeper commitment to trade unionism was a key question asked in Judy Wajcman's interviews in 1975, whilst the *Observer* described the occupation as 'something of an education in politics and production for the women', claiming that the majority of them had voted for the Conservatives at the last election but would not be doing so again.[63] Yet it was clear from Marees' testimony that she understood it more as a personal transition, as opposed to a 'political awakening'. She told a similar story to that of Peggy from Brentford in the previous chapter:

> I got told that I was a communist once and I didn't even know what that meant. This was when the sit-in was going on and I got told I was a communist and I said 'what's a communist?' and nobody seemed to know. It was somebody who came to visit us must have said it, called us communists, and I thought: 'what on earth is he talking about?' I still don't really know the difference between that or being a bit more labour than not labour I guess [laughs] I'm not political, I'm not a political person.... I [occupied the factory] cos I wanted to keep my job. That's really the main reason ... other people may have had their ideas but mine was just to keep my job.[64]

The Fakenham workers were ambivalent towards their own union and trade unionism in general, both retrospectively and at the time, which is unsurprising because their union undermined them and failed to support the occupation. These sentiments echoed Wajcman's findings in 1975, which led her to conclude the women continued to share similar conservative political views with their husbands, despite the 'obvious opportunity for political development'.[65] She argued that the very real constraints they faced in both the domestic economy and paid employment created a sense of powerlessness, which meant that they accepted the inequalities they faced as natural and adopted views that justified their oppression.[66] These pessimistic conclusions were criticised by Veronica Beechey for emphasising the ideology of domesticity and giving weight only to the women's experiences within the family, therefore losing sight of how their attitudes towards paid work had changed after working in the co-operative.[67] The present analysis shows that the occupation affected the women as individuals – by giving them greater confidence and independence, which permits for a more complex view of the impact of such action on the women's political attitudes. It also raises questions around the assumption that 'workers' control' would equate with leftist political views.

The women I interviewed were keen to stress that they were 'not political' and emphasised their 'ordinariness'. My respondents' desire to represent themselves as 'ordinary' is unsurprising, as British sociologists find that working-class and middle-class people have preferred to describe themselves in this manner as 'a means of refusing both a stigmatised and pathologised identity ... at the same time that it refuses a privileged position'.[68] Beverley Skeggs argues that white working-class women are likely to experience their class position as particularly denigrated and are therefore most likely to 'dis-identify' with class in this manner.[69] Savage is sceptical of this argument because it risks positing a correct manner in which working-class women should identify themselves. Instead, he argues that the theme of 'ordinariness' relates to people's desire to assert their personal 'authenticity' and 'naturalness', and avoid snobbishness which involves insincere judgements of people based on their 'social position' rather than as 'primordial individuals'.[70] In both cases, 'ordinariness' assumes a political guise because it intimates common interest with other people, against non-ordinary people.

The Fakenham women's personal testimony can be read in this way – an assertion of common interests. But it could also be understood as an attempt to claim their own voice from a fuzzy mix of 'non-ordinary' people: the company who 'treated us like dirt'; or the union who 'forgot about us' and just expected us to find another job'; or 'the people who came to visit us' and 'called us communists'; or 'the Fakenham people' who treated them like a 'curiosity at the zoo'. In this sense, their identification as 'ordinary' was connected to an individual assertion of their authenticity, as much as an identification of collective interests.

Also, identifying and understanding oneself as 'ordinary' is not entirely the same as identifying and understanding oneself as 'not political'. In this context, the women's description of the occupation as 'non-political' should be understood as a means of claiming ownership of the dispute and distancing it, and themselves, from what they perceived as external 'political' causes and 'ideas' of other people who supported them. They identified the dispute as non-political to show that it was generated from everyday conditions and that they possessed natural and authentic motivations for occupying their factory. Nancy McGrath explained in an interview in 1976: 'The main support that we got was from ... people in universities and things like this. And a lot of ordinary people when they began to find out what it was all about and that we were really serious and it wasn't just a stunt or something.'[71] The Fakenham women differentiated themselves from the 'people in universities' and developed political identities around convincing other people that they were ordinary as a means of justifying their collective action and asserting their right to work.

Feminist support and influence

The lack of assistance the women received from their trade union left a space for the emerging WLM to play a prominent role in supporting the occupation. Thousands of donations, letters and orders for leather goods were sent to the women from fellow workers expressing solidarity. WLM groups in particular offered their support, including Pat Sturdy, a Lucas worker from Burnley, who set up the short-lived Women's Industrial Union the previous year.[72] A letter from Liz Burke of Brighton WLM informed the Fakenham workforce, 'You're in the front line of the industrial struggle and women workers everywhere are relying on you.'[73] Beryl Foster wrote on behalf of the Glasgow Women in Action group to say, 'We are encouraged up here to read about your occupation of your factory. ... We realise you have taken on two battles, one at work and one in the home and we hope you win both.'[74] After receiving a leaflet from the Colchester Women's Lib group, Jill Walker of the East Manchester and Stockport Women's Lib group asked the Fakenham women to send a catalogue so they could find local shops to stock the co-operative's products.[75] Such letters show how Fakenham Enterprises received significant support from an emerging network of feminist groups, and was conceptualised as being part of wider feminist awakening that activists perceived to be taking place across England and Scotland.

On a national level, feminist groups publicised the occupation and appealed for donations and orders on behalf of the women in various journals and newsletters. The occupation was discussed and a collection was held at the 1972 Women's Liberation conference in Manchester.[76] Cinema Action Group, a collective committed to filmmaking as a form of political activism, made a film about the occupation. The director 'wanted to make a film about women who had done something that could be shown to other groups of both men and women who might be on the verge of some kind of political commitment'.[77] This raised the profile of the occupation and enabled the women to raise the necessary funds to form a co-operative.[78]

Local feminist groups in East Anglia also supported the occupation. Norwich had its own women's centre and a separate women's liberation group, which paid regular visits to the factory and joined the women for demonstrations outside the local NUFLAT and DSS offices in April.[79] Sheila Bell, a member of the Norwich women's liberation group, discussed how important it was for WLM groups to support the Fakenham women in light of 'union disregard for women's jobs':

> I think that these women are putting up a jolly courageous fight. If men's jobs were involved then there would probably have been a strike but because they are women's jobs they are not counted as very important. Although the NUFLAT union has mostly women members, it is ran by men who the women feel are just embarrassed by the whole situation.[80]

As a result of this support, the occupation was publicly portrayed in a feminist context by the local and national press, which raised the profile of some key issues affecting working-class women. This included the sexual discrimination they faced from their union, the importance of women's wages and their treatment as a disposable form of labour.

The Fakenham case, similar to Trico, is a revealing example of how WLM groups attempted to engage with working-class women and trade unions in this early period of the movement. The support the women received from feminist groups was an example of a wider historical phenomenon taking place at the time. Whilst middle-class female social investigators had been concerned with working-class women's experience of factory work since the nineteenth century, the interest shown by WLM groups, academics and filmmakers during the 1970s was part of a wider transnational social movement that developed new research practices and mediums in the forms of participant observation ethnographies and film, but also problematised and attempted to redefine the relationship between women and paid work in a different way.[81] Wajcman's study should be seen in a similar context to Anna Pollert's *Girls, Wives, Factory Lives* and Miriam Glucksman's *Women on the Line* (discussed in Chapter 1).[82] Both writers were WLM activist and students who ended up in factories undertaking similar participant observation studies with female workers. Judy Wajcman (now Professor of Sociology at London School of Economics) described to me her own feminist trajectory from a poor Jewish immigrant community in Melbourne to a leather factory in Norfolk, via Cambridge University. Her testimony reveals the wider opportunities open to some young women during the post-war period, and the impact of this on her understanding of class and gender relations in a manner that led her to Fakenham:

> As a sociologist I would just say, and you'll just laugh if I go through all the characteristics ... I have a classic feminist trajectory. I'm exactly the right age; I was brought up by a Jewish immigrant family who valued education ... I went to do a degree in politics, and then I got very involved in the anti-Vietnam demonstrations. I had a political science education in Marxism ... and it was only around the end of that when feminist inklings started to emerge around the communist party and something kind of clicked! It was like a flash, like one of those gestalt things, where I just thought: 'oh yeah!'
>
> But I became involved in Fakenham through the women's movement actually. I was in Cambridge studying for a PhD and I was absolutely going to do it on work – I was really interested in work and pay and stuff – and you know it was the beginning of the kind of second-wave stuff, so you know I got very involved with the women's movement in the university and in the town. I got very involved in particular with the socialist feminist bid, like I didn't get involved with domestic violence and those things. I was absolutely involved with the trade union orientated, women's work, equal pay, socialist feminist thing. ... Then the word was out that there was this occupation, it was in Norfolk. ... And so I think I went up and visited with a mate of mine in Cambridge to try and help ... and we thought that we would try and get them some orders for stuff to keep them going. I had lots of trips up there ... and my supervisor just said well given that's where you're spending your time and you haven't yet organised to go anywhere else, why don't you just do your PhD on that? So that was what I was going to do. And nobody at Cambridge was doing anything to do with women's work, it was all male dominated themes ... like it was completely a topic that nobody was doing and I can remember people who are now famous and have done stuff on women's work just saying to me 'well what's interesting about women's work?' and 'what a stupid topic!'[83]

Wajcman was acutely aware that her 'typical feminist' trajectory meant that she had very different experiences of work and education than the women she worked alongside and interviewed in the summer of 1975. She went on to talk about her initial impressions of working at the factory, but also of her awareness at the time that the women did not see their struggle in the same socialist feminist frame of reference as herself, and also of her (and the WLM's) limited capacity to influence their wider political outlook:

> I remember when I arrived that they had incredibly thick Norfolk accents, and they thought I had a really strong Australian accent ... it was just such a foreign world to me in a whole lot of ways ... I just did

> not understand that feudal England was alive and well in Norfolk ... like when I met some of the husbands and went to do interviews and they were in tied-Cottages ... so it was quite an extraordinary world to have fallen into. ... It was rural poor and I had never seen that before because I had come from a cosmopolitan background I was aware that I was at Cambridge and incredibly privileged, and I would never have dreamt of patronising them, or suggesting stuff ... I suppose we [WLM campaign] didn't try and influence them because, I am a real structural Marxist, and if you can't give people the conditions in which they can live out different lives then what the hell are you doing going around and telling them to be different.[84]

Wajcman's testimony illustrates the dynamic relationship between theory and practice within academic feminism, and how feminist research was both informed and inspired by local activism. However, there was also a clear distinction of the meaning of Fakenham Enterprises between the WLM groups that provided support and the women who actually organised it. Whilst the former generally interpreted it as part of a wider stirring of working-class women's consciousness, the latter understood their action as a direct attempt to save their jobs and alter the power relations within the specific context of their workplace.

The workforce at Fakenham was aware that their action was being publicly conceptualised as a fight for women's rights. Sexual difference was central to their own understanding of how their occupation had evolved and how other people responded to them. Nancy believed their co-operative received little support from their union and the government because they were women. She said in an interview in 1976,

> If we had half a dozen men in there strutting about telling us what to do I'm quite sure they'd be prepared to help us. Because most of those people in government circles ... like Tony Benn sent a man down. He didn't send a woman down – he sent a man down. He approached it from a man's viewpoint. He wasn't interested in us because we're women but I'm quite sure that it had a bearing on the outcome of his visit, the fact that we were women. And most of the men think women don't know what they're about anyway.[85]

Similarly, the women believed the co-operative's economic failure could also be explained by sexual difference. A worker named Isabel discussed how 'vulnerable' they were: 'Because we are an all-woman factory and people are inclined to lean on us a bit heavy' or 'people try and rip you off all the time'.[86] They also discussed how married women felt under pressure from their husbands to find more stable work. In 1976, Nancy explained how one worker left the co-operative after her husband 'almost bodily dragged her from the place'.[87] She went on:

> **NANCY:** I know one husband who told his wife that rather than work here for, what was it, about £15 a week, she could go to the laundry and get £28 or nearly £30 at Fakenham laundry. And he created quite a fuss because she didn't go there. But her health wouldn't stand up to it with the steam and the chemicals and everything else. And he was a husband who I would never in my wildest dreams have envisaged saying that sort of thing. But they had economic pressures on them.
> **INTERVIEWER:** And you think it's economic the reason why …
> **NANCY:** I think it must be. I can't see what other reason there is, can you? Can you think of another reason? I mean people aren't avaricious, are they? Not from choice.[88]

Whilst the above passage shows that male behaviour was not necessarily understood as the primary cause of women's exploitation, it was clear the women felt their experiences of work and trade unionism were shaped by gender and their relationships with individual men. In response, the workers reorganised their work in different ways. The practice of weekly meetings and participation in shared decision making represented a fundamental break from the past in the women's experiences of paid work. In the 1976 interviews, one woman compared their meetings to 'group therapy', where everybody 'talked', 'shouted' and 'aired their grievances'.[89] They allowed working mothers to synchronise their working hours with their childcare responsibilities. Nancy pointed out, 'I haven't known of anywhere else, at least not around here anyway, where it is possible to do this sort of thing, where women cater specifically for women with women's problems'.[90] Nancy suggested that the male directors they dealt with from Scott Bader 'haven't understood what it's all about. They haven't understood basically that it's an all-woman concern. And they haven't been able to integrate into the system we have there which is a peculiarly feminine or female approach to it.'[91]

My interview respondents retrospectively emphasised the significance of this 'peculiarly female' collective culture and practices they developed working at Fakenham Enterprises. Margaret remembered:

> Well, it was important that we were women … I used to take my baby, Cathleen, with me. Sometimes I'd stay there until about 8 o'clock at night, but I used to take everything with her and you know everyone took it in turns to feed her and that … . It was like a family really. We all worked together, we never used to fall out, everyone got on and we

stuck together. When we used to make a decision, we all stuck by it and that was it. But nowadays that doesn't happen; people say one thing and do another.⁹²

For Marees,

> I definitely enjoyed it ... we were a very close knit, friendly lot. And em ... I think I have grown up thinking that I should stick up for myself as well. When I was voted as a director, I thought, 'why would they pick me?' you know 'why bother' because I suppose this was the first time in my adult life that somebody had actually thought that I was worth listening to! Yeah I got confidence from the fact that somebody had voted for me yeah, and that people wanted me to have a say, yeah. Definitely, that did make me feel a bit better about myself, but until then I was just one of the girls.⁹³

The women remembered the collective culture they fostered that enabled them to assume their own voice, or 'have a say'. However, whilst gender difference was central to how they made sense of their collective action, they were reluctant to identify themselves as 'feminists' either at the time, or retrospectively.

At the time, the workers welcomed 'the right kind of support' from feminist groups on a practical level, but they did not associate themselves with that wider movement and differentiated themselves from the women they encountered during their occupation.⁹⁴ Nancy McGrath made it clear: 'We do not necessarily agree with all of the images projected by women's lib and did not make a request for their backing. But we are glad of their support that they are giving to our specific fight.'⁹⁵ Marees was more explicit about her attitude towards feminism. I originally asked her if she felt her action had been influenced by feminism, to which she responded, 'I don't know, I'm not really sure, it might have done because I have been told constantly that I was a feminist.' Although she did not necessary identify herself as a feminist, the fact that she emphasised how other people identified her in this manner is important. She went on to talk about her surprise at the solidarity and wider support they received at the time, again in a similar manner to Peggy in the previous chapter:

> Em, I was surprised that people sent us money for the fighting fund, I was thinking, 'why did these strangers send us anything?' why would they be interested in helping us?! Well I suppose I come from a family where you work for what you get and you don't get it if you don't work so I suppose if somebody was helping somebody else outside of the family, I was thinking, why are they? ... I was very surprised that

anybody who was outside of our little group what we were sitting in, or people around here, would be interested in us.⁹⁶

She pointed out that she felt that the occupation had been identified with the wider feminist movement, although she said that she would never have identified with that herself.

> A lot of money came from feminist groups, and ... I got the feeling that people thought that's what we were, but I was ... I wasn't a 'woman's woman' sort of person. I did sometimes feel that because there was a lot of feminists and people like that, I did feel that that's what they thought we were but ... I didn't feel the same as them no, because I was a married woman having a baby! That's why, it's silly, really silly, but yeah ... some of the ladies we met were very sort of strong and outspoken types of people. Not how I thought I was; I probably am now, but not how I was then. That's probably why ... I just thought a lot of people probably did think that's what we were, not just ordinary housewives and mothers. I was just an ordinary housewife and mother to be. I didn't think of myself as being anything special.⁹⁷

Marees was not involved in WLM groups and did not adopt a 'feminist' identity after the occupation had finished. However, she did identify the occupation as a turning point for her personally. In her narrative, she constructed her pre-strike self as shy and embarrassed, to having become a strong independent woman, willing to stick up for herself, in the present. Whilst she did not necessarily feel comfortable with explicitly identifying herself as a feminist – to avoid representing herself as 'anything special' – she was keen to point out that other people identified her in this manner. She was uncomfortable with the term, but she also associated it with being strong and independent. She reflected on the personal effects of the occupation:

> I can now see how it impacted on me, but I just buried it all, I didn't ever think about it, I think I was always a bit embarrassed by it! I used to be quite embarrassed by people looking at me because I wasn't a very confident 22 year old, I was very shy ... I didn't speak out a lot, no I was quiet ... but during the occupation, there was a lot of people who supported you and we would speak to people down the market and the store holder would say 'go on! well done girls', and that sort of thing. ... So I didn't think it had affected me until this come up, I didn't think much about it, but I think it probably did because I always sort of ... especially in recent years, and I know because people have said to me that I do stick up for myself now ... you know so yeah I think I am

quite independent, and that possibly is from going back to then, which was quite important really.⁹⁸

Margaret similarly discussed the occupation in relation to her own personality and strength of character as an individual. Rather than suggesting that the occupation represented a turning point in her life that was influenced by feminism, she suggested that she had been brought up to be a strong woman, unafraid to stand up to men and defy expected gender norms in the first place. Her participation in the occupation was only used as an example to further demonstrate these characteristics she identified with herself, and downplay the significance of 'external' political influences.

> Well, it was important that we were women; I think we were the first ones ever for women to actually stick up and say 'yeah we're going to take over the factory!' But I think I had always thought 'why should we women be treated differently from men?' from before the occupation, because them days women were treated differently. I remember like the men used to be up the pub ... and them were the days what when women didn't used to go in pubs. But I used to go to the pubs on my own but they'd look at you like there was something wrong with you. But I used to always say: 'well if I want a drink I'll go up the pub' ... so I had always been like that. You know people saying that you should do this or shouldn't do that, because you're a woman. ... But I didn't. I come from a family where there was eight of us, four boys and four girls. And I was brought up sort of tough, you know? With 10 of us in the family and I'd never give in ... so I suppose I have always stuck up for myself ... and so that's why I am quite loud really! Well I don't mean nasty loud, I just mean that I was one who was willing to fight for the factory and help them in every way.⁹⁹

Although Margaret did not identify the occupation as a turning point in her life, it was clear she felt it had influenced her on a personal level and represented her own fearlessness to stand up for her rights as an individual woman, which was something she felt she had learned from her childhood. Both Marees and Margaret told stories about their personalities when they spoke about their motivations and the impact of the occupation. This recalls Michael Roper's suggestion that subjectivity is not simply composed by ideological formations, but is a matter of personality formed through lived experience and emotional responses to these experiences.¹⁰⁰ In this respect, the Fakenham workers did not necessarily identify themselves as feminists, but framed their experiences around feminist values in terms of emphasising the importance of their self-worth and individual autonomy.

Conclusion

Wajcman argued that the women at Fakenham doubted their political efficacy because they were unable to improve their material conditions by forming a co-operative. However, focusing on oral history and personal testimony allows for a broader view of the various criteria with which the women themselves judged their experience of 'self-management'. In 1976, Nancy McGrath reflected,

> If the worst comes to worst and it folds up ... it's been a good four years and I wouldn't have changed it. I wouldn't give it up for anything, not the experiences that I've gone through. ... Maybe somebody else will learn from it. Maybe we can put our knowledge or experience at somebody else's disposal.[101]

In my oral history interviews, respondents generally reflected that working at Fakenham Enterprises was a positive experience, particularly in comparison to their subsequent experiences of work in low-paid service industries. The women I interviewed judged the effects of their brief experiences of self-management on their individual sense of self. They emphasised the importance of the economic and subjective value of their work, the alternative working arrangements they developed as a co-operative and their encounters with workers and political activists outside Fakenham. Whilst their political identity was by no means radicalised, this should not mean we overlook the personal significance of self-management for the protagonists who identified it as a break from the past. This is reflected in their handling of the co-operative where they claimed their own voice and leadership as women.

Whilst the Fakenham women's influence on feminist activists can clearly be seen from Wajcman's testimony, the influence of the WLM on the women themselves is less obvious. They felt the occupation had not led to wider critiques of class and gender relations across society. Instead of telling stories about 'gestalt moments' or feminist epiphanies, in the context of deindustrialisation, they told stories of personal strength, independence and learning to stick up for themselves as individual women. This raises questions about the diffuse socio-cultural influences of feminist campaigns in the 1970s, which may not have transformed working-class women's political orientations, but may have provoked them to ask questions about their personal autonomy and experiences of work.

Notes

1 MRC, Fakenham Enterprises Limited, MSS.30, 'Unions Ready for a Fight', *Eastern Evening News*, 1 March 1972.
2 'Angry Women Demonstrate Over Loss of Jobs', *Eastern Daily Press (EDP)*, 12 March 1972.
3 'Staff to Take over Doomed Shoe Factory', *EDP*, 18 March 1972.
4 For a narrative of the key events that occurred during the occupation, see Wajcman, *Women in Control*, Chapter 3.
5 'Women's Lib and Shoe Workers in Demo', *EDP*, 6 April 1972.
6 Wajcman, *Women in Control*, pp. 50–51.
7 'Sit-in's Happy Ending', *Guardian*, 17 July 1972, p. 5; G. Sheridan, 'Work in Work On', *Guardian*, 18 July 1973, p. 11.
8 MRC, FAK, MSS.30, 'Work-In Group Has Own Factory', *EDP*, 17 July 1972; 'Work-in Women form New Firm', *EDP*, 23 June 1972; E. Grand, 'Love at the Work-In' (untitled and undated article). See also Wajcman, *Women in Control*, pp. 53–55.
9 For a full account of how the Fakenham Enterprises functioned as a co-operative see Wajcman, *Women in Control*, Chapters 3 and 4.
10 C. Cockburn, 'Review of Wajcman, "Women in Control"', *Marxist Review* (March 1984), p. 40.
11 For an account of these disputes see K. Coates (ed.), *The New Worker Co-Operatives* (Nottingham: Spokesman Books, 1976).
12 Letters of Support are available in MRC, FAK, MSS.30/3/1.
13 L. Segal, 'Slow Change or No Change?: Feminism, Socialism and the Problem of Men', *Feminist Review*, no. 31 (Spring 1989), p. 9; Rowbotham, *The Past is Before Us*, p. 200.
14 M. Cerna, J. Davis, R. Gildea and P. Oseka, 'Revolutions' in R. Gildea, J. Mark and A. Warring (eds), *Europe's 1968: Voices of Revolt* (Oxford: Oxford University Press, 2013), pp. 125–126.
15 Wajcman, *Women in Control*, p. 183.
16 *New Earnings Study*, 1976 and *Small Towns Study*, Cambridgeshire and Ely County Council, 1972 in Wajcman, *Women in Control*, p. 38 and p. 196.
17 Wajcman, *Women in Control*, pp. 38–39.
18 'Fakenham Occupation', *Libertarian Struggle*, February 1973, pp. 4–5.
19 Wajcman, *Women in Control*, pp. 41–43.
20 M. Holland, 'Women give Shoe Firm the Boot', *Observer*, 7 May 1972, p. 3.
21 Figures from Department of Unemployment in Irene Bruegel, 'Women as a Reserve Army of Labour: A Note on Recent British Experience', *Feminist Review*, no. 3 (1979), pp. 12–23.
22 Figure from F. Field, *Are Low Wages Inevitable?* (Nottingham: Spokesman Books, 1976), quoted by Wajcman, *Women in Control*, p. 196; P. Symon, 'Life or Death in Rural Norfolk?' *The Times*, 14 December 1972, p. 16.
23 P. Symon, 'Life or Death in Rural Norfolk?' *The Times*, 14 December 1972, p. 16.
24 M. Holland, 'Women give Shoe Firm the Boot', *Observer*, 7 May 1972, p. 3.
25 Wajcman, *Women in Control*, p. 193.

26 MRC, MSS.30B/7/1, Fakenham, Misc., Dianne Glass, Fakenham Film, Transcripts, Tape 31, c. 1976: Interview with Roger Spiller, divisional officer of ASTMS (undated).
27 See A. Beckett, *When the Lights Went Out: Britain in the 1970s* (London: Faber and Faber, 2010), pp. 65–86 or Sandbrook, *State of Emergency*, pp. 118–133.
28 K. Coates, *Work-ins, Sit-ins, and Industrial Democracy: The Implications of Factory Occupations in Great Britain in the Early Seventies* (Nottingham: Spokesman, 1981).
29 'Open-Day Plan for Factory Work-In', *Dereham and Fakenham Times*, 10 April 1972.
30 MRC, MSS.30B/7/1, c. 1976. Tapes 37–38, interview with Nancy McGrath at her home on 17 March 1976.
31 Wajcman, *Women in Control*, p. 41.
32 Interview with Margaret in Fakenham, 15 April 2013.
33 Interview with Marees in Fakenham, 15 April 2013.
34 *New Earnings Study*, 1976 and *Small Towns Study*, Cambridgeshire and Ely County Council, 1972 in Wajcman, *Women in Control*, p. 39.
35 K. McCreery, 'We Want to Work: The Shoemaking Women of Fakenham', *ASTMS Journal* (August 1972).
36 MRC, MSS.30B/7/1, c. 1976: Tapes 34–36, transcripts of group discussion at Fourth Anniversary Party of Occupation on 17 March 1976.
37 'Fakenham Occupation', *Libertarian Struggle*, February 1973, pp. 4–5.
38 Ibid.
39 MRC, MSS.30, S. Shapiro and T. Van Gelderen, 'Fakenham: Danger Women at Work' in *Socialist Women* (undated).
40 MRC, MMS.30/3/3, Correspondence about the early organisation of Fakenham Enterprises, Report for ICOM, 30 July 1972.
41 Interview with Marees in Fakenham, 15 April 2013.
42 Interview with Patricia in Fakenham, 15 April 2013.
43 'Work-in Plan for Sexton's as Receiver Appointed', *EDP*, 1 March 1972; 'Sexton Girls Hope to See Receiver Today', *EDP*, 21 March 1972.
44 'Angry Women Demonstrate Over Loss of Jobs', *EDP*, 12 March 1972; 'Sleep in by Women Workers at Sexton's', *Norwich Evening News*, 18 March 1972; *EDP*, 'Bid to Move Plant', *EDP*, 20 March 1972; J. Windsor, *Guardian*, 'No Nonsense with Women's Enterprise', 7 April 1972.
45 MRC, MSS.30B/7/1, c. 1976, Interview with Arthur Ellsegood, Branch Secretary of NUFLAT, Norwich (undated).
46 'Angry Women Demonstrate Over Loss of Jobs', *EDP*, 12 March, 1972.
47 'Fakenham Occupation', *Libertarian Struggle*, February 1973, pp. 4–5.
48 McCreery, 'We Want to Work'.
49 'Sexton Girls Hope to See Receiver Today', *EDP*, 21 March 1972.
50 'Under Worker's Control', *Guardian*, 15 June 1972.
51 Wajcman, *Women in Control*, p. 48.
52 'Fakenham Occupation', *Libertarian Struggle*, February 1973, pp. 4–5.
53 See Appendix 1: Timeline for other examples of female workers occupying their workplace during this period.
54 Interview with Patricia in Fakenham, 15 April 2013.

55 *Ibid.*
56 K. Sayer, *Women of the Fields: Representations of Rural Women in the Nineteenth Century* (Manchester: Manchester University Press, 1995), pp. 126–135 and p. 180.
57 MRC, MSS.30B/7/1, c. 1976, Diane Glass interview with Eric Sexton, former owner of Sexton Everard and Managing Director of Meadows Company, Norwich, 11 March 1976.
58 MRC, MSS.30/3/1, Letters of support to Fakenham Workers, Letter from NUFLAT Members of Ballys (undated).
59 MRC, MSS.30/3/1, Letters of support to Fakenham Workers, Letter from Wycombe Trades Council dated 28 April 1972.
60 MRC, MSS.30/3/1, Letters of support to Fakenham Workers, Letter from Ealing Branch of AUEW, 28 August 1972.
61 Interview with Marees in Fakenham, 15 April 2013.
62 *Ibid.*
63 Mary Holland, 'Women give Shoe Firm the Boot', *Observer*, 7 May 1972.
64 Interview with Marees in Fakenham, 15 April 2013.
65 Wajcman, *Women in Control*, pp. 157–182.
66 *Ibid.*
67 V. Beechey, 'What's So Special about Women's Employment? A Review of Some Recent Studies of Women's Paid Work', *Feminist Review*, no. 15 (1983), pp. 23–45.
68 M. Savage, 'Working-Class Identities in the 1960s: Revisiting the Affluent Worker Study', *Sociology*, 39 (2005), pp. 929–946, at p. 938.
69 B. Skeggs, *Formations of Class and Gender: Becoming Respectable* (London: Sage Publications, 1997).
70 Savage, 'Working-Class Identities', pp. 939–942.
71 MRC, MSS.30B/7/1, c. 1976. Tapes 37–38, interview with Nancy McGrath at her home on 17 March 1976.
72 MRC, FAK, MSS.30/3/37, Letters of Support. For discussion of Women's Industrial Union see Boston, *Women Workers*, pp. 294–295.
73 MRC, FAK, MSS.30/3/147, Letters of Support.
74 MRC, FAK, MSS.30/3/155, Letters of Support.
75 MRC, FAK, MSS.30/3/171, Letters of Support.
76 'Factory Work-In Gains Support', *EDP*, 4 April 1972.
77 'Under Worker's Control', *Guardian*, 15 June 1972.
78 'Sexton Women's Plea to PM', *EDP*, 5 April 1972.
79 'Women's Lib and Shoe Workers in Demo', *EDP*, 6 April 1972.
80 'Factory Work-In Gains Support', *EDP*, 4 April 1972.
81 Examples of social investigators with an interest in women's work include L. Bell, *At the Works: A Study of a Manufacturing Town* (London: Virago, 1985) or M. Spring Rice, *Working-Class Wives: Their Health and Conditions* (London: Virago, 1981).
82 Pollert, *Girls, Wives, Factory Lives*; Glucksmann, *Women on the Line*.
83 Interview with Judy Wajcman in London, 22 April 2013.
84 *Ibid.*

85 MRC, MSS.30B/7/1, c. 1976. Tapes 37–38, interview with Nancy McGrath at her home on 17 March 1976.
86 MRC, MSS.30B/7/1, c. 1976. Tapes 27–29 are interview with Isabel Gilder at her home in Fakenham and her husband Basil (undated).
87 MRC, MSS.30B/7/1, c. 1976. Tape 3 and Tape 4 are from an Interview with Nancy McGrath in the office of Fakenham Enterprises, 10 March 1976.
88 Ibid.
89 MRC, MSS.30B/7/1, c. 1976. Tapes 34–36, transcripts of group discussion at Fourth Anniversary Party of Occupation on 17 March 1976.
90 MRC, MSS.30B/7/1, c. 1976. Tapes 37–38, interview with Nancy McGrath at her home on 17 March 1976.
91 Ibid.
92 Interview with Margaret in Fakenham, 15 April 2013.
93 Interview with Marees in Fakenham, 15 April 2013.
94 'Women's Lib and Shoe Workers in Demo', EDP, 6 April 1972.
95 'Factory Work-In Gains Support', EDP, 4 April 1972.
96 Interview with Marees in Fakenham, 15 April 2013.
97 Ibid.
98 Ibid.
99 Interview with Margaret in Fakenham, 15 April 2013.
100 Roper, 'Slipping Out of View: Subjectivity and Emotion in Gender History'.
101 MRC, MSS.30B/7/1, c. 1976. Interview with Nancy McGrath at her home, 17 March 1976.

5

The Ford Sewing machinists' strike, Dagenham, 1984–85

This final chapter returns to Ford, Dagenham, to analyse the second strike that was organised by female sewing machinists for skill recognition in the winter of 1984–85. Chapter 2 illustrated the tensions between public representations of the 1968 Ford sewing machinists as a 'historic' victory for equal pay, and the personal memory of the individual actors. Whilst the strike was optimistically hailed as a turning point symbolising a new era of gender equality, the sewing machinists were dissatisfied because the skilled nature of their work was not recognised. The women I interviewed remembered the strike as a defeat and had not accepted the wider impact of the dispute on equal pay legislation until the feature film *Made in Dagenham* was made in 2010. This was because the company and unions involved continued to rely on legal and managerial definitions of the sewing machinists' work; they preserved the gendered hierarchy of labour in the factory by offering the sewing machinists equal pay on a formal basis, instead of recognising their specific skills as women. The failure of employers and trade unions to recognise the subjective value of paid work to women persistently characterised the experiences and memories of the workers involved in the case studies that followed. For the women at Ford, the underlying grading grievance and the sense of injustice that led to the 1968 dispute continued to shape their experiences of work and trade unionism for the next seventeen years.

This dispute marks an appropriate place to begin to draw some broader conclusions about women's experiences of workplace activism between 1968 and 1985. The Ford sewing machinists' eventual success in winning their grading intimates that a transition had occurred in the way women's work was valued in the intervening seventeen years between the strikes – at least within the Ford factory. Drawing on contemporary representations of the dispute and interviews with women involved, this final chapter considers whether the women themselves believed that the strike represented a change in attitudes towards female workers. It considers women's explanations of their motivations for going on strike in relation to their broader experiences of work and trade unionism, as well as their personal understandings of feminism.

Context

As was shown in Chapter 2, the Ford sewing machinists were unhappy with the equal pay resolution that brought an end to their strike in 1968. Although the dispute was a catalyst leading directly to the passage of the Equal Pay Act in 1970, the sewing machinists continued to earn 92 per cent of the unskilled male B grade until the act was implemented in 1975. More importantly, the women were dissatisfied because they did not have the skilled nature of their work recognised. The sewing machinists continued to demand skill recognition and had claims to be regraded rejected by the Ford National Joint Negotiating Committee in 1970, 1974, 1981, 1982 and 1983.[1]

The strike in 1984 was provoked by legislative change. In 1983, the European Court of Justice pressured the British government to add an Equal Value amendment to the Equal Pay Act. This entitled women to equal pay where they performed 'like work' and 'work rated as equivalent' and where work was considered to be of 'equal value' to that of male co-workers in the same employment. The Ford sewing machinists responded to this legal change in April 1984 by taking their claim to an industrial tribunal. With support from the TGWU, they argued that their jobs were of equal value to Grade C manual jobs performed by Eastman Cutters and paint spray operators.[2]

The tribunal was organised in a manner where the women had to prove the original job evaluation scheme in 1967 had discriminated against them on the basis of sex. The male assessors from the consultancy firm Urwick Orr and Partners had ranked the women's hand-eye coordination and manual dexterity as exceptional, yet rated them as thirty-ninth of fifty-six jobs in the factory.[3] In spite of this, the women were unable to provide concrete evidence showing that sex discrimination was the reason for this anomaly, and the tribunal ruled in favour of the company. The TGWU appealed against the judgement by arguing that the burden lay with Ford to prove they did not discriminate.[4]

The sewing machinists themselves were no longer willing to wait and voted to strike on 21 November 1984. They felt they had been lied to and treated with a lack of respect by the company. They formed a strike committee and issued the following statement:

For 16 years we sewing-machinists have sought recognition for our skills. We are skilled and experienced sewing-machinists – that is what the advert said when we came here. Everybody knows the skill involved in sewing the seat covers and upholstery – it would take an unskilled worker years of training to reach the standard of skill we have. Two years ago the company pledged that our skill would be recognised. The plant manager said this is a promise that has been made and it will be fulfilled. Like lambs we believed it. Now they have gone back on their promise and they have refused us. They stuck two fingers at us. We followed all the procedures – we waited 16 years. But enough is enough.[5]

Although the 1984 strike was over the same issue of skill recognition that concerned the sewing machinists in 1968, it is important to recognise some differences between the two strikes. First, the Equal Pay Act had been passed in 1970, and there was no space for confusing the women's demands, as occurred in 1968. Second, the shop stewards Rose Boland and Lil O'Callaghan who led the 1968 strike were no longer alive and had been replaced by a new group of shop stewards, who, according to my interviewee Dora, had less experience and confidence. Finally, the NUVB, the main union involved in the 1968 dispute, was incorporated into the TGWU in 1972. The main continuity between the two strikes was the instigation of both by trade unionists at a grassroots level and the influence of Bernard Passingham, who was involved in the 1968 dispute as the NUVB deputy convenor for the River Plant and by 1984 had taken over as the plant convenor.

Passingham helped instigate the 1984 dispute by refusing to sign the company's annual wage agreement in protest against the industrial tribunal's failure to regrade the women. This delayed annual pay increases of 7 per cent for 40,000 Ford workers one month before Christmas and placed greater pressure on the company and union officials involved to negotiate a resolution to the strike.[6] The women organised a twenty-four-hour picket of the factory and once again brought Ford's production to a halt.[7] By the beginning of December, the company were reported to have laid off 10,000 production workers in factories in Dagenham, Merseyside and Southampton. Ford attempted to resolve the situation by suggesting that 'independent' assessors examine the sewing machinists' claim. But the sewing machinists were no longer willing to take the company's offers seriously and demanded a comparative job review from the Advisory, Conciliation and Arbitration Service (ACAS) instead.[8]

After nine weeks, the strike was brought to an end when Ford agreed for ACAS to independently reassess the women's grade. At Dagenham,

150 women voted overwhelmingly to end the strike. At Halewood, sixty-seven to thirty-four workers voted in favour of returning to work. Some feared that history would repeat itself; the Merseyside shop steward Kathy McGovern said, 'You can't help but have a lot of mistrust about arbitration after 16 years. A lot of women are not happy about it. A lot of them feel we have sacrificed six weeks' pay.'[9] However, the ACAS enquiry revisited and regraded the key characteristics from the original job evaluation scheme carried out in 1967. After observing 'benchmark jobs' across Ford's UK plants, the panel changed the original assessments on a number of ratings including hand-eye coordination, visualisation of shapes and spatial relations.[10] On 26 April 1985, the Ford sewing machinists were recognised as skilled workers after seventeen years of struggle. The company defended themselves in light of the independent panel's conclusions by arguing that many of the original benchmark jobs had disappeared after 1967. Conversely, Mick Murphy, the TGWU national officer, acknowledged 'the original decision not to regrade the women as skilled workers amounted to discrimination'. He felt the 1984 strike represented progress and predicted it would have an impact throughout British industry and at Ford plants across Europe.[11]

It is important to recognise that the workforce included a new generation of female workers who had not been involved in the original dispute, yet who held the same grievance as those who went on strike in 1968. The women I interviewed in Chapter 2 had not been involved in the 1984 dispute. In 2015, I interviewed Pam and Dora, who had both played an active role in organising the strike in 1984. Dora was a shop steward, and Pam stood on the picket line every night for seven weeks during the strike.

Both of my interviewees thought their victory was significant. Pam explained, 'You got your grading and you got what you was entitled to, which was all you wanted really. To be recognised that you had a skill.'[12] Similarly, Dora remembered, 'In actual fact we nearly went to D grade. We weren't far off D grade then but you can't do that. We were skilled and that's what we wanted.'[13] Whilst they clearly thought it was significant to have their ability finally recognised, my interviewees also had doubts about the wider impact of the dispute for two reasons. First, the women were moved from the River Plant to the Paint, Trim and Assembly (PTA) plant shortly after the strike, which eventually closed in 1992. The majority of both male and female workers at Ford were made redundant from the late 1980s onwards.[14] Pam explained, 'It went along for a while okay. But then I think they might have started to think about shutting the place down.'[15] The second reason for their doubts about the dispute's long-term impact was they seemed exasperated at how it had only been recognised more recently, rather than at the time. Dora said,

> The Wainwright Trust [an equal opportunities charity] called us up to um ... they had a thing up there ... like for what we did. That was the first time that we were really recognised for doing anything. And you know, they wait until I'm 77, and then they want to, oh well I was about 70 then and they want to do all these things ... I mean I never thought about it, we never went on strike to get publicity. ... No one thought anything about it at all really. And I didn't. I certainly didn't. It was just that what you've got to do you know? You've got to stand up for women.[16]

Dora felt that the publicity from the *Made in Dagenham* film and musical had changed the way their strike was remembered. She pointed out, 'It's because of *Made in Dagenham* because that was only the 1968 strike. They didn't mention the 84.'[17] Dora thought the 1968 strike had been recognised ahead of the 1984 dispute because the issue of equal pay 'involves all women'.[18] She was also keen to stress that for the sewing machinists in 1968, equal pay 'wasn't what they wanted' but it was 'better than nothing'.[19] She felt that the 1984 strike had been ignored because 'when you come to recognition of skill it don't come to so many women, does it?'[20] She said, 'No one really knows about the 84 strike' and explained she often felt angry after attending events to commemorate the disputes where she was always asked '"what happened in 84?"... they didn't even know. That's not good. I mean it's still history for women.'[21] When the disputes had been remembered publicly, Dora suggested they had been remembered in a manner that trivialised the main issues. She explained,

> I got a phone call from Paul O'Grady to go on there [television programme]. But to me – I don't mind Paul O'Grady, don't get me wrong – but he's a comedian. And that's not funny. That's the story and it's not funny is it? I mean you can laugh about different things of it but I thought no, he's gonna take the P.[22]

My interview respondents felt their memory of the strike did not fit with the way it was being publicly remembered. As Dora pointed out, it was about standing up for women, but it was 'lots of different things as well'.[23] It was not a joke.

The rest of this chapter considers these broader tensions, between individual and public memory, and the memory of the 1968 strike as a victory for equal pay and the relative absence of the 1984 strike from public memory. Following Chapter 2, it highlights the problems with triumphant narratives that represent the 1968 strike as a moment of change and illustrates the continued sense of injustice and conflict that characterised the sewing machinists' experiences of work and trade unionism at Ford. It aims to move beyond thinking about these strikes as events signifying women's 'arrival' within trade unions and develop a better understanding of what the dispute meant for the women involved.

Experiences of work

In 1984, there was no confusion over the issue of equal pay; the sewing machinists' motivations for going on strike were conceptualised and articulated as demands for skill recognition by the workers. The women emphasised that the dispute was over a 'moral' principle, rather than 'economic' gain. A shop steward called Lil Thompson told the *Guardian*, 'The strike is not about the £6.50 extra, but recognising women's skills.' She said, 'The reason we are in this grade is simple, it's because we are women.'[24] A worker named Joan explained, 'This dispute goes back a long time. We've waited for years for recognition that we are skilled workers. The girls just aren't going to put up with it any more. It's not the money that's important – it's the principle.'[25] Another worker told the *Guardian* it would take five years to become a skilled machinist: 'Once you cross the Ford threshold you're deemed unskilled. For six months I was transferred to spot welding and did the job, but a spot welder couldn't do my job and yet he's grade C, and I'm grade B.'[26] A shop steward named Doreen Cook pointed out,

> No, it's exactly the same as in '68 when we were 85% of the male pay and it got twisted to equal pay. Equal pay was fine for the skilled grade or C grade but we would have preferred the skilled grade because equal pay would have followed anyway. It's the principle of the thing.[27]

From a feminist perspective, an article in *Spare Rib* explained, 'The Ford's strike clearly shows the undervaluing of women's role in industry … this results from the general belief that difficult, fiddly and repetitive work, such as sewing, is the "natural" ability of women and as such requires little or no training.'[28]

The sewing machinists also had to contend with patronising attitudes from the Ford management and local press. The sewing machinists' foreman said their work could be performed by a 'banana.'[29] The *Barking and Dagenham Post* also appeared sceptical about the value of the women's work. Contrary to the sewing machinists' explanation of their incentives, they described the dispute as a 'pay row' and suggested that the women wanted their '£128 weekly wage brought in line with higher skilled workers'.[30] Such reporting diverted attention from the grading issue and sought to undermine the legitimacy of the women's demand by focusing on the issue of higher pay. It was suggested that the women were in a lower grade because 'men's work is heavier and requires more expertise'.[31] The local newspaper also emphasised that the strike had blocked a 9 per cent pay rise for 40,500 workers and laid off 8,000 men.[32]

In an oral history interview conducted by the TUC in 2006, Dora explained how unfair it felt being paid less than men whose work the women perceived to be less skilled.

> The cutters used to cut by hand, like with scissors and all that and then they brought the machine in and they, they just stood there – the machine cut it! ... they still had women sitting on a machine and doing her work, but they fetched a machine in just to cut and they were C grade, and they'd just stand there watching a thing go round.[33]

This was very similar to the way Sally described the situation at Trico in Chapter 3, and shows how women drew on their personal experience of and sense of injustice in watching men *not* working and being paid higher wages, whilst they were denied such personal freedom for themselves. A worker named Maureen told a similar story in the 2006 TUC interview when she spoke about the injustice of women being able to perform men's work, but men being unable to perform women's work. She said,

> If our work built up and they didn't need so many car seats, they would say to some of the girls, 'Oh, we'd like you to go over to the door panels, because they're a bit short-staffed', and the girls would go over there and get stuck in and do the door panels, or in the tank shop; they would find you work over there, but when we were very busy and there was quite a few spare machines, they could never say to the men, 'Would you come over and do a bit of machining?', because, you know, the men would never have a clue how to even thread a needle, I shouldn't think, rather than do machining, and in the end the women started talking amongst their selves and saying, 'Well, this is not on; we can sort of turn our hands to anything but the men can't', which is, which seemed very unfair to us. So I think that was the start of us digging our heels in.[34]

A worker named Geraldine reflected 'I think we was like a fraction away from getting D grade, but I think if they'd have given us D grade then it would have proved that they'd have been wrong all them years ago. Women, everything you wanted you really had to fight for.'[35] At the surface, the strike was about skill recognition. But the women's testimony shows the strike was perceived and understood as challenging an unequal hierarchy in the factory between men and women. In my own oral history interviews, women located these moments in their life stories in broader narratives about asserting their independence and taking control over their own lives in the face of power relations which disadvantaged them.

Dora was born in 1938. She grew up in Custom House in East London. She moved to Dagenham with her family when she was thirteen years old, but worked in a range of jobs in London's East End after leaving school at the age of fifteen. She got married when she was nineteen and moved to nearby Ilford with her husband, who was a docker. Dora started working at Ford in 1971 when she was thirty-four years old. Ford was her first 'proper job' after she had spent the previous eight years producing curtains at home whilst she looked after her three children. She chose to work at Ford 'because it was better money'.[36] Pam was born in Dagenham in 1954. Her mother did 'indoor ironing', and her father worked in the PTA at Ford and later became a janitor. Like the women interviewed in Chapter 2, she emphasised how much she enjoyed growing up in Dagenham and reflected on the sense of decline since the closure of the Ford factory. Talking about growing up there, she said,

> I loved it ... everybody knew everyone up the road. You know you could go into each other's houses, have a cup of tea and everything. But times have changed now. And I've lived here [Romford] 28 years and I know one couple of up there and that's about it really. But living in Dagenham, because you've got Fords as well and everybody worked there so you knew everybody.[37]

Pam was sixteen years old when she left school and started work. Her early experiences of work were characterised by 'horrendous' pay and bronchitis.

> I went into machining, I started making nurses' uniforms at Goodmayes. No [I did not enjoy it]. The money was horrendous, it was so ... well, you didn't get a lot of money. I can't remember how much it was but it weren't a lot and then I decided I don't want to do that and so I went down the road for another job ... and so I left and then I went into Fergusons, to make televisions and radiograms, that was in Hainault, and then I done that for four years. ... But I had to leave because I got bronchitis because of the flax off all the soldering and wiring. Yeah, and I couldn't breathe and I was on a pump ... I was just so ill that I thought 'I can't work here no more'.[38]

Pam moved to Ford in 1975 when she was twenty-one years old. Like the women interviewed in Chapter 2, working at Ford appealed to her because of the high wages and sense of stability it offered by comparison to other machining and manufacturing jobs. She said,

> Oh it was much better rewards. I really can't remember how much it was. … But it was the best pay around really. … And you knew that it was a factory that was going to be there for a while and so if you stayed there longer you would get your pension and things like that. It had more going for it really. It wasn't just pay, but it was the machining itself and the sense of security.[39]

Pam actively chose to work at Ford because she thought it would give her more control over her life. After the strike, she became a supervisor and explained that she wanted to 'better herself'.[40] It was clear that paid work was important to her self-understanding and was not just a temporary stage of her life. Dora, too, retrospectively connected the sewing machinists' motivations for going on strike to a concern to have the personal and material significance of paid work for women recognised. She spoke about the importance of women's wages at the time of the strike and having to contend with the persistent notion that women worked for pin money.

> It was about time women stood up for themselves and like as I'd said the men used to say 'pin money' but there was a lot of women in there that were widowed, divorced, had children – I mean they didn't turn out for pin money. I mean okay I could of lived without working at Fords, like he [my husband] was at work, but I wouldn't have had what I've got today if I hadn't. And you want to be recognised. You want to be earning the rate you should be earning. And also, when you got C grade it goes on your pension when you retire, so that makes a difference as well.[41]

The point here was that the sewing machinists all faced different circumstances outside work – some women had to work at Ford to survive, whilst others like Dora felt they could have lived without working there. However, none of the women was dependent, or understood themselves as dependent on anyone else other than themselves. Regardless of their circumstances, they were working there to improve their lives and felt this basic 'fact' was being ignored on the basis of their sex.

As well as emphasising the importance of women's wages and security, both Pam and Dora spoke about how much they enjoyed work due to their friendships and work culture. The work itself was not particularly enjoyable; Pam explained, 'It was very repetitive.'[42] But she liked working there because 'you had a load of different people who were very strong in character ... and it was just silly things really, you know what I mean – always laughing and joking about. But I loved it there. It was good.'[43] Dora also repeatedly emphasised throughout her interview how she enjoyed work: 'I liked it in Fords, I enjoyed what I did' or 'I enjoyed it and I know it was aggro at times but that passed, you know? You'd get annoyed at the time and then it's gone. ... But I enjoyed what I did. I enjoyed going to work.'[44] Neither woman strongly identified with the labour process itself, but both enjoyed working at Ford because it was better pay than their previous (and in Pam's case, subsequent) jobs, because it felt secure, and because of the good atmosphere created by the women themselves.

Although Dora and Pam both stressed that they enjoyed work, their accounts were also characterised by an unequal dynamic of power between men and women. This took the form of general observations: for example, Pam explained to me, 'It was always, men always got more money, and they always did. I don't know why, but they did.'[45] But it was also expressed in more specific anecdotes; for example, Dora told me a story about 'having a battle' with a male shop steward representing workers in the engine plant who believed the women 'were taking men's seats in the canteen'.[46] She pointed out, 'if that had been men they would have just took no notice of it', and suggested it was just one of 'all sorts of things you come across because we were women'.[47] Similar to my interviewees in Chapter 2, Pam drew on the leitmotif of being 'angry with the janitors sweeping around your feet' and went on to explain how her dad became a janitor and 'he was still earning more than me and I was sitting there machining!'[48] She also remembered, 'I thought I'll get another job as a stack truck driver because that was C grade and they blocked it and they put it on to night work because they knew you didn't want night work.'[49] She thought management did this 'because you was women! They weren't going to do [allow] that were they?'[50] Dora remembered the first time the union pressured the management to pay the workforce sick pay, 'all barring pregnant women', and felt this was a good example of 'how they treated women'.[51] Both Dora and Pam enjoyed work but felt they were treated differently because of their sex in ways that limited their wages and undermined their social status within the factory. Although the strike centred on the issue of skill recognition, my interviewees connected it to their broader experiences of paid work, which were characterised by conflict between men and women in the factory. Women felt they were at the bottom of an unequal hierarchy based on their gender, and they sought to challenge this when they went on strike in 1984.

Experiences of trade unionism

The strike was not treated as novel and unexpected by the unions involved in the same way as the other case studies considered in this book, which was obviously because it was a revival of the concerns surrounding the 1968 dispute. There was evidence of some opposition from male trade unionists reported at the time. The chairman of the Halewood joint shop stewards' committee was not prepared to support the strike because he did not want to 'polarise issues that were too complicated to express as right or wrong'.[52] He said, 'We could never say that the girls have not got a case but there are many other grievances. We have a grading system that dates back to the 1960s and is just not capable of coping with the structure of a modern car plant.'[53] The body plant convenor at Halewood said, 'They have a good case but other people could present just as good a case. The men don't know much about it because the women have played their cards closed to their chest.'[54] The president of the AUEW said the women's regrading would have a destabilising impact on the Ford wage structure.[55]

Although the women's case was perceived by some as 'too complicated' to fit within a 'modern' car plant, the TGWU fully supported the strike and made it official after two weeks.[56] The strike occurred at a time when the TGWU perceived itself to be changing its relationship with its female members. Shortly after the strike, an article in the union's national newspaper claimed, 'The TGWU is firmly committed to the greater involvement of women in the union, the Living Wage Campaign and the fight for equal rights for women in the workplace and society at large.'[57] The journal suggested that a 'breakthrough' had occurred in 1979, when they organised regional women's advisory committees. In 1983, they established a national women's advisory committee. They held their first ever women's shop stewards course in 1980, and held five national courses for women between 1984 and 1985. The General Council elected its first woman member in 1984. In 1985, the union produced special booklets on equal pay, sexual harassment and other 'issues of specific importance to women'.[58]

At the time, it was reported that male workers within the factory had changed their attitude towards women since the 1968 strike. The *New Statesmen* claimed, 'The women's case is accepted by the men who work at Ford, and attitudes have changed since 1968.'[59] A TGWU district official explained, 'We have argued the job is harder, that the women are susceptible to joint strain that leads to tenosynovitis and that the job evaluation scheme should have rated the markings for physical effort and eye and co-ordination higher.'⁶⁰ The TGWU demanded an independent re-evaluation of the women's grading by ACAS and celebrated a victory for the women when they finally achieved their grading in April 1985.

In the strike's aftermath, the TGWU issued a commemorative plate that assumed ownership of the victory. The plate paid tribute to the 'Ford Sewing-Machinists' historic contribution to the advancement of women's rights at the workplace in Britain.' The plate was accompanied by a written 'brief history' of the 1968 and 1984–85 disputes, which described them as 'the most important industrial struggle by a group of British women since the Bryant and May Match girls strike of 1888'. The 'brief history' misremembered the unions' position in the 1968 dispute:

> Throughout the 17 year period of struggle, the Ford River Plant's Joint Shop Stewards' Committee at Dagenham was the main centre of Trade Union support. It gave encouragement and unqualified assistance to the sewing-machinists. The committee provided the 'know how' of struggle and the links with the Labour and Trade Union Movement both nationally and locally, without which a successful outcome would not have been possible. ... All concerned won themselves an honoured place in British Labour history.⁶¹

Herein lies the contradiction that characterised women's experiences of trade unionism during this period. Trade unions had a crucial role to play in improving the conditions of female workers, and it was more difficult for women to fight without them; however, the 'know how' and positions of power within the union remained unequally distributed between male and female workers. Female workers did not necessarily want to be 'provided' with 'know how', but wanted to speak for themselves. The consequence on the shop floor was that many women had to organise themselves without the support of their union and subsequently defined their interests in opposition to those of their trade union officials. It is important to acknowledge that whilst union support was crucial for female workers' success, the force of change came from the women themselves. Lumping the strikes together and commemorating them collectively ignores the fact the strikes actually involved different women with different experiences and memories.

The commemorative plate memorialising the strikes issued by the TGWU illustrates this point in itself. The plate has a 'scroll of honour' that pays tribute to sixteen male union officials involved in the 1984 dispute, and six female sewing machinists. Dora, who played an active role in the dispute as a shop steward, said.

My name's not on it because they forgot. I said to Bernard Passingham. Well, I didn't take no notice at first, it didn't bother me ... but there were a lot of men on that plate and they shouldn't have been there. That was a woman's plate ... so I didn't agree with it to be honest.[62]

The union issued the plate to cement their role into a triumphant narrative about winning improved conditions for their female members. In memorialising the role of the male union officials involved, the plate cast an institutional shadow over the women themselves, like Dora and Pam, who had given up their time and money to actually instigate and lead the strike. The focus on success misrepresents the strike's leadership; it implies closure and gender harmony; and it smoothes over the complexities of the individual actors' motivations and sense of injustice that continued to characterise female workers' experiences of trade unionism before and after the strike. Fundamentally, it ignores a whole different level of conflict between women and men in the workplace and against gender hierarchies in work and industrial action.

The women involved in the 1984-85 strike retrospectively emphasised the importance of being in the union at Ford in a similar manner to my interviewees who were involved in the 1968 strike. In the 2006 TUC interview, a worker named Geraldine remembered joining the union when she first started working at Ford:

> When I started, I think there was – I think I started with about twelve or thirteen of us; we went and sat round this big table and it was Lil O'Callaghan again; and she said, 'Right, you've got to join this union', and she, you know, she just put you right and said, 'You've got to join this union, because you'll need us behind you', and we really did actually.[63]

Dora and Pam had quite distinct memories of their experiences of trade unionism from one another, but both women characterised working at Ford with industrial conflict. Speaking about her upbringing, Pam said, 'There was no politics, but my Dad, because he worked in the PTA he was always on strike, so we was always out with him when I started.'[64] Pam didn't remember the 1968 strike, which took place when she was fourteen years old, but she knew about it because, 'Well you worked there and people talked about it and all, "what we done" and "what we didn't do"'.[65] She remembered a sense of antagonism in the build up to the strike in 1984: 'I think it was just the unrest with it all. ... And then you just thought "well people are earning more money than you", really, it was just unease, unease really.'[66] Pam also spoke about the strike possessively and distinguished her interests from those of male workers in a comparable manner to the women interviewed in Chapter 2: 'I wasn't involved in any strikes before our one ... we was only put out when the men went out at the PTA really ... you was in the union so you sort of had to come out, you can't really sit in there.'[67] The 1984 strike was different to her previous experiences of being on strike because it was for the women themselves.

Dora also spoke about the high frequency of strikes within the factory, and intimated that female workers generally felt they lacked control in a lot of these situations:

> I was only there for a week and then they went out on strike [laughs]. ... But there was always strikes. I mean the women always came out with the men. ... And they weren't always happy about it because the men had a lot of them sort of things.[68]

Dora was eventually voted shop steward in 1984, and it was clear from her testimony that she had played a central role in the union and the union was an important part of her life. Although she did not join the TGWU until she was thirty-four years old, and was not voted shop steward until she was in her forties, she explained she had always taken an interest in her previous jobs and linked this to her individual character and sense of justice:

> I was always interested and I always sort of got involved with the stewards. Because I've always been very outspoken. And I mean some people deceit people all the time, always, but not me. Because some [stewards] didn't think you should tell people the truth, but ... if I was in a meeting and they didn't want me to tell the girls, I would go back and tell them. I would take them in because it's their livelihood as well as mine and like they didn't want them to know what was going on.[69]

Dora connected her role as shop steward to her personal characteristics: her outspokenness, her honesty and her authenticity. These were individual characteristics she felt aligned with her role as shop steward, where she was responsible for other people's wellbeing as well as her own.

Although Dora 'always' took an interest in the union, she did not put herself forward to be elected as a shop steward until 1984, when she had a personal conflict with a foreman. She explained,

> I'd had to have a hysterectomy and so they put me on the job where I took work off the bottom, and it was heavy work, and oh it was really bad, actually so I went to see the doctor and he went 'you can't go back on that job'. He said they'll have to give you a light job for a while. I get

back, of course they put me on that job. Oh and I just thought 'I've had enough'. They didn't like me because I argued with them.[70]

When Dora became shop steward, she put in a complaint about the foreman, who was also having an affair with a woman on the assembly line, and he was moved to a different section of the factory. She reflected, 'So that was my main aim to be honest with you, you know when I first went in, but I didn't want another woman treated how I was treated.'[71] This story reflects a blurring of individual and collective interests. Dora's interest and commitment to trade unionism evolved from her personal experiences of victimisation and her sense of injustice. However, she linked these individual concerns to the wider wellbeing of other, predominantly female workers in the factory.

Dora became very involved in the union for the rest of her working life and spent the majority of the interview describing the challenges she felt she had faced due to sex discrimination. She spoke about fighting for maternity pay. She also spoke about fighting the sense of injustice when male workers were allowed to claim compensation for deafness induced by the noise of the machinery, whilst women were not. She emphasised the challenges she felt she had faced in having women's voice heard with the union. She said,

> **DORA:** We had to fight for everything we wanted and you know it was the union, as I said, it wasn't the management at Fords.
> **JONATHAN:** Why do you think that was?
> **DORA:** Well they was all men. Always. You look at the union all those years ago, you never had no … we had one woman officer and that was it. Now when I look back I think how bad the union was to women as well. I mean I've been to other meetings now and they say like 'has it got better for the women?' Well, I don't think so. I think women are still left out of a lot of them. I mean in the union now haven't got many women officers.[72]

Although Dora found it challenging operating as a shop steward, she also emphasised the importance of this role within her life and the impact she had in the factory by talking about her reputation. She compared herself to a 'doctor' and spoke about how people used to 'come into my office with all sorts of personal things'.[73] She used to get called in to the factory in the middle of the night to resolve other people's problems. When she retired, she described how 'the management couldn't get me out quick enough', whilst her former workmates still used to call her up asking for help. I asked her if she was sad to leave and she replied, 'Not first of all, but I was. I really missed it. I really missed it. I used to see people going to work and think I wish that was me.'[74]

The union had played an important part in Dora's working life and led her to join the Labour Party later on in the 1980s. However, like the majority of women in this study, she actively identified herself, her involvement in the union and the strike as not political. She had joined the Labour Party so she could sell commemorative plates for the strike at their annual conference. She pointed out, 'I didn't join it out of choice. Because I've never been politically minded. I don't want to get into that, you know?'[75] I asked if she did not see her own involvement in the union as political but she replied, 'No, not really, no I don't. Well, you fight for your rights and other people's rights. And I suppose I could be a little bit ... no I don't think I am. I don't think I am.'[76]

Dora left the Labour party after she retired. She also left the TGWU after they amalgamated to become Unite in 2007 and closed her local branch. Having been in the TGWU for thirty years, she told me that she now got up when she attended meetings 'to say how rubbish the unions are now'.[77] For Dora, the problem was the people who she perceived to have taken over the labour movement like Len McCluskey, the general secretary of Unite. She said,

> You've got to have somebody with a bit of guts and not just for themselves. All their politics and all this ... McCluskey is in the union for what he can get out of it – not what he can do for other people. I mean years ago, you took old Jack Jones and that, they didn't get the money and everything they get today, and they were all for the workers. But this lot ain't. They are only out for what they can get for their self. ... No but I like people with principles. They were there because they wanted to fight for the people, for the working class if you like. And they done a good job, but as time's gone on, no. I don't belong to a union now.[78]

Dora associated 'politics' with people like Len McCluskey and Tony Blair – people who she perceived to be self-serving and possessed ulterior motives other than helping other workers. Whilst her testimony could be described as nostalgic – an oversimplified and romanticised account of trade union leaders being 'better' in the past (which does not actually fit with her personal experiences of trade unionism) – it also offers a significant clue towards explaining her own reluctance to identify herself as political. Throughout the interview, she emphasised her individuality when explaining her role as shop steward. She said, 'People say to me: "you've got to be a certain person", like a different person to take a meeting like that. Like it's got to be in you to do it.'[79] Dora felt she was that 'certain person' because she 'listened to people', but also,

> Well I like people to be treated fair. I think, and I like getting into debates. Not just an argument but debating and learning, if you like? Because when I first went there, I went to meetings I wouldn't speak because I didn't know what I was talking about, but then as soon as I learned ... I liked it and I enjoyed it ... I think it was always in me to be honest. I've always been outspoken. ... You can't learn it, it's there isn't it? ... I just wish that like one of my granddaughters would, or one of my daughters would have got involved in women's lib things really, you know? But they haven't been really interested. It's a shame really, but then I love athletics and they don't – so you know?[80]

This quote reflected a common means by which the women interviewed in this book appeared to retrospectively make sense of their workplace activism. Dora described herself as not politically minded and turned her attention inward as she sought an explanation for her behaviour. By rejecting a 'political' identity, she (like many of the other women interviewed for this book) dis-identified herself from the formal institutions connected with the labour movement, which had let her down and were perceived to possess external motivations. Instead, she emphasised what appeared to her as an inherent way of being – her outspokenness, her sense of justice and her authenticity. These were all characteristics necessary for her to assume her own voice and look after both herself and her fellow workmates in an environment that sought to undermine their dignity on the basis of their sex.

Pam had not been as involved in the union as Dora, but she identified herself in a related fashion of being not political. She had little to say about her trade unionism. Talking about herself at the time of the strike, she explained that she had not been involved in the union because 'I was young, I was too busy going out at night and I wasn't really bothered about politics or things really.'[81] She also explained her role in the strike by emphasising her individuality. However, she distinguished her experience of working at Ford by emphasising the importance of the collective solidarity shared among the workforce, which she felt was lacking in her subsequent jobs in other factories and a school kitchen. She said,

> **PAM:** I've always been a strong person and I've always believed in what's right. So I think that sort of kept going through my years ... but it just sparked it off I suppose.
> **JONATHAN:** Sparked it off? The strike or working in Fords?

> **PAM:** I think working in Fords, seeing the difference between what people do. You know but when I went to other factories, you saw it there, but obviously they didn't have stewards or anything so they can't do nothing about it. ... Yeah because [at Ford] we was in numbers, we made an effect that I think if you work in an office or anything like that and you've got a dispute, you've only got yourself and you're easier to get rid of.
>
> **JONATHAN:** Did you feel like that happened working in your other jobs after Ford then?
>
> **PAM:** You sort of just got your head down really and got on with that you had to do, because like in the kitchen I think there was about eight or nine of us, but there was nothing that come up that made you want to do anything really. You just done it, you know? It wasn't that environment to think about someone else getting more money than you.[82]

Pam did not associate the strike with a transition in the relationship between female workers and trade unions. She retrospectively related her involvement in the strike with her strength of character and personal resilience. However, she also felt she developed such qualities from working in an 'environment' where the workforce possessed collective strength and solidarity and had representatives with the ability to exert an 'effect' on how their work was organised. She felt it was more difficult for workers, in particular female workers, to assert the value of their work in the present:

> Like because there were so many of us, you could stop it. But like when we went to that meeting the other night, there was all women complaining about other things, like nurses and that, you know, talking about going out on strike, but they're in another situation ... it's different making a car and looking after a person who is really ill. You know?[83]

Dora offered a very similar explanation for women's workplace militancy in the past and felt it occurred in a manner that no longer happened in the present. She said,

> It is more difficult today, like they've not got big factories no more, like at Fords we had so many women in there and so many men, you've got an army going in you know, but it's different today, and especially when they take a member in out of like a supermarket say, and then don't support them, I mean bleeding hell![84]

Pam and Dora did not remember the strike as a 'breakthrough' for female workers improving their working conditions and position in the labour movement – as it was understood at the time. Pam felt the strike had a limited personal impact because she left Ford after she had children. She explained that she went back for one year, but was unable to afford childcare and so got another job in a school canteen because the hours were more convenient. Pam liked working in the school kitchen, because there 'was a lot nice girls there', but pointed out it was 'definitely hard work and the money wasn't as good as Fords'.[85] She also suggested that the strike had a limited impact due to economic decline. She said,

> I don't think [women] have got anywhere really, because there's still women who are not happy. You know? Like there's still meetings everywhere and things so I don't think it changed anything really. I think that for workers in general really because when I look at the pay for my sons and that I think its rubbish you know what I mean? You know it's not good is it? All the bills go up and everything goes up but there's not many places now that gives you rises.[86]

For Pam, the strike for skill recognition was part of a different era.

> Yeah you had choice. Yeah you could always leave one job and get another one, but I don't think you can do it now. Well I ain't had a job for years so I don't know. But it is a dying trade machining.[87]

My interviewees drew upon this narrative of industrial decline and economic instability to explain the limited impact of their dispute. They had fought to assert the value of a trade that nearly no longer existed. Pam was not particularly active in the union and felt it was dominated by men, but she also associated working in the factory as a space where she was able to 'stand her ground'. They were able to temporarily improve their situation at Ford, but they felt they were unable to transform the broader manner in how women's work was valued, which was evidenced by their own personal experiences, as well as the persistence of grievances among other women in the present.

Attitudes towards feminism

At the time, the successful outcome of the strike was connected to a wider story about 'women's rights' outside the factory. The *T&G Record* proclaimed,

> Amid wild scenes of jubilation Ford women sewing-machinists celebrated a famous victory last month in ending 17 years of sex-discrimination. The battle for women's rights will have wide ranging

effects through British industry – wherever the struggle for equal pay is being waged.⁸⁸

A TGWU national officer claimed, 'The Ford fight against all the odds will be a beacon of light for all other women trade unionists.'⁸⁹ The decision to regrade the women was seen by some as representative of a societal change in attitudes towards female workers. *Spare Rib* suggested the very fact there were two women on the arbitration committee indicated change and meant 'they were able to look at the situation with greater awareness of sex discrimination than there had been in the 1968 strike'.⁹⁰ The victory was connected to women's struggles elsewhere as ACAS received seventy-eight applications for upgrading of women's work on the basis of equal pay in the first three months of 1985.⁹¹ For *Spare Rib*, 'It seems that the Fords women's major victory is only one of some new inroads made in undervaluing women's work.'⁹² At the TGWU Annual Conference, the sewing machinists were discussed in relation to 'the heroic role of women at Greenham Common and fighting alongside miners' who had 'highlighted how active women could be'.⁹³

However, for the women who actually worked at Ford, they were less inclined to relate their strike to these external struggles and were unconvinced that a change had occurred in the way their work was valued. The sewing machinists articulated their grievance as a consequence of an unequal gender hierarchy. A shop steward called Doreen Cook explained,

> We just see it as sex discrimination. We're sure it's because we're women. Had it been men this would have been settled long ago. Had it been a male dominated job it would never have been graded as it was. They seem to think women haven't got any skills but we have – they may be different skills but they're skills nevertheless and they're just as important to industry.⁹⁴

The perception of the women's lack of ability was inseparable from a moral judgement about women as legitimate social actors. The factory was described as 'a man's world', and it was suggested 'women are nothing at Ford'.⁹⁵ In this way, whilst the women's sense of injustice was not directed specifically at male workers, their collective action was conceptualised as an assertion of their own distinct voice within a male-dominated environment.

As one can see from the testimony in the previous sections, my interview respondents characterised their experiences of work and trade unionism with unequal relations between men and women. They perceived this relationship as unfair and reconstructed the strike as an attempt to redefine it. But, similarly to the other women interviewed in this study, they did not identify themselves as feminists. Dora said, 'I believe in justice for women, but no I'm not a feminist.'[96] She explained that it was important to her that Bernard Passingham's role in supporting the women was not forgotten, and suggested this was evidence that she was not a feminist:

> I want to involve Bernard, if I was a feminist, see then I wouldn't. And them women that went to meetings were all women and they don't want to know [about Bernard]. As soon as you mention a man's name, they don't want to know, they don't want to think about him, yeah so no I'm not a feminist. If anyone does good, I'll say so.[97]

Pam offered a parallel explanation of her motivations and involvement in the strike.

> I think it is just what is right and what is wrong really. I've never been a feminist. I've been to a lot of meetings with women who are feminists but I still think women are women and I'd like the door opened for me, so it's not down them lines of being a feminist. It's about sticking up for what is right. ... Yeah we never burned our bras or nothing. ... You was just doing it because you were being treated unfairly.[98]

Both Pam and Dora appeared to be operating with a definition of feminism that positioned male and female interests in direct opposition to one another. They rejected this position and represented themselves in a manner that emphasised universal values. They claimed to believe in 'justice' – what was 'right or wrong' – and they felt they judged people as individuals, rather than as categories of men or women. Nevertheless, both women believed that men had privileged access to knowledge and resources in terms of how their work was valued and their position within the labour movement. Speaking about trade unions, Dora said,

> Women should get involved more, but the men won't let them. That is true. The men don't want them and it is that simple. Like they didn't want me. But I persisted – [another] woman put down for steward, she got it but the other stewards made it so awkward for her, she had to pack it in. ... So it's not that women won't come forward, in a big environment like that, the men don't want them.[99]

Both Dora and Pam drew on a cultural model that emphasised male dominance (at least in public institutions) where 'men are governors'; 'men always earned more money' and 'men wouldn't allow' women to do things – such as play an active role in the union, or apply to become a stack truck driver. Drawing on their personal experiences, they appeared to assume this was an inevitable aspect of life that continued to the present. As a consequence, they did not perceive their strike in 1984 as an emancipatory moment that led to a positive transformation in women's experiences of work and trade unionism. Rather, it was seen as a limited concession resulting from the determination and resilience of the sewing machinists themselves after seventeen years of struggle.

Their identity and perception of their experience and the world around them was bound between emphasising their individual agency, whilst also accounting for the gender and class constraints on their ability to affect how women's work was collectively organised. They believed that a feminist approach to this tension would dogmatically hold men responsible for the devaluation of their labour and subsequently rejected this on the grounds that it was inauthentic – or untrue to their personal morality and experience. They retrospectively understood the strike as a collective act challenging institutional injustice, but they did not see their beliefs as political, or their behaviour as politically motivated. Instead, they preferred to emphasise the importance of the informal bonds shared between the workers at the time. In this sense, they also represented the strike as a moral act of personal courage and virtue that illustrated women's independence and self-reliance. For my interviewees, their militancy was not understood as driven by external 'feminist' ideas or by their participation in the TGWU; instead it was seen as an 'authentic' assertion of their self-worth in response to the devaluation of their labour. The paradox here was that women rejected feminism as a label, as they simultaneously emphasised the distinctiveness of women's experience and adopted feminist principles of equality, autonomy, self-representation and self-fulfilment to make sense of their resistance to sex and class inequality in the past.

Conclusion

The experiences of the Ford sewing machinists in Dagenham illustrate the continued salience of the value of women's work throughout the period considered in this book. The 1968 strike was publicly conceptualised as a turning point in societal attitudes towards women's right to equal pay. However, the triumphant narrative of the strike as a victory for equal pay served to disguise the underlying grievance that continued to affect many women throughout Britain during this period and beyond. The women at Ford continued to be perceived to possess less ability than male workers due to their sex. They were subsequently paid lower wages and occupied a lower social status within the factory. The sewing machinists' eventual victory in 1985 was swiftly explained as a consequence of a societal change in attitudes towards female workers. Yet as this chapter illustrates, the dispute was instigated by a largely different group of women in response to the same sense of indignity and injustice affecting those who went on strike in 1968. Thus the sewing machinists were not simply passive beneficiaries of abstract social change, but actively sought to change the way their work was valued themselves.

Notes

1 'Striking Machinists Revive Spirit of 1968', *Guardian*, 7 December 1984, p. 6.
2 TUC, 'A Woman's Worth: The Story of the Ford Sewing-Machinists' (2006), www.unionhistory.info/equalpay/display.php?irn=651 (accessed 1 July 2015).
3 MRC, MSS.126/TG/193/1/64, 'Taking Equal Pay to Top', *T&G Record*, November 1984, p. 3.
4 *Ibid.*
5 MRC, MSS.126/TG/193/1/64, 'Ford Sewing-Machinists Walk Out', *T&G Record*, December 1984.
6 'Striking Women Put Ford Pay Deal at Risk', *Guardian*, 22 November 1984, p. 4.
7 *Ibid.*
8 'Ford Strike Leads to More Lay-offs', *Guardian*, 6 December 1984, p. 3.
9 'Ford Machinists End Pay Strike', *Guardian*, 29 December 1984, p. 1.
10 TUC, 'A Woman's Worth: The Story of the Ford Sewing-Machinists' (2006), www.unionhistory.info/equalpay/display.php?irn=651 (accessed 1 July 2015).
11 'Seamstresses at Ford Win Skilled Workers' Status', *Guardian*, 26 April 1985, p. 3.
12 Interview with Pam in Romford, September 2015.
13 Interview with Dora in Dagenham, August 2015.
14 Ford eventually stopped production in Dagenham in 2002 and has since established new plants in Brazil, Venezuela and India. See 'When the Wheels Came Off the Dream', *Guardian*, 25 February 2009.
15 Interview with Pam in Romford, September 2015.
16 Interview with Dora in Dagenham, August 2015.
17 *Ibid.*
18 *Ibid.*
19 *Ibid.*
20 *Ibid*
21 *Ibid.*
22 *Ibid.*
23 *Ibid.*
24 'Striking Machinists Revive Spirit of 1968', *Guardian*, 7 December 1984, p. 6.
25 'Shut Down at Ford As Women Walk Out', *Barking and Dagenham Post*, 21 November 1984.
26 'Striking Machinists Revive Spirit of 1968', *Guardian*, 7 December 1984, p. 6.
27 'It's a Man's World at Ford's', *Spare Rib*, no. 115, 1985, p. 17.

28 *Ibid.*
29 MRC, MSS.126/TG/193/1/65, 'Ford Women Crash the Sex Barrier', *T&G Record*, May 1985.
30 'Ford Women: The Strike Goes On', *Barking and Dagenham Post*, 28 November 1984.
31 *Ibid.*
32 'Ford's Pay Rise Halted', *Barking and Dagenham Post*, 5 December 1984; 'Ford Women Say No', *Barking and Dagenham Post*, 19 December 1984.
33 Interview with Dora Challingsworth, Pamela Brown, Maureen Jackson and Geraldine for film produced by Sarah Boston for TUC in 2006. Film available at TUC Archives, London Metropolitan University. Full transcript of interview was unavailable.
34 Interview with Dora, Pamela, Maureen and Geraldine for TUC, 2006.
35 *Ibid.*
36 Interview with Dora in Dagenham, August 2015.
37 Interview with Pam in Romford, September 2015.
38 *Ibid.*
39 *Ibid.*
40 *Ibid.*
41 *Ibid.*
42 Interview with Pam in Romford, August 2015.
43 *Ibid.*
44 Interview with Dora in Dagenham, August 2015.
45 Interview with Pam in Romford, August 2015.
46 Interview with Dora in Dagenham, August 2015.
47 *Ibid.*
48 Interview with Pam in Romford, September 2015.
49 *Ibid.*
50 *Ibid.*
51 Interview with Dora in Dagenham, August 2015.
52 'Striking Women Put Ford Pay Deal at Risk', *Guardian*, 22 November 1984, p. 4.
53 *Ibid.*
54 *Ibid.*
55 'Seamstresses at Ford Win Skilled Workers' Status', *Guardian*, 26 April 1985, p. 3.
56 MRC, MSS.126/TG/193/1/65, 'Ford Strike', *T&G Record*, January 1985.
57 MRC, MSS.126/TG/193/1/65, 'Women make Breakthrough', *T&G Record*, September 1985.
58 *Ibid.*
59 '16-year Fight of Ford Sewing-Machinists', *New Statesman*, 14 December 1984.
60 *Ibid.*
61 MRC, MSS.572/150, Papers of Ron Todd, Miscellaneous Papers, 1911–1998, 'Brief History of the Ford Sewing-Machinists disputes' (undated).
62 Interview with Dora in Dagenham, August 2015.
63 Interview with Dora, Pamela, Maureen and Geraldine for TUC (2006).
64 Interview with Pam in Romford, September 2015.
65 *Ibid.*

66 *Ibid.*
67 *Ibid.*
68 Interview with Dora in Dagenham, August 2015.
69 *Ibid.*
70 *Ibid.*
71 *Ibid.*
72 *Ibid.*
73 *Ibid.*
74 *Ibid.*
75 *Ibid.*
76 *Ibid.*
77 *Ibid.*
78 *Ibid.*
79 *Ibid.*
80 *Ibid.*
81 Interview with Pam, Romford, September 2015.
82 *Ibid.*
83 *Ibid.*
84 Interview with Dora, Dagenham, August 2015.
85 Interview with Pam, Romford, September 2015.
86 *Ibid.*
87 *Ibid.*
88 MRC, MSS.126/TG/193/1/65, 'Ford Women Crash the Sex Barrier', *T&G Record*, May 1985.
89 *Ibid.*
90 'Ford Women Victorious At Last', *Spare Rib*, no. 155, 1985, p. 9.
91 *Ibid.*
92 *Ibid.*
93 MRC, MSS.126/TG/193/1/65, 'Heroic Role of Women', *T&G Record*, July 1985.
94 'It's a man's world at Ford's', *Spare Rib*, no. 115, 1985, p. 17.
95 *Ibid.*
96 Interview with Dora in Dagenham, August 2015.
97 *Ibid.*
98 Interview with Pamela, Romford, August 2015.
99 Interview with Dora, Dagenham, August 2015.

Conclusion

By listening to the voices of women who fought for equal pay, skill recognition and the right to work, this book contributes a fresh understanding of the relationship between feminism, workplace activism and trade unionism during the years 1968–85. The industrial disputes analysed in the preceding chapters show that women's workplace militancy was not simply a direct response to women's heightened presence in trade unions and second-wave feminism. The women involved in these disputes were more likely to understand their experiences of workplace activism as an expression of the economic, social and subjective value of their work and an assertion of their personal autonomy. Their political subjectivity was caught between emphasising their individual agency and rights as independent women and the gender and class constraints on their everyday experiences of paid work and trade unionism.

Industrial disputes involving female workers have been conceptualised as evidence of changing attitudes towards women within male-dominated trade unions, and shifting attitudes among working-class women themselves. Existing accounts of women's experiences within the labour movement have mapped where change has occurred at an institutional level in terms of the growing number of female trade unionists and the growing commitment of trade unions to recognising the specific interests of female workers.[1] Other accounts have described this development as a consequence of second-wave feminism and women's growing participation in the labour force after the Second World War.[2] The starting point for this book was to draw attention to female workers' voices and interpretations of their experiences, which had hitherto been largely absent from this existing story.

Focusing on individual subjectivity unsurprisingly complicates the story of women playing a more active role within the labour movement during this period. It is difficult to establish patterns that illustrate when,

CONCLUSION

how and why women's experiences of workplace protest were different to men's from personal accounts. But this was not the aim of the study. The nature of the research – the concentration on individual case studies and individual women's experiences – provides snapshots of the everyday transitions in thought and behaviour that lay behind women's workplace militancy. These snapshots provide clues as to how and why female workers' experiences differed from those of men. But each case study provides richer and more nuanced evidence of how women ascribed meaning to their past experiences and how they constituted themselves as political subjects. The focus has thus been more on understanding and appreciating how differences between men and women affected the beliefs and values of the individual actors in these specific situations, rather than explaining the processes that lay behind such differences. This approach means each case study contributes fresh insights into the gendered division of labour and women's experiences of, and attitudes towards, trade unionism and feminism.

Each case study reveals the central importance of paid work to working-class women's everyday lives after 1945. Women's propensity to work part-time clearly meant that women presented themselves on the labour market on different terms to men and that women's relationship with paid work changed at different points of the life cycle. Further research is required to fully explain women's subjective experiences of part-time work. Yet the preceding case studies suggest that paid work was central to women's' claims to citizenship. The women involved in these disputes possessed specific skills and ability, which were closely tied to their sense of self and political identity. The majority of my respondents shared similar work trajectories, and all worked for most of their lives from school-leaving age through bringing up children and proceeding to work until retirement. Work was certainly not interpreted as a temporary stage in these women's lives, nor was it simply a means of complementing a husband's income to meet the growing consumer desires of an increasingly affluent society.[3] All of my respondents emphasised the economic value of their work and their role as economic providers in their families – from when they began work after leaving school to contribute to their family income to after they had married, bought homes or had children of their own. These women felt that they had worked out of economic necessity, to build better lives for themselves with further opportunities for their own families.

Yet paid work was not always a positive experience. Whilst women emphasised elements of their work they enjoyed, such as the camaraderie, solidarity and friendships they shared with workmates, their relationship with their employers was frequently characterised by conflict. Respondents suggested they felt 'persecuted', 'treated with contempt' or like 'dogs'. Gender was a critical explanatory factor behind this sense of inadequacy. In both contemporary representations of each dispute, as well as the oral history interviews, women spoke about having to justify their action in the face of pervading notions of 'pin money'. The women who went on strike for equal pay and skill recognition obviously spoke about having their ability devalued on the basis of their sex. The women who occupied their factory felt they were perceived as weaker and more expendable by their employers who made them redundant. It is no surprise that the majority of interviewees spoke fondly about their female-centred work culture, which provided them with the means to informally influence how their work was organised.

The coherence of women's work identity was also refracted through the lens of deindustrialisation, which influenced how they reinterpreted the meaning of their activism some decades later. Whilst respondents were generally enthusiastic and eager to stress the importance of their jobs at the time of the disputes they were involved in, they had much less to say about their later experiences of work, which were predominantly in similarly low-paid, undervalued service sector jobs such as retail, catering or care work. These 'silences' reflected the persistence of gender and class structures that my interviewees felt constrained their own, as well as their friends' and family members' choices of work in the years following the disputes they were involved in. It was not that my interviewees had stopped being the 'strong women' they associated with their sense of self at the time of each dispute; rather the decline of heavy and manufacturing industry, stable employment and trade unions' power, and the persistence of unequal pay and the gendered division labour made them doubt their political efficacy and the wider meaning of the disputes they were involved in.

The point is that women's experiences of paid work had a crucial effect on their understanding of the world and their place within it. But the significance of paid work within these women's lives should not be conflated with the notion that work represented an emancipatory experience. Women interviewed in this book perceived themselves to be at the bottom of a gender hierarchy (an intersectional analysis focusing on the experiences of women of colour would reveal how these hierarchies were also racialised) in their workplaces, which they believed was unfair and which they sought to change. The fact that they took action and challenged these hierarchies is the crucial point here. Yet it is also vital to think about how the persistence of occupational segregation and unequal pay at the time of the interviews led women to doubt their political efficacy.[4] Their struggle to transform the way their work was valued says more about the forces with which they had to contend than the women themselves.

Although each dispute occurred in a different industrial sector and involved different unions, the women involved shared similar experiences and memories of their trade union engagement. The majority of women involved in each case study were all unionised prior to each dispute, but they had minimal contact with their trade union officials and their experience of trade unionism and industrial struggle was generally limited. Each dispute considered in this book was represented as novel and an anomaly at the time by the unions involved, and the local and national press. The lack of connection between union officials and female workers on the shop floor meant that respondents saw the role of their union as largely irrelevant to their own decision to engage in collective action and saw their interests as isolated from the wider movement, which also created space for alternative forms of action, as demonstrated by the Fakenham case study.

The women involved in the 1968 strike at Ford 'believed in unions' and were well organised, but distinguished their strike as their 'own' and separate from the interests and struggle of male workers in their factory. Although they appreciated the support of their union, there was resentment expressed at the time, and in the oral history interviews, at how their NUVB officials had steered them away from their grading grievance and encouraged them to demand equal pay instead. At Fakenham the women received no support and had nothing but contempt for NU-FLAT, which was expressed at the time and in retrospect, and meant that the union was viewed as completely irrelevant to the lives of the women interviewed in the present. The exception was the women at Trico who were well supported by their local branch of the AUEW; many of the female workers became more involved in the union once their dispute was over. Yet even in this case, it is important to remember that the strike for equal pay was initiated by the women themselves and that their relationship with the union was cut short after the factory closed the following decade. The Dagenham sewing machinists who went on strike in 1984 received support from the TGWU that was crucial to their success, yet the women involved characterised their relationship with the union as sexist. The image that emerged of women's relationship with their trade unions was one where they felt as if they had to 'fight for everything'.

The women involved in these disputes did not necessarily want to play a more active role within their unions; rather they wanted to be leaders of their own action, to represent themselves and have a say in how their work was organised. The diversity in experience shows that, whilst trade unions' response to female workers' everyday interests was generally insufficient, the situation varied within factories depending on local factors, such as the nature of a union's district branch or full-time officials, as well as attitudes within the local community. Thus, the book also indicates the need to look beyond trade unions' official policies towards female workers, as women's experience of trade unionism was most likely to be affected by how their union was organised at a grassroots level.

Whilst the disputes unfolded in different ways, and respondents offered various opinions about trade unions' significance, each case study was similar in that the women involved initially organised themselves independently of their union. The result of this was that the majority of women saw their membership as irrelevant to their militancy and the manner in which they thought about their rights and themselves as political subjects. Marees from Fakenham described her union membership as 'a waste of money'.[5] Dora from Dagenham played an active role in the TGWU throughout her working life, but was reluctant to suggest that the union influenced her values and beliefs. She, like many of the women interviewed in this book, continually emphasised how her 'political' understandings came from within.

Although 'more was written about women and unions in the decade between 1975 and 1985 than the previous century' and the emergence of new structures within the TUC and individual unions, such as separate women's groups and officers, demonstrated a desire to hear and reflect women's voice within the labour movement, I would argue that such changes represented the influence of women's workplace militancy on the organisation and priorities of trade unions, rather than the converse.[6] Women's ambivalence towards their trade union membership was explained by their direct experiences of sex discrimination, isolation and the lack of space to have their voice heard within their factories and at a local level. These experiences reflected the failure and reluctance of unions to alter the uneven balance of power between female workers and male-dominated executive committees at a national level. The initial success achieved by the women at Trico highlighted the necessity of trade union support for sustaining women's action. Whilst the TGWU celebrated its role in the Dagenham sewing machinists' eventual victory in 1985, it is important to recognise that women did not want to depend on trade unions, but wanted to speak with their own voice and to be listened to within them.

CONCLUSION

Each case study also offers a deeper insight into the relationship between working-class women and the WLM. Whilst the Dagenham sewing machinists' strike preceded the formation of WLM groups across Britain, the disputes analysed in this book represented sites of convergence between working-class women seeking to alter the relations of power within their workplace and WLM activists hoping to extend the social composition of the movement by raising the consciousness of working-class women. Feminist support for female workers was also driven by the personal motivations of individual members who, in the words of Sheila Rowbotham, 'wanted to involve working-class women and do things about women's oppression rather than just discuss it'.[7] Feminist support was crucial for raising the public profile of women's militancy and could provide essential moral and financial backing for women who were not supported by their union, such as the workers at Fakenham.

Historians of second-wave feminism often write about how the WLM changed the way people in Britain thought and spoke about women during the 1970s.[8] This book shows how female workers, who did not identify themselves with the WLM, contributed to this process. Women who engaged in industrial disputes did not passively internalise feminist ideas; instead, they were actively changing the way they thought and constituted themselves as political subjects in response to their everyday experiences. The women I interviewed did not feel they had been directly influenced by the WLM, which can be explained by both the material reality of the limited presence of the movement within these women's workplaces and communities, and negative portrayals of the movement in public memory. Throughout the interviews, respondents made reference to 'burning bras' or being 'anti-men', which drew on negative and sexist stereotypes that have been idly equated with the movement by the British media since.[9] Whilst the women did not necessarily express negative views towards feminism, it was not an identity that they adopted themselves. This common distinction between WLM activists and their own (various) identity(ies) was demonstrated most clearly by Marees from Fakenham when she explained, 'Some of the ladies we met were very sort of strong and outspoken types of people. Not how I thought I was; I probably am now, but not how I was then.'[10] This piece of testimony encapsulated the manner in which the majority of my respondents spoke about feminism, workplace activism and their sense of self. Whilst they did not adopt a feminist identity or associate their action with the WLM, they spoke about themselves and their militancy in a manner that emphasised feminist values of equality, autonomy and self-worth.

Although respondents did not interpret their activism as 'gestalt moments' like Judy Wajcman experienced, nor the epiphanies common in the narratives of WLM activists or middle-class women, there was a sense that they appealed to a 'feminist script' in an attempt to achieve coherence in the process of the oral history interview, which aligned their militancy to fit with an image of themselves they felt comfortable with in the present.[11] Thus, although the women I interviewed did not describe themselves as feminists, the majority of respondents used their militancy as a symbol to evidence their independence as women and their refusal to be treated unequally with men. Some women, like Sheila from Dagenham, fitted this into a narrative about individually resisting inequality or managing adversity throughout their life. Other women, like Sally from Brentford, discussed how they gained greater confidence during their disputes, which they related to other events that had taken place in their lives, including buying their own homes, fighting against the poll tax, raising children independently or applying for jobs previously restricted to men in their factory. Such events were connected to wider notions of independence, confidence and personal autonomy, and offer a new example of women adopting this narrative structure to talk, not just about positive opportunities for education and career advancement, but also experiences of resisting inequality in the past.

Identifying the women's action as feminist is complicated by the issue of interpretive authority. Revisiting the disputes from a historical perspective enables one to see how these women were both indirectly influenced by and contributed towards the development of British feminism. Women's attempts to redefine how their work was valued and to speak with their own voice within the labour movement challenged gender norms and can be described as feminist. These attitudes and behaviours had similarities to what Annemarie Hughes describes as a 'rough kind of feminism' developed by working-class women in interwar Scotland in response to their dual experience of sexual and class antagonism.[12] In some ways, these findings fitted with recent calls to broaden the definition of feminism to include the practical activism of women who did not identify with explicitly feminist groups or organisations. They certainly connect to Molony and Nelson's call to think of women's activism as 'women in movement' rather than 'women's movements', which views feminism as growing organically from activist responses to marginalisation, rather than activism being prompted by feminism as an ideology.[13] However, it is less clear that the women involved in these disputes developed a 'strong feminist consciousness' whilst participating in workplace protest. Considering how much of this book has focused on how women defined

CONCLUSION

themselves, labelling them as feminists seems inappropriate when this did not fit with their own self-understanding. It is important to recognise and respect that this is not how the majority of women identified themselves at the time or in my interviews.

It is crucial to think about why the women interviewed did not see themselves or their behaviour as either feminist or political. In some ways, it is unsurprising that my interviewees felt reluctant to identify themselves as feminists, considering the negative imagery and stereotypes surrounding feminism in the present. But the rejection of a feminist and political identity also stemmed from a desire to justify their behaviour and assert their authenticity – the idea they were being true to themselves. As Mike Savage has shown, people in Britain have increasingly sought to identify themselves as 'ordinary' as a means distancing themselves from social fixing, avoiding stigmatised class or privileged identities.[14] As a result, people seek to avoid class when forming political judgements about their self and others (in public) and more commonly articulate a 'naturalistic' and 'individualistic' ethic instead. The evidence in this book suggests that people seek to avoid gender in a similar manner. In each dispute considered in this book, women's behaviour was perceived by observers as novel, 'historic' or extraordinary. But the women involved did not think of themselves as extraordinary, and rather understood their behaviour as a legitimate and justified response to their very real, 'ordinary' experiences of class and gender inequality. The women involved in these disputes were reluctant to identify themselves as feminist for fear it would imply they were acting out of ulterior and inauthentic motives. As one of the Fakenham women explained at the time, 'They were not pulling a stunt.' The majority of the interviewees stressed how they judged people as individuals rather than as categories. For many of the women, being feminist implied being 'anti-men', and they disavowed it on the grounds that it would involve judging people on the basis of their sex.

In a parallel fashion, many of the women said they were not political, and stressed their personal characteristics and internal sense of justice when they explained their involvement in each dispute. They thought of themselves as practising ethics rather than politics, and stressed their individual or natural qualities in contrast to external political ideas as a means of making sense of the world and their place within it. They blurred boundaries between individual and collective interests by emphasising personal qualities such as authenticity, resilience and strength of character to explain why they were good at looking after both themselves and each other. In this sense, their political identity was influenced by public feminist narratives about being strong, autonomous women who believed in equality and women's rights. Yet it also drew on and emphasised the importance of their 'internal' values and beliefs derived from their personal experiences. These political understandings arguably present difficulties for aggregating shared interests and sustaining collective action.

The women's political identity and experiences of activism were also influenced and differentiated by their locality, family and age. Each dispute occurred in markedly different contexts, in terms of region and also factories with their own specific history and culture of industrial relations. Ford was a much larger company with a well-organised workforce in comparison to Sexton's shoe factory located in rural East Anglia, whilst Brentford was a racially diverse, metropolitan area with a progressive labour movement. These local circumstances distinguished the social and economic context from which the women came as well as individual women's experiences and political identity in each case study. Yet, importantly, women were taking similar action to one another across Britain, in a range of industries and both urban and rural locations, which is illustrated by the timeline in the Appendix.

Whilst respondents did not discuss their militancy in relation to their family in great detail, it was clear that family relationships also had a significant influence on women's sense of self and political identity. Sally from Brentford claimed to have a 'Tory upbringing' and emphasised that she had just split up with her husband before she went on strike for equal pay, which meant that she felt increasingly aware of and incensed at the differential between male and female wages.[15] Marees was married and pregnant when she occupied the factory in Fakenham, which she felt distinguished her from the strong, outspoken types of women from the WLM she met during the occupation.[16] Relationships within families also had an important influence on how a dispute was conducted. In every case study, there was discussion in the press of the disruption that women's militancy had allegedly caused to family life, especially during occupations where women spent nights away from home in the factory. The workers at Dagenham and Trico both suggested that it was very difficult for women with unsympathetic husbands to stay out on strike. By contrast, nearly all of the women who were married emphasised the importance of the support they received from their husbands during their disputes and how they shared similar political views.

The experiences presented in this book are those of white working-class women. However, race relations clearly had a significant impact on women's experiences of work and trade unionism during this period; the women at Trico discussed the informal racial segregation of the workforce prior to their dispute and suggested that industrial action could

CONCLUSION

break down racial barriers within workplaces, in a similar manner to the claims made by the labour movement during the Grunwick dispute between 1976 and 1978. However, McDowell *et al.* have shown that the relationship between workers' protest and race relations was often much more complex than this, and it is an issue that needs further research.[17]

These variances in personal circumstances show that the women interviewed in this book, and by extension working-class women more generally, did not necessarily express a common identity, neither at the time of their activism nor in the present. However, they did share similar experiences of gender and class inequality. The economic necessity of work had shaped their lives in a manner that they felt inhibited their aspirations and opportunities for further education or careers. The majority remembered having unequal power relationships with male bosses which they challenged and sought to change. They differentiated their own interests from those of the trade union that was supposed to represent them. Whilst this experience was not uncommon and would have been shared with working-class men, it was distinguished by the fact that their work was devalued because it was performed by women. Male workers never had to fight to have the value of their work recognised and appropriately remunerated on the basis of their sex.

The overall implications of the book are that female workers' experiences of work, trade unionism and workplace activism were distinguished by an unequal relationship between men and women. A comparative study that explored differences between men and women's workplace militancy quantitatively and discursively would provide more 'concrete' answers to when, how and why this was the case. But the women's stories examined here, actively and creatively generated from memory, contribute towards a better understanding of how such differences affected women's everyday experiences and sense of self. Being judged to have less ability than men meant women felt that they were taken less seriously as legitimate social actors within the workplace and trade unions. Women's workplace activism during this period should be understood as a direct response to this everyday sense of injustice and a demand to be judged as independent women, speaking with their own voice and seeking greater control over their own lives.

Notes

1 Boston, *Women Workers*; Cunnison and Stageman, *Feminizing the Unions*.
2 Rowbotham, *The Past is Before Us*; Coote and Campbell, *Sweet Freedom*.
3 Roberts, *Women and Families*, p. 235.

4 In 2014, the Fawcett Society found the mean gap between male and female wages (part-time and full-time) was 19.1 per cent. Women accounted for 82 per cent of those working in 'caring leisure and other service industries', 77 per cent of those in 'admin and secretarial' and 63 per cent in sales and customer service. The predominance of women in low-paid sectors meant that 62 per cent of workers earning below the living wage were women. The Fawcett Society's Gender Pay Gap Briefing (November, 2014), p. 4 and p. 6. https://www.fawcettsociety.org.uk/gender-pay-gap-briefing-november-2014 (accessed 1 December 2014).
5 Interview with Marees in Fakenham, 15 April 2013.
6 Boston, *Women Workers*, p. 311.
7 Rowbotham, 'Jolting Memory: Nightcleaners Recalled' in Maria Ruido (ed.), *Plan Rosebud: On Images, Sites and Politics of Memory* (Santiago de Compostela: Xunta de Galicia, 2008), p. 7.
8 Rowbotham, *The Past is Before Us*; Browne, *Women's Liberation Movement in Scotland*.
9 Abrams, *Oral History Theory*, p. 98.
10 Interview with Marees in Fakenham, 15 April 2013.
11 Abrams, 'Liberating the Female Self', p. 32.
12 Hughes, *Gender and Political Identities*.
13 B. Molony and J. Nelson (eds), *Women's Activism and 'Second Wave' Feminism: Transnational Histories* (London: Bloomsbury, 2017), Introduction.
14 Savage, 'Working-Class Identities'.
15 Interview with Marees in Fakenham, 15 April 2013.
16 Interview with Peggy, Phyllis and Sally in London, 10 April 2013.
17 McDowell *et al.*, 'Striking Narratives'.

Appendix

Timeline of Women's Workplace Militancy in Britain, 1968–85

Date	Company and Location	Dispute Details
Feb 1968	Fishermen's Wives Campaign, Hull.	Women lead campaign in Hull for safety improvements on fishing boats.
May–Jun 1968	Grading dispute at Ford, Dagenham and Halewood.	187 sewing machinists strike for improved grading at Ford, Dagenham.
Jan 1969	Renold Ltd, Coventry and Manchester.	1,000 women strike for equal pay in chain-making factory.
Feb–Mar 1970	Clothing workers' strike, Leeds (also spread to factories in south Yorkshire and Teesside).	14,570 clothing workers from factories across Leeds, the majority of whom are women, strike for 4 weeks after the NUTGW negotiates a national wage agreement without their consent.
Sep 1970–Dec 1972	Campaign to unionise night cleaners, London.	The Cleaners' Action group encouraged night cleaners to join NUTGW or CSU.
Jan–Mar 1971	Post office workers' strike, nationwide.	Women play active role in strike for 15 per cent wage rise.
Sep 1971	Lucas, Burnley.	Pat Sturdy organises women-only breakaway union – Women's Industrial Union – in protest against sexist treatment from GMWU officials.
Feb–Jul 1972	Sexton's Shoe Factory, Fakenham, Norfolk.	45 women occupy factory and successfully resist redundancy.
Jul 1972	Equal pay strike, Goodman's Loudspeaker factory, Havant, Hampshire.	Women strike for union recognition and equal pay.
Jul 1972	General Electric Company (GEC), Erith, south London.	Female workers demand equal pay as part of a national engineering claim.
Sep 1972	Coops Clothing, Wigan, Lancashire.	Women strike in protest at sacking of a shop steward.
Sep 1972	Ever Ready Electrical Company, Wolverhampton.	Mostly Asian women involved in grading dispute.

(cont.)

APPENDIX

(cont.)

Date	Company and Location	Dispute Details
Oct 1972	Plessey Electronics, London.	Women sit-in after the sacking of senior shop steward.
Oct 1972	Courtaulds' Deeside Mill, Flint, Wales.	120 women on strike for a month over bonus dispute.
Nov 1972	Morriston Hospital, Swansea.	80 women domestic workers, mainly cleaners, strike over a pay dispute.
Nov 1972	South London Hospital.	Hospital ancillary workers demonstrate outside hospital for £8 claim. Nationally there is a 1-day stoppage of hospital workers on 4 November.
Nov 1972	Mansfield Hosiery Mill, Loughborough.	Asian hosiery workers strike against racial discrimination and for higher pay. 80 women at Clarence St Works come out in sympathy with them.
Nov 1972	St Anne's College, Oxford.	Cleaners go on strike for union recognition (NUPE).
Nov 1972	Easterbrook and Allcard tool factory, Sheffield.	Women machinists strike for the reinstatement of a sacked trade union convenor.
Dec 1972	Granada Publishing, London and St Albans.	ASTMS members on strike for union recognition.
Dec 1972	Barbour Rainwear Factory, South Shields.	60 women strike for union recognition and wage rise.
Jan 1973	British Leyland Combine, Birmingham.	Women workers walk out in Christmas holiday pay dispute.
Jan 1973	Warwick University.	Cleaners and catering staff on strike for £2.40 weekly wage rise.
Jan 1973	Baird's Television Factory, Bradford.	4,000 mostly female workers demand 40 per cent wage increase.
Feb 1973	Grunwick Processing Lab, Willesden, London.	Women involved in struggle for the reinstatement of a sacked worker.
Feb 1973	Empire Pools, Blackpool.	65 women on strike for union recognition.
Mar 1973	Tillotsons Print Company, Bolton, Lancashire.	700 print workers, men and women, protest against the sacking of shop stewards and redundancies.

APPENDIX

(cont.)

Date	Company and Location	Dispute Details
Apr 1973	Watney Mann Brewery, Whitechapel, London.	Women strike with men in defiance of wage freeze.
Apr–May 1973	Stirmur Manufacturing Company, Paisley.	100 printers strike in support of pay increases for 25 women workers.
Apr–May 1973	Baxters Bolt and Rivet Works, Birmingham.	Women in the AUEW walk out in support of sacked convenor.
Apr–May 1973	Nu-Swift Fire Extinguisher Factory, Elland, Yorkshire.	Women office workers strike for substantial pay increases. Joined by canteen workers and draughtsmen.
May 1973	Alligator Rainwear Factory, Stockport.	Women strike to reinstate a sacked machinist and guarantee job security.
Jun 1973	Wyuna Garment Factory, Southall, west London.	Asian women workers wage rise and union recognition.
Jun 1973	Croft Seafood Factory, Liverpool.	Female shellfish packers in GMWU strike against the casual labour system and demand a pay rise.
Jun 1973–Jul 1973	GEC Salford Electrical Instruments, Eccles and Heywood, Greater Manchester.	90 female office workers demand that the difference between the male and female rates be reduced by one-third as a step towards equal pay.
Jun 1973	GEC Turbine Generators, Rugby, Warwickshire.	Women clerical workers in APEX walk out because company refused to bring women's rates up to 90 per cent of men's by 1 August 1973.
Jun 1973	Supreme Overall Services, Wednesbury, Staffordshire.	350 laundry workers, mostly women, strike for 5 days for a 5p per hour increase on their 32p wage.
Jul–Aug 1973	GEC Spon Street Works, Coventry.	200 women workers earning a basic £13 per week strike after introduction of new materials brings piece rates down. They fight not only the company but the AUEW convenor, who was reported to have said, 'I'm not having my men laid off by a bunch of silly girls.'
Jul 1973	Chelsea Quilt Factory, Barnstaple, Devon.	24 women in 2-week strike over management attempt to alter wage differentials.

APPENDIX

(cont.)

Date	Company and Location	Dispute Details
Sep 1973	Slumberland Beds, Paisely.	Office and supervisory staff in 10-week strike for ASTMS union recognition.
Sep 1973	Crompton Parkinson Electrical Manufacturing, Dundee.	400 women strike over management pay offer to increase male differential by £1.80.
Sep 1973	Seiko, Kilburn, London.	Women strike for 5 weeks for union recognition. Followed by occupation against poor conditions and piece-rate system.
Oct 1973	Adwest Engineering, Reading.	400 male and female workers occupy factory to save from closure.
Oct 1973	Pressed Steel, Cowley, Oxford.	Women office workers go on strike for equal pay. Men in office support them with work to rule, overtime ban and 1-day sit-in.
Oct 1973	Rotaprint, Willesden, London.	450 assembly line workers strike as management attempt to divide women by paying some male rates and others low unskilled rates.
Nov 1973	Hawker Siddeley, Chadderton and Woodford, Lancashire.	Women on strike demanding a £1.50 weekly wage increase.
Nov 1973	Biro-Bic, Reading.	70 women in dispute for union recognition of AUEW.
Dec 1973	Babcock and Wilcox, Renfrew, Glasgow.	200 women clerical workers win settlement for equal pay.
Dec 1973	Maclaren Controls, Glasgow.	300 mostly female workers strike for 5 weeks, followed by factory occupation to win £5 wage increase.
Jan 1974	Rank Radio International, Camborne, Cornwall.	Women shop stewards organise successful campaign to reorganise working week.
Jan 1974	Armstrong Patents, Beverley, Yorkshire.	80 men and women walk out after TGWU female convenor sacked for refusing to accept 3-day week. TGWU fails to support the pickets. 100 female workers leave the firm.

APPENDIX

(cont.)

Date	Company and Location	Dispute Details
Mar 1974	GEC, Coventry.	200 women strike to defend jobs as management try to re-deploy women to secondary factory in attempt to break union.
Mar 1974	Timex, Dundee.	3-week strike by 500 mostly female workers in opposition to closure. AUEW call off official support.
Mar 1974	Bonar Long, Dundee.	500 workers walk out and strike against productivity agreement.
Mar 1974	Lucas, Birmingham.	2,000 mostly female production workers walk out over announcement of redundancies.
Apr 1974	Lentheric, London.	290 women strike because they receive £8 less than lowest male weekly rate. They win increase of £2.25.
Apr 1974	British Domestic Appliance, Peterborough.	1,300 workers, 400 of whom are women, strike for equal pay.
Apr 1974	Auto-Machinery, Coventry.	190 men and women demand equal wages with factory in Stoke. Women demand equal pay and achieve 95 per cent of men's rate.
Apr 1974	Jonas Woodhead, Yorkshire.	Part-time women workers on evening shift in shock absorber plant gain recognition of AUEW and elect shop stewards.
May 1974	Renold Gear Division, Milnrow, Lancashire.	100 clerical workers strike for equal pay.
May 1974	Imperial Typewriters, Leicester.	700 male and female, mostly Asian, workers strike over productivity agreement without support of TGWU.
May 1974	Nurses' Strike for wage rises in Teesside, Liverpool and Nottingham.	COHSE members organise marches and 1-hour lightning strikes.
May 1974	National Switch Factory, Keighley, Yorkshire.	400 women strike for 8 days when management reneges on national wage agreement.
Jun 1974	Wingrove and Rogers, Old Swan, Liverpool.	250 mostly female workers strike at electrical engineering factory for 5 weeks over low pay.

APPENDIX

(cont.)

Date	Company and Location	Dispute Details
Jun 1974	Easterbrook and Allcard, Sheffield.	600 workers strike against low pay.
Jun 1974	London Hospitals.	Female technicians and radiographers join nurses in strike for 30 per cent wage rise.
Jun 1974	Smiths Industries, Cricklewood, London.	177 female workers occupy speedometer factory for 2 days after being laid off.
Jun 1974	Kenilworth Components, Leicester.	Asian women hold 2-day strike against low pay and receive support from female workers from Imperial Typewriters in Leicester.
Sep 1974	Persona Razorblades, Hillingdon, Glasgow.	2-week strike for equal pay with women earning £6 per week less than men.
Sep 1974	Vauxhall, Luton.	Women office cleaners, TGWU members strike for 3 weeks over low pay and gain 10p per hour increase and 1 week extra holiday.
Oct 1974	Salford Electrical Instruments, Heywood, Lancashire.	40 women AUEW members occupy switchboard as part of equal pay dispute. They are undermined by male AUEW members, and management removes them with security guards.
Oct 1975	Bronx Engineering, Brierley Hill, West Midlands.	Women receive support from male engineering workers for dispute with management.
Nov 1975–Jan 1976	Newton Derby engineering firm, Derbyshire.	20 female APEX members strike for 13 weeks for skill recognition and equal pay.
Mar 1976	Louis Newmark, Ipswich.	Female office workers strike for equal pay in engineering firm.
Mar 1976	Cockburns Valves, Glasgow.	Female members of TASS strike at engineering firm for equal pay.
May–Oct 1976	Trico-Folberth, Brentford.	Successful 21-week strike for equal pay led by 400 female assembly workers at windscreen wiper factory.
Aug 1976–Jul 1978	Grunwick Processing Lab, Willesden, London.	Dispute for union recognition at photo-processing plant involving mostly female Asian workers.

(cont.)

Date	Company and Location	Dispute Details
May 1977	Laird Portch, East Kilbride.	400 women NUTGW members in 6-week unofficial strike for equal pay.
Jul 1977	Essex International, Kilwinning, Ayrshire.	Female workers occupy electronics factory due to differential between female wage rates in Irish and Scottish factories.
Dec 1978–Feb 1979	'Winter of Discontent'.	Public sector workers involved in strikes across Britain against wage freeze and incomes policy.
Oct 1979	Mass demonstration again Corrie Bill, London.	Thousands of women participate in demonstration organised by TUC to protest against John Corrie's private members' bill aiming to amend 1967 Abortion Act.
Feb–Sep 1981	Lee Jeans factory occupation, Greenock.	240 female workers resist redundancy by occupying jeans factory for 7 months.
Jan 1982	Lovable Lingerie, Cumbernauld, Lanarkshire.	Women occupy factory in a bid to resist redundancy.
Mar–May 1982	Plessey Capacitors, Bathgate, West Lothian.	220 mostly female workers occupy engineering factory for 8 weeks in bid to save factory from closure.
1984–85	Women Against Pit Closures, nationwide.	Women's groups play active role in mining communities across Britain during the miners' strike.

Sources: 'Striking Progress 1972–1973', *Red Rag*, no. 5 (August 1973); 'Striking Progress, 1973–1974', *Red Rag*, no. 8 (February 1975); Sheila Rowbotham and Beatrix Campbell, 'Class Struggle in Britain', *Radical America*, vol. 8, no. 5 (1974); Sheila Rowbotham, *The Past is Before Us* (London: Pandora Press, 1989); Sarah Boston, *Women Workers and the Trade Unions*, 2nd edn (London: Lawrence and Wishart, 1989).

Bibliography

Oral history interviews

Interview with Pam Brown in Romford, 16 September 2015.
Interview with Dora Challingsworth in Dagenham, 4 August 2015.
Interview with Gwen Davis, Sheila Douglass, Eileen Pullen and Vera Sime in Rainham, Essex, 21 June 2013.
Interview with Gwen Davis and Eileen Pullen, 11 August 2015.
Interview with Marees Dewing in Fakenham, 15 April 2013.
Interview with Peggy Farmer, Phyllis Griffin and Sally Groves in London, Wednesday 10 April 2013.
Interview with Patricia Howling in Fakenham, 15 April 2013.
Interview with Barbara Humphries in London, 16 April 2013.
Interview with Margaret Rahm in Fakenham, 15 April 2013.
Interview with Sheila Rowbotham in Bristol, 14 June 2013.
Interview with Sally Groves in London, 19 June 2013.
Interview with Judy Wajcman in London, 22 April 2013.

Additional oral history

Interview with Dora Challingsworth, Pamela Brown, Maureen Jackson and Geraldine Dear for film produced by Sarah Boston for TUC in 2006. Film available at TUC Archives, London Metropolitan University.
Interview with Violet Dawson, Sheila Douglas and Vera Sime for film produced by Sarah Boston for TUC in 2006. Film available at TUC Archives, London Metropolitan University.
Interview with Sally Groves by David Welsh and Rima Joebear on 25 March 2013 for TUC, Britain at Work Oral History Project.
Interview with Bernard Passingham for film produced by Sarah Boston for TUC in 2006. Film available at TUC Archives, London Metropolitan University.

Unpublished primary sources

Modern Records Centre, University of Warwick:
MSS. 30, Fakenham Enterprises Ltd Collection.
MSS.126/TG/193/1/64, T&G Record, January–December 1984.
MSS.126/TG/193/1/65, T&G Record, January–December 1985.
MSS.126/TG/466/A1/1/2/6, TGWU, Ford National Joint Negotiating Committee, Notes of Proceedings.
MSS. 178/17, Ford Motor Company Limited: dispute with the National Union of Vehicle Builders about the grading of women sewing machinists (inquiry held in June and July 1968) in Papers of Jack Scamp (1913–1977).

BIBLIOGRAPHY

MSS.259/AEU/6/3/SL/3/43, AEEU Southall District Branch Papers, Trico-Folberth Ltd, 1970–1978.
MSS.539/4/17, Trico Equal Pay Dispute in Papers of Alan Clinton.
MSS.572/150, Papers of Ron Todd, Miscellaneous Papers, 1911–1998.

The National Archives, Kew:
PREM 13/2412, STRIKES AND INDUSTRIAL DISPUTES. Strike of female sewing-machinists at Fords, Dagenham: intervention by Prime Minister. June–July 1968.
LAB 10/3312, Court of Inquiry into strike of Sewing-machinists employed at Dagenham Plant of Ford Motor Co Ltd: transcripts of evidence (London: HMSO, 1968).

TUC Library Collections, London Metropolitan University:
HD 6061, AUEW Official Trico Equal Pay Strike Bulletins, sixteen produced from Wednesday 29 June to Monday 18 October 1976.
HD 9710.6, Report of a Court of Inquiry under Sir Jack Scamp into a dispute concerning sewing-machinists employed by the Ford Motor Company Limited (London: HMSO, 1968).
HD 6661, TUC Women's Conference Annual Reports, 1968–1981.
The Garment Worker, Official Journal of NUTGW.
AUEW Engineering Section Journal.

Official publications

Annual Report of the Equal Opportunities Commission (London: HMSO, 1976).
Annual Report of the Equal Opportunities Commission (London: HMSO, 1981).
Equal Opportunities Commission, 'Women and low incomes: a report based on evidence to the Royal Commission on Income Distribution and Wealth' (London: HMSO, 1977).
HC Deb 11 March 1947 vol. 434 col. 1150 (Hansard).

Newspapers and periodicals

Barking and Dagenham Post
Brentford and Chiswick Times
Daily Mail
Daily Mirror
Daily Telegraph
Dereham and Fakenham Times
Eastern Daily Press
Eastern Evening News
Evening Mail
Ford Bulletin
Guardian

Leicester Mercury
Libertarian Struggle
Middlesex Chronicle
Militant
Morning Star
New Society
Northants Post
Norwich Evening News
Observer
Romford Times
Red Rag
Shrew
Socialist Women
Socialist Worker
Spare Rib
Spectator
Sun
Sunday Telegraph
Sunday Times
The Times
Time Out
Women's Voice
Women's Weekly

Contemporary articles, books and pamphlets

Beechey, V., 'What's So Special about Women's Employment? A Review of Some Recent Studies of Women's Paid Work', *Feminist Review*, no. 15 (Winter 1983), pp. 23–46.

Beynon, H., *Working for Ford* (London: Penguin, 1973).

Breitenbach, E., 'A Comparative Study of the Women's Trade Union Conference and the Scottish Women's Trade Union Conference', *Feminist Review*, vol. 7 (1981), pp. 65–86.

Brown, R., 'Women as Employees: Some Comments on Research in Industrial Sociology (and Postscript)' in D. Leonard and S. Allen, *Sexual Divisions Revisited* (London: Macmillan, 1991), pp. 153–178.

Bruegel, I., 'Women as a Reserve Army of Labour: A Note on Recent British Experience', *Feminist Review*, vol. 3 (1979), pp. 12–23.

Castle, B., *Fighting All the Way* (London: Macmillan, 1993).

Clutterback, D., 'Lady Leather Workers Mind Their Own Business', *International Management* (November 1973), MRC, MSS. 30, Fakenham Enterprises Ltd Collection.

Coates, K. (ed.), *The New Worker Co-Operatives* (Nottingham: Spokesman Books, 1976).

Coates, K., *Work-ins, Sit-ins, and Industrial Democracy: The Implications of Factory Occupations in Great Britain in the Early Seventies* (Nottingham: Spokesman, 1981).

Cockburn, C., 'Review of Wajcman, "Women in Control"', *Marxist Review* (March 1984), p. 40.

BIBLIOGRAPHY

Coultas, V., 'Feminists Must Face the Future', *Feminist Review*, no. 7 (1981), pp. 35-48.

Crine, S., and C. Playford, *From Rags to Rags: Low Pay in the Clothing Industry* (Report by Low Pay Unit, November 1982).

Dromey, J., and G. Taylor, *Grunwick: The Workers' Story* (London: Lawrence and Wishart Press, 1978).

Eliot, R., 'How Far Have We Come? Women's Organization in the Unions in the United Kingdom', *Feminist Review*, vol. 16 (1984), pp. 64-73.

Friedman, H., and S. Meredeen, *The Dynamics of Industrial Conflict: Lessons from Ford* (London: Croom Helm, 1980).

Glucksmann, M., *Women on the Line* (London: Routledge and Keegan Paul, 1982).

Hardy, C., 'Responses to Industrial Closure', *Industrial Relations Journal*, vol. 16, no. 1 (1985), pp. 16-24.

Hobsbawm, E., 'The Forward March of Labour Halted', *Marxism Today* (September 1978), pp. 279-286.

Hunt, P., *Gender and Class Consciousness* (Basingstoke: Macmillan, 1980).

James, S., *The Perspective of Winning* (London: London Wages for Housework Committee and Falling Wall Press, 1976).

James, S., *Women, The Unions and Work ... or What Is Not to be Done* (London: London Wages for Housework Committee and Falling Wall Press, 1972).

Layard, R., and S. Nickell, 'Unemployment in Britain', *Economica*, New Series, vol. 53, no. 210, Supplement: Unemployment (1986), pp. 121-169.

Mann, M., *Consciousness and Action among the Western Working Class* (London: Humanities, 1973).

Martin, J., and C. Roberts, *Women and Employment: A Lifetime Perspective* (London: Department of Employment and Office of Population Censuses and Surveys, HMSO, 1984).

McCreery, K., 'We Want to Work: The Shoemaking Women of Fakenham', *ATMS Journal* (August 1972), MRC, MSS. 30, Fakenham Enterprises Ltd Collection.

Pollert, A., *Girls, Wives, Factory Lives* (Basingstoke: Macmillan, 1981).

Ramdin, R., *The Making of the Black Working Class in Britain* (Aldershot: Ashgate Publishing, 1987).

Rogaly, J., *Grunwick* (Harmondsworth: Penguin, 1977).

Rowbotham, S., (ed.), 'The Beginnings of Women's Liberation in Britain' in *Dreams and Dilemmas: Collected Writings* (London: Virago, 1983), pp. 32-44.

Rowbotham, S., and B. Campbell, 'Class Struggle in Britain', *Radical America*, vol. 8, no. 5 (1974), pp. 55-77.

Turner, G., *The Car Workers* (London: Pelican, 1963).

Wajcman, J., *Women in Control: Dilemmas of a Workers' Cooperative* (Milton Keynes: Open University Press, 1983).

War On Want Pamphlet, *For a Few Dollars More: Lee, the Ultimate Rip-off* (London: WOW Publications, 1981).

Willmott, P., *The Evolution of a Community: A Study of Dagenham After Forty Years* (London: Routledge and Kegan Paul, 1963).

BIBLIOGRAPHY

Published secondary sources

Abrams, L., 'Liberating the Female Self: Epiphanies, Conflict and Coherence in the Life Stories of Post-War British Women', *Social History*, vol. 39, no. 1 (2014), pp. 14–35.

Abrams, L., 'Mothers and Daughters: Negotiating the Discourse on the "Good Woman" in 1950s and 1960s Britain' in N. Christie and M. Gauvreau (eds), *The Sixties and Beyond: Dechristianisation in North America and Western Europe, 1945–2000* (Toronto: University of Toronto Press, 2013), pp. 60–80.

Abrams, L., *Oral History Theory* (Abingdon: Routledge, 2010).

Abrams, L., *The Making of Modern Woman 1989–1918* (Harlow: Pearson 2002).

Abrams, L., 'The Unseamed Picture: Conflicting Narratives of Women in the Modern European Past', *Gender and History*, vol. 20, no. 3 (2008), pp. 628–643.

Aldcroft, D., and M. Oliver, *Trade Unions and the Economy: 1870–2000* (Aldershot: Ashgate Publishing, 2000).

Alexander, S., *Becoming a Woman: And Other Essays in 19th and 20th Century Feminist History* (London: Virago Press, 1994).

Alexander, S., 'Women's Work in Nineteenth-Century London: A Study of the Years 1820–50' in J. Mitchell and A. Oakley (eds), *The Rights and Wrongs of Women* (Harmondsworth: Penguin, 1976).

Alexander, S., and A. Davin, 'Feminist History' (editorial) *History Workshop Journal*, vol. 1, no. 2 (1976), pp. 1–4.

Alexander, S., A. Davin and E. Hostettler, 'Labouring Women: A Reply to Eric Hobsbawm', *History Workshop Journal*, vol. 8, no. 1 (1979), pp. 174–182.

Alt, J. E., 'The Politics of Economic Decline in the 1970s' in L. Black, H. Pemberton and P. Thane (eds), *Reassessing 1970s Britain* (Manchester: Manchester University Press, 2013), pp. 25–38.

Anderson, K., and D. Jack, 'Learning to Listen: Interview Techniques and Analysis' in R. Perks and A. Thomson (eds), *Oral History Reader* (London: Routledge, 1998), pp. 157–172.

Anitha, S., R. Pearson and L. McDowell, 'Striking Lives: Multiple Narratives of South Asian Women's Employment, Identity and Protest in the UK', *Ethnicities*, vol. 12, no. 6 (2012), pp. 654–775.

Beaumont, C., *Housewives and Citizens: Domesticity and the Women's Movement in England, 1928–1964* (Manchester: Manchester University Press, 2013).

Beckett, A., *When the Lights Went Out: Britain in the 1970s* (London: Faber and Faber, 2010).

Black, L., *Redefining British Politics: Culture, Consumerism and Participation* (Basingstoke: Palgrave Macmillan, 2010).

Blackburn, S., 'Working Class Attitudes to Social Reform: Black Country Chainmakers and Anti-Sweating Legislation, 1880–1930', *International Review of Social History*, vol. 33, no. 1 (1988), pp. 42–69.

Bornat, J., 'A Second Take: Revisiting Interviews with a Different Purpose', *Oral History*, vol. 31, no. 1 (2003), pp. 47–53.

Boston, S., *Women Workers and the Trade Unions*, 2nd edn (London: Lawrence and Wishart, 1989).

BIBLIOGRAPHY

Bouchier, D., *The Feminist Challenge: The Movement for Women's Liberation in Britain and the United States* (New York: Schocken Books, 1984).

Bracke, M., 'Between the Transnational and the Local: The Origins and Trajectories of the Wages for Housework Campaign in 1970s Italian Feminism', *Women's History Review*, vol. 22, no. 3 (2013), pp. 625–642.

Bracke, M., 'From Politics to Nostalgia: The Transformation of War Memories in France During the 1960-1970s', *European History Quarterly*, vol. 41, no. 1 (2011), pp. 25–49.

Bracke, M., *Women and the Reinvention of the Political: Feminism in Italy, 1968-1983* (London: Routledge, 2014).

Bradley, H., *Gender and Power in the Workplace: Analysing the Impact of Economic Change* (London: Macmillan Press, 1999).

Bradley, H., *Men's Work, Women's Work: A Sociological History of the Sexual Division of Labour in Employment* (Cambridge: Polity Press, 1989).

Brooke, S., 'Gender and Working Class Identity in Britain During the 1950s', *Journal of Social History*, vol. 34, no. 4 (2001), pp. 773–795.

Brooke, S., *Sexual Politics: Sexuality, Family Planning and the British Left from the 1880s to the Present Day* (Oxford: Oxford University Press, 2011).

Brown, C., and H. W. Fraser, *Britain Since 1707* (Harlow: Pearson, 2010).

Brown, T., and B. Vidal (eds), 'Editors Introduction' in *The Biopic in Contemporary Film Culture* (London: Routledge, 2014).

Browne, S., *The Women's Liberation Movement in Scotland* (Manchester: Manchester University Press, 2014).

Bruley, S., 'Consciousness-Raising in Clapham; Women's Liberation as "Lived Experience" in South London in the 1970s', *Women's History Review*, vol. 22, no. 5 (2013), pp. 717–738.

Bruley, S., *Women in Britain Since 1900* (Basingstoke: Palgrave Macmillan, 1999).

Callander, C., 'Redundancy, Unemployment and Poverty' in C. Glendinning and J. Millar (eds), *Women and Poverty in Britain* (Brighton: Whitesheaf, 1987), pp. 137–159.

Cerna, M., J. Davis, R. Gildea and P. Oseka, 'Revolutions' in R. Gildea, J. Mark and A. Warring (eds), *Europe's 1968: Voices of Revolt* (Oxford: Oxford University Press, 2013).

Clifford, R., 'Emotion and Gender in Oral History: Narrating Italy's 1968', *Modern Italy*, vol. 17, no. 2 (2012), pp. 209–221.

Cohen, S., 'Equal Pay – or What? Economics, Politics and the 1968 Ford Sewing-Machinists' Strike', *Labor History*, vol. 53, no. 1 (2012), pp. 51–68.

Cook, J., and S. Watt, 'Racism, Women and Poverty' in C. Glendinning and J. Millar (eds), *Women and Poverty in Britain* (Brighton: Wheatsheaf, 1987), pp. 53–73.

Coote, A., and B. Campbell, *Sweet Freedom: Struggle for Women's Liberation* (Oxford: Basil Blackwell, 1987).

Crompton, R., *Women and Work in Modern Britain* (Oxford: Oxford University Press, 1997).

Cronin, J., *Labour and Society in Britain, 1918-1979* (London: Batsford Academic, 1984).

Cunnison, S., and J. Stageman, *Feminizing the Unions* (Aldershot: Avebury, 1993).

Davis, A., *Modern Motherhood: Women and Family in England, 1945-2000* (Manchester: Manchester University Press, 2012).

BIBLIOGRAPHY

Davis, M. (ed.), *Gender and Class in the British Labour Movement* (London: Merlin Press, 2012).

De la Mare, U., 'Necessity and Rage: The Factory Women's Strikes in Bermondsey, 1911,' *History Workshop Journal*, vol. 66, no. 1 (2008), pp. 62–80.

Della Porta, D., and M. Diani, *Social Movements: An Introduction* (Oxford: Blackwell, 2005).

Dex, S., *The Sexual Division of Work: Conceptual Revolutions in the Social Sciences* (Brighton: Harvester Press, 1985).

Edgerton, D., *The Rise and Fall of the British Nation: A Twentieth Century History* (St Ives: Allen Lane, 2018).

Fielding, S., *The Labour Governments 1964–1970 Vol 1: Labour and Cultural Change* (Manchester: Manchester University Press, 2003).

Fraser, H., *A History of British Trade Unionism 1700–1998* (Basingstoke: Macmillan Press, 1999).

Fraser, K. *Same or Different: Gender Politics in the Workplace* (Aldershot: Ashgate, 1999).

Frisch, M., *Shared Authority: Essays on the Craft and Meaning of Oral and Public History* (New York: SUNY Press, 1990).

Gall, G., 'Contemporary Workplace Occupations in Britain: Motivations, Stimuli, Dynamics and Outcomes', *Employee Relations*, vol. 33, no. 6 (2011), pp. 607–623.

Gall, G., 'Resisting Recession and Redundancy: Contemporary Worker Occupations in Britain', *Working USA*, vol. 13, no. 1 (2010), pp. 107–132.

Gallie, D., 'The Labour Force', A. H. Halsey and J. Webb (eds), *Twentieth-Century British Social Trends* (Basingstoke: Macmillan Press, 2000).

Gazely, I., and A. Newall (eds), *Work and Pay in Twentieth Century Britain* (Cambridge: Cambridge University Press, 2007).

Giddens, A., *The Constitution of Society: Outline of the Theory of Structuration* (London: Polity Press, 1984).

Glucksmann, M., *Women Assemble: Women Workers and New Industries in Inter-war Britain* (London: Routledge, 1990).

Gordon, E., *Women and the Labour Movement in Scotland, 1850–1914* (Oxford: Clarendon Press, 1991).

Grant, M., 'Historicising Citizenship in Post-War Britain', *The Historical Journal*, vol. 59, no. 4 (2016), pp. 1187–1206.

Green, A., 'Individual Remembering and "Collective Memory": Theoretical Presuppositions and Contemporary Debates', *Oral History*, vol. 32, no. 2 (2004), pp. 34–44.

Grele, Ron (ed.), *Envelopes of Sound: The Art of Oral History* (New York: Praeger, 1991).

Groves, S., and V. Merritt, *Trico: A Victory to Remember: The 1976 Equal Pay Strike at Trico Folberth, Brentford* (London: Lawrence and Wishart, 2018).

Hakim, C., 'Five Feminist Myths about Women's Employment', *The British Journal of Sociology*, vol. 46, no. 3 (September 1995), pp. 429–455.

Hay, C., 'Narrating the Crisis: The Discursive Construction of the Winter of Discontent', *Sociology*, vol. 30, no. 2 (May 1996), pp. 253–277.

Hinton, J., *Nine Wartime Lives: Mass Observation and the Making of the Modern Self* (Oxford: Oxford University Press, 2010).

Hobsbawm, Eric, 'Man and Woman in Socialist Iconography', *History Workshop Journal*, no. 6 (1978), pp. 121–138.

BIBLIOGRAPHY

Holloway, G., *Women and Work in Britain Since 1840* (London: Routledge, 2005).

Honeyman, K., *Well Suited: A History of the Leeds Clothing Industry, 1850–1990* (Oxford: Oxford University Press, 2000).

Howell, C., *Trade Unions and the State: The Construction of Industrial Relations Institutions in Britain* (New Jersey, NJ: Princeton University Press, 2005).

Howell, D., 'Editorial', *Labour History Review*, vol. 60, no. 1 (1995), pp. 1–7.

Hughes, A., *Gender and Political Identities in Scotland, 1919–1939* (Edinburgh: Edinburgh University Press, 2010).

Hughes, C., *Young Lives on the Left: Sixties Activism and the Liberation of the Self* (Manchester: Manchester University Press, 2015).

Hunt, C., *The National Federation of Women Workers, 1906–1921* (Basingstoke: Palgrave Macmillan, 2014).

Hunt, J., 'A Woman's Place Is in Her Union' in J. West (ed.), *Work, Women and the Labour Market* (London: Routledge and Kegan Paul, 1982), pp. 154–172.

Hyman, R., *Strikes* (Basingstoke: Macmillan Press, 1989).

Inglehart, R., *The Silent Revolution: Changing Values and Political Styles Among Western Publics* (Princeton, NJ: Princeton Legacy Library, 1977).

Kirk, N., 'Challenge, Crisis, and Renewal? Themes in the Labour History of Britain, 1960–2010', *Labour History Review*, vol. 75, no. 2 (2010), pp. 162–180.

Langhamer, C., 'Feelings, Women and Work in the Long 1950s', *Women's History Review*, vol. 26, no. 1 (2017), pp. 77–92.

Langhamer, C., 'Love and Courtship in Mid-Twentieth-Century England', *The Historical Journal*, vol. 50 (2007), pp. 173–196.

Lawrence, J., 'Social-Science Encounters and the Negotiation of Difference in Early 1960s England', *History Workshop Journal*, vol. 77, no. 1 (2014), pp. 215–239.

Laybourn, K., *A History of British Trade Unionism, 1800–1990* (Stroud: Sutton Publishing, 1992).

Lee Downs, L., *Manufacturing Inequality: Gender Division in the French and British Metalworking Industries, 1914–1939* (Ithaca, NY: Cornell University Press, 1995).

Lewenhak, S., *Women and Trade Unions: An Outline History of Women in the British Trade Union Movement* (London: Benn, 1977).

Lewis, J., 'Women and Social Change in Britain, 1945–1995' in J. Hollowell (ed.), *Britain Since 1945* (Oxford: Blackwell Publishers, 2003), pp. 260–279.

Lewis, J., *Women in Britain Since 1945* (Oxford: Wiley Blackwell, 1992).

Lewis, J., *Women in England 1870–1950: Sexual Divisions and Social Change* (Brighton: Wheatsheaf, 1984).

Liddington, J., and J. Norris, *One Hand Tied Behind Us: The Rise of the Women's Suffrage Movement* (London: River Oram Press, 2000).

Linde, C., *Life Stories: The Creation of Coherence* (Oxford: Oxford University Press, 1993).

Lockyer, B. 'An Irregular Period: Participation in the Bradford Women's Liberation Movement', *Women's History Review*, vol. 22, no. 4 (2013), pp. 643–657.

Lonsdale, S., 'Patterns of Paid Work' in C. Glendinning and J. Millar (eds), *Women and Poverty in Britain* (Brighton: Whitesheaf, 1987).

Martin R., and J. Wallace, *Working Women in Recession: Employment, Redundancy, and Unemployment* (Oxford: Oxford University Press, 1984).

Martin-Lopez, T., 'The Beginning of Labour's End? Britain's "Winter of Discontent" and Working-Class Women's Activism', *International Labour and Working Class History*, vol. 75, no. 1 (2009), pp. 49-68.

Martin-Lopez, T., *The Winter of Discontent: Myth, Memory, and History* (Liverpool: Liverpool University Press, 2014).

McCarthy, H., 'Gender Equality' in P. Thane (ed.), *Unequal Britain: Equalities in Britain Since 1945* (London: Bloomsbury, 2010).

McCarthy, H., 'Social Science and Married Women's Employment in Post-War Britain', *Past and Present*, vol. 233, no. 1 (2016), pp. 216-217.

McCarthy, H., 'Women, Marriage and Paid Work in Post-War Britain', *Women's History Review*, vol. 26, no. 1 (2017), pp. 44-61.

McDowell, L., *Working Lives: Gender, Migration and Employment in Britain, 1945-2007* (Hoboken: Wiley, 2013).

McDowell, L., S. Anita and R. Pearson, 'Striking Narratives: Class, Gender and Ethnicity in the "Great Grunwick Strike," London, UK, 1976-1978', *Women's History Review*, vol. 23, no. 4 (2014), pp. 595-619.

McGowan, J., 'Dispute, Battle, Siege, Farce? – Grunwick 30 Years On', *Contemporary British History*, vol. 22, no. 3 (2008), pp. 383-404.

McKibbin, R., *Classes and Cultures: England 1918-1951* (Oxford: Oxford University Press, 1998).

Mcllellan, J., 'The "Problem of Women" in Post-War Europe', *English Historical Review*, vol. 130, no. 545 (July 2015), pp. 934-944.

Mcllroy, J., 'Strikes and Class Consciousness in the Early Work of R. Hyman', *Capital and Class*, vol. 36, no. 1 (2012), pp. 53-75.

Mcllroy, J., and A. Campbell , 'The High Tide of Trade Unionism: Mapping Industrial Politics, 1964-1979' in J. McIlroy, N. Fishman and A. Campbell (eds), *British Trade Unions and Industrial Politics: The High Tide of Trade Unionism, 1964-1979* (Aldershot: Ashgate Publishing, 1999), pp. 93-133.

McIvor, A., *Working Lives: Work in Britain Since 1945* (London: Palgrave Macmillan, 2014).

Meehan, E., 'British Feminism from the 1960s to the 1980s' in H. Smith (ed.), *British Feminism in the Twentieth Century* (London: Edward Elgar, 1990).

Minister, K., 'A Feminist Frame for the Oral History Interview' in S. B. Gluck and D. Patai (eds), *Women's Words: The Feminist Practice of Oral History* (London: Routledge, 1991), pp. 27-40.

Molony, B., and J. Nelson (eds), *Women's Activism and 'Second Wave' Feminism: Transnational Histories* (London: Bloomsbury, 2017).

Navickas, K., 'What Happened to Class? New Histories of Labour and Collective Action in Britain', *Social History*, vol. 36, no. 2 (2011), pp. 192-204.

Oerton, S., 'Exploring Women Workers' Motives for Employment in Cooperative and Collective Organizations', *Journal of Gender Studies*, vol. 3, no. 3 (1994), pp. 289-290.

Offen, K., 'Defining Feminism: A Comparative Historical Approach', *Signs*, vol. 14, no. 1 (1988), pp. 119-157.

Offen, K., 'Understanding International Feminisms as "Transnational" – An Anachronism?' in O. Janz, and D. Schonpflug (eds), *Gender History in a Transnational Perspective: Networks, Biographies, Gender Orders* (Oxford: Berghan Books, 2014).

Passerini, L., 'Work, Ideology and Consensus under Italian Fascism', *History Workshop Journal*, vol. 8 (1979), pp. 82–108.

Pearson, R., S. Anitha and L. McDowell, 'Striking Issues: From Labour Process to Industrial Dispute at Grunwick and Gate Gourmet', *Industrial Relations Journal*, vol. 41, no. 5 (2010), pp. 408–428.

Phillips, J., *Collieries, Communities and the Miners' Strike in Scotland, 1984–85* (Manchester: Manchester University Press, 2012).

Portelli, A., *The Death of Luigi Trastulli and Other Stories: Form and Meaning in Oral History* (Albany, NY: State University of New York Press, 1991).

Pugh, M., *Women and the Women's Movement, 1914–1999* (Basingstoke: Macmillan, 2000).

Raw, L., *Striking a Light: The Bryant and May Matchwomen and Their Place in History* (London: Continuum, 2011).

Reid, A., *United We Stand: A History of British Trade Unionism* (London: Penguin, 2005).

Rees, T., *Women and the Labour Market* (London: Routledge, 1992).

Roberts, E., *A Woman's Place: An Oral History of Working-Class Women, 1890–1940* (Oxford: Blackwell, 1984).

Roberts, E., *Women and Families: An Oral History 1940–1970* (Oxford: Wiley Blackwell, 1995).

Robinson, E., C. Schofield, F. Sutcliffe-Braithwaite and N. Thomlinson, 'Telling Stories about Post-War Britain: Popular Individualism and the "Crisis" of the 1970s', *Twentieth Century British History*, vol. 28, no. 2 (2017), pp. 268–304.

Roper, M., 'Oral History' in B. Brivati, J. Buxton and A. Seldon (eds), *The Contemporary History Handbook* (Manchester: Manchester University Press, 1996), pp. 345–352.

Roper, M., 'Re-remembering the Soldier Hero: The Psychic and Social Construction of Memory in Personal Narratives of the Great War', *History Workshop Journal*, no. 50 (2000), pp. 181–204.

Roper, M., 'Slipping Out of View: Subjectivity and Emotion in Gender History', *History Workshop Journal*, vol. 59, no. 1 (2005), pp. 57–72.

Rose, S., 'Gender Antagonism and Class Conflict: Exclusionary Strategies of Male Trade Unionists in Nineteenth-Century Britain', *Social History*, vol. 13, no. 2 (1988), pp. 113–131.

Rowbotham, S., 'Cleaners' Organising in Britain from the 1970s: A Personal Account', *Antipode: A Radical Journal of Geography*, vol. 38, no. 3 (2006), pp. 608–625.

Rowbotham, S., *Hidden from History: 300 Years of Women's Oppression and the Fight Against It* (London: Pluto Press, 1973).

Rowbotham, S., 'Jolting Memory: Nightcleaners Recalled' in M. Ruido (ed.), *Plan Rosebud: On Images, Sites and Politics of Memory* (Santiago de Compostela: Xunta de Galicia, 2008).

Rowbotham, S., *The Past is Before Us: Feminism in Action Since the 1960s* (London: Pandora Press, 1989).

Sandbrook, D., *State of Emergency: Britain 1970–1974* (London: Penguin, 2011).

Sangster, J., 'Telling Our Stories: Feminist Debates and the Use of Oral History', *Women's History Review*, vol. 3, no. 1 (1994), pp. 5–28.

Saunders, J., 'The Untraditional Worker: Class Re-Formation in Britain 1945–65', *Twentieth Century British History*, vol. 26, no. 2 (2015), pp. 225–248.

Savage, M., *Identities and Social Change in Britain Since 1940: The Politics of Method* (Oxford: Oxford University Press, 2010).

Savage, M., 'Working-Class Identities in the 1960s: Revisiting the Affluent Worker Study', *Sociology*, vol. 39 (2005), pp. 922–946.

Sayer, K., *Women of the Fields: Representations of Rural Women in the Nineteenth Century* (Manchester: Manchester University Press, 1995).

Schwartz, L., 'Rediscovering the Workplace', *History Workshop Journal*, vol. 74, no. 1 (2012), pp. 270–277.

Scott, J., 'Gender: A Useful Category of Historical Analysis', *The American Historical Review*, vol. 92, no. 5 (1986), pp. 1053–1075.

Scott, J., S. Dex, H. Joshi, K., Purcell and P. Elias 'Introduction' in J. Scott *et al.* (eds), *Women and Employment: Changing Lives and New Challenges* (Cheltenham: Edward Elgar, 2009).

Segal, L., 'Jam Today: Feminist Impacts and Transformations in the 1970s' in L. Black, H. Pemberton and P. Thane (eds), *Reassessing 1970s Britain* (Manchester: Manchester University Press, 2013), pp. 149–167.

Simonton, D., *A History of European Women's Work: 1700 to the Present* (London: Routledge, 1998).

Smart, C., *The Ties that Bind* (London: Routledge, 1984).

Smith, G., 'Beyond Individual/ Collective Memory: Women's Transactive Memories of Food, Family and Conflict', *Oral History*, vol. 35, no. 2 (2007), pp. 77–90.

Smith, H. L., 'The Women's Movement, Politics and Citizenship, 1960s–2000' in I. Zweiniger-Bargielowska (ed.), *Women in Twentieth Century Britain* (Harlow: Pearson, 2001).

Smith-Wilson, D., 'A New Look at the Affluent Worker: The Good Working Mother in Post-War Britain', *Twentieth Century British History*, vol. 17, no. 2 (2006), pp. 206–229.

Soldon, N. C., *Women in British Trade Unions, 1874–1976* (Dublin: Gill and Macmillan, 1978)

Spender, S., *Gender, Work and Education in Britain in the 1950s* (Basingstoke: Palgrave Macmillan, 2005).

Summerfield, P., 'Culture and Composure: Creating Narratives of the Gendered Self in Oral History Interview', *Cultural and Social History*, vol. 1 (2004), pp. 65–93.

Summerfield, P., *Reconstructing Women's Wartime Lives: Discourse and Subjectivity in Oral Histories of the Second World War* (Manchester: Manchester University Press, 1998).

Summerfield, P., 'Women in Britain Since 1945: Companionate Marriage and the Double Burden' in P. Catterall and J. Obelkevich (eds), *Understanding Post-War British Society* (London: Routledge, 1994).

Summerfield, P., *Women Workers in the Second World War: Production and Patriarchy in Conflict* (London: Crook Helm, 1984).

Sutcliffe-Braithwaite, F., *Class, Politics, and the Decline of Deference in England, 1968–2000* (Oxford: Oxford University Press, 2018).

Tarrow, S., *Power in Movement: Social Movements and Contentious Politics*, 3rd edn (Cambridge: Cambridge University Press, 2011).

Taylor, B., and A. Phillips, 'Sex and Skill: Notes towards a Feminist Economics', *Feminist Review*, no. 6 (1980), pp. 79–88.

Thane, P., 'Women and the 1970s: Towards Liberation?' in L. Black, H. Pemberton and P. Thane (eds), *Reassessing 1970s Britain* (Manchester: Manchester University Press, 2013), pp. 167–187.

Thomlinson, J., 'De-industrialisation not Decline: A New Meta-Narrative for Post-War British History', *Twentieth Century British History*, vol. 27, no. 1 (2016), pp. 76–99.

Thomlinson, N., *Race, Ethnicity and the Women's Movement in England, 1968–1993* (Basingstoke: Palgrave Macmillan, 2016).

Thomson, A., 'Putting Popular Memory Theory into Practice in Australia' in R. Perks and A. Thomson (eds), *The Oral History Reader* (London: Routledge, 2006), pp. 300–311.

Tilly, L., and J. Scott, *Women, Work and Family* (London: Routledge, 1987).

Todd, S., 'Affluence, Class and Crown Street: Reinvestigating the Post-War Working Class', *Contemporary British History*, vol. 22, no. 4 (2008), pp. 501–518.

Todd, S., 'Class, Experience and Britain's Twentieth Century', *Social History*, vol. 56, no. 4 (2014), pp. 489–508.

Todd, S., 'Domestic Service and Class Relations in Britain 1900–1950', *Past and Present*, vol. 203, no. 1 (2009), pp. 181–204.

Todd, S., *The People: The Rise and Fall of the Working Class 1910–2010* (London: John Murray, 2014).

Todd, S., *Young Women, Work and Family, 1918–1950* (Oxford: Oxford University Press, 2005).

Tuckman, A., 'Factory Occupation, Workers' Cooperative and Alternative Production: Lessons from Britain in the 1970s' in M. Atzeni (ed.), *Alternative Work Organisations* (Basingstoke: Palgrave Macmillan, 2012), pp. 25–48.

Turner, A., *Crisis? What Crisis? Britain in the 1970s* (London: Aurum Press, 2008).

Walby, S., *Patriarchy at Work* (Cambridge: Cambridge University Press, 1986).

West, J. (ed.), *Women, Work and the Labour Market* (Routledge: London, 1982).

Wright, V., 'Education for Active Citizenship: Women's Organisations in Interwar Scotland', *History of Education*, vol. 38, no. 3 (2009), pp. 419–436.

Wrigley, C., *British Trade Unions Since 1933* (Cambridge: Cambridge University Press, 2001).

Wrigley, C., 'Industrial and Labour Relations' in J. Hollowell (ed.), *Britain Since 1945* (Oxford: Blackwell, 2003).

Wrigley, C., 'Industrial Relations' in N. Crafts, I. Gazeley and A. Newell (eds), *Work and Pay in Twentieth Century Britain* (Oxford: Oxford University Press, 2007).

Wrigley, C., 'Women in the Labour Market and in the Unions' in J. McIlroy, N. Fishman and A. Campbell (eds), *British Trade Unions and Industrial Politics: The High Tide of Trade Unionism, 1945–1979* (Aldershot: Ashgate Publishing, 1999), pp. 43–70.

Young, H., 'Hard Man, New Man: Re/composing Masculinities in Glasgow, c. 1950–2000', *Oral History*, vol. 35, no. 1 (2007), pp. 71–81.

Young, J. D., *Women and Popular Struggles: A History of Scottish and English Working-Class Women, 1500–1984* (Edinburgh: Mainstream Publishing, 1985).

Talks and presentations

Paterson, L., 'Part-Time Work and Working Motherhood, c. 1951–1981', paper presented at the North American Conference of British Studies, November 2017.

Unpublished theses

Homans, H., 'Visions of Equality: Women's Rights and Political Change in 1970s Britain' (Unpublished PhD Thesis, University of Bangor, 2014).

Setch, E., 'The Women's Liberation Movement in Britain, 1969–79: Organisation, Creativity and Debate' (Unpublished PhD Thesis, Royal Holloway, 2001).

Internet resources

British Library Sisterhood and After Project website, www.bl.uk/learning/histcitizen/sisterhood/clips/activism/campaigns-and-protests/143934.html (accessed 12 April 2014).

Grigg, J., and B. Humphries, 'Labour Heritage in west London', *Labour Heritage Bulletin* (Spring 2010), www.labour-heritage.com/spring-2010.php (accessed 21 May 2013).

Longman, P., 'Restarting Our Women's Work', Alliance of Worker's Liberty, www.workersliberty.org/node/8199 (accessed 12 December 2013).

'Pay Gap Widens as Women's Standing in the Economy Further Undermined', *Fawcett Society*, www.fawcettsociety.org.uk/gender-pay-gap-briefing-november-2014 (accessed 8 September 2014).

The Fawcett Society's Gender Pay Gap Briefing (November 2014), www.fawcettsociety.org.uk/gender-pay-gap-briefing-november-2014 (accessed 10 November 2015).

'Trade Union Membership 2013: A Statistical Overview' (May 2014), available online www.gov.uk/government/uploads/system/uploads/attachment_data/file/313768/bis-14-p77-trade-union-membership-statistical-bulletin-2013.pdf (accessed 18 August 2014).

TUC, *Winning Equal Pay*, www.unionhistory.info/equalpay/voices.php (accessed 12 October 2013).

Index

abortion 7, 35, 39
Abortion Act (1967) 35, 181
Advisory, Conciliation and
 Arbitration Service 141–142,
 150, 158
Alexander, Sally 38
Amalgamated Union of Engineering
 and Foundry Workers 56, 67,
 70, 73
Amalgamated Union of Engineering
 Workers 82, 83, 85, 87, 93–99,
 104–106, 148, 167
Association of Cinematograph,
 Television and Allied
 Technicians 35
Association of Professional,
 Executive, Clerical and
 Computer Staff 35, 45,
 117, 180
Association of Scientific Technical
 and Managerial Staffs 111,
 114, 115, 119
authenticity 125, 152, 155, 171

BBC *Women's Hour* 113
Benn, Tony 113, 129
Bermondsey 5
bi-modal work pattern 2
Blair, Tony 154
Boston, Sarah 5, 34
Brentford 82, 84–86
Brown, Richard 32
Bryant and May matchstick girls
 strike 5, 150

Cambridge University 127
Campbell, Beatrix 36
Canada 15
Castle, Barbara 56, 91
childcare 3, 6, 34, 39, 64, 119,
 130, 157
Cinema in Action 126

citizenship 9, 50–51, 165
Civil Service Union 34
collective memory 19, 105
Conservative Party 3, 43, 75, 113,
 116, 124
Coote, Anna 36
Cradley Heath 5

Dagenham 59–62, 146
decline of deference 10
deindustrialisation 10, 31, 134, 166
Department of Social Security 111
Desai, Jayaben 45
Domestic Violence Act (1976) 43
Dundee 5

East Africa 15
East Anglia Economic Planning
 Council 115
Electrolux dispute, Luton 98
Equal Opportunities Commission 32,
 43, 91
equal pay 27–31, 42–44, 56–57,
 66–77, 82–106, 139–144, 149,
 158, 160, 166, 167, 172
Equal Pay Act (1970) 3, 12, 27, 33,
 42, 43, 56, 57, 74, 77, 82, 83,
 84, 89–91, 98, 106, 140, 141
Equal Pay Campaign Committee 34
European Court of Justice 140

Fakenham 114–116, 118
Fawcett Society 43
feminism 7–9, 13, 16, 35, 36–42, 43,
 72–76, 99–105, 113, 116,
 126–134, 157–160, 164,
 169–172
First World War 11
Foot, Michael 113
Ford National Joint Negotiating
 Committee 140
Ford Sewing machinists

INDEX

1968 strike 1, 12, 56–77, 167
1984–85 strike 12, 139–161, 167
Halewood 56, 142, 149
Friedman, Henry 72

General and Municipal Workers' Union 35, 175, 177
Glucksmann, Miriam 32, 40–42, 127
Goodmans equal pay strike, Havant 39
Greater London Association of Trade Union Councils 93, 95
Greenham Common 158
Grunwick 1, 14–15, 16–17, 45, 173

Hobsbawm, Eric 49
Housing Act (1980) 61
Hunt, Pauline 32
Hyman, Richard 10–11, 49

Imperial Typewriters Dispute, Leicester 46–48
Indian Workers Association 47, 48
Industrial Relations Act (1971) 115
International Common Ownership Movement 112, 119
International Marxist Group 75, 90–91
International Socialists 39, 86

James, Selma 36
Jones, Jack 154

Kenilworth Components dispute, Leicester 47
King's Lynn 114

Labour Party 3, 34–36, 43, 76, 84, 85, 86, 112, 154
Labour Party Young Socialists 84, 85, 103
Lee Jeans Dispute, Greenock 121
Linde, Charlotte 17–18
Living Wage Campaign 149

London Trades Council 34
Low Pay Unit 118
Lucas Industries Dispute, Birmingham 121

Made in Dagenham 57, 143
Mansfield Hosiery Mill dispute 46
masculinities 19
Mass-Observation 11
McCluskey, Len 154
McGrath, Nancy 111, 114, 115, 118, 120, 125, 129–131, 134
Merseyside 56, 112, 141–142
motherhood 3, 27, 31

National Federation of Women Workers 5
National Front 47, 85, 94
National Joint Action Campaign Committee for Women's Equal Rights 34, 74–75
National Union of Hosiery and Knitwear Workers 46
National Union of Public Employees 35, 176
National Union of the Footwear, Leather and Allied Trades 111, 114, 115, 119–126, 127
National Union of Vehicle Builders 56, 69, 70, 71, 106, 141, 167
night-cleaners campaign 1, 38
Norwich 111, 114, 120–121, 122

O'Callaghan, Lil 58, 66, 73, 141
oral history 8, 9, 13–20
ordinariness 125, 132, 171

part-time work 2–3, 5, 11, 27, 31, 32 50, 51, 165
Passingham, Bernard 71, 141
Plessey Electronics Dispute, London 121
political identity 9–11, 156, 160, 165, 166, 171–172

INDEX

Pollert, Anna 6, 32, 41, 127
pronatalism 31

race, racism 4, 44–48, 85, 172
Race Relations Act 46
Roberts, Elizabeth 3
Rowbotham, Sheila 7, 36, 37, 38, 43, 75, 169

Scanlon, Hugh 94
Scotland 7, 14
Scott Bader 112, 118–119, 130
second-wave feminism 7–9, 13
Second World War 2–3, 5, 11, 17, 164
Sex Discrimination Act (1975) 3, 42–44, 72
Sexton Son and Everard shoe factory occupation, Fakenham, Norfolk 12, 41, 111–134, 167
sexual division of labour 27–31
Sexual Offences Act (1977) 43
Six Point Group 43
Skeggs, Beverley 125
Socialist Workers' Party 36
Southall District Trades Council 85, 93–99
Southampton 141
South Asian women's activism 44–48
Status of Women Committee 75
subjectivity 9, 11, 75, 95, 97, 133, 164
Summerskill, Shirley 73–74

Technical, Administrative and Supervisory Section 35, 91, 101, 180
Thatcher, Margaret 10, 61, 87
Thatcherism 9
Trades Union Congress 6, 34, 35, 36, 45, 64, 168

trade unionism 5–7, 11
  experiences of 68–72, 93–99, 110–126, 149–157
  and women 34–36
Transport and General Workers Union 46, 47, 65, 69, 140, 141–142, 149–150, 152, 154, 158, 160, 167, 168
Trico-Folberth Equal Pay Strike, Brentford 12, 82–106, 167

unemployment 5, 10, 32, 90, 114–115, 123
Union of Shop, Distributive and Allied Workers 37
Unite 154
Upper Clyde Shipbuilders 112, 115–116

Wainwright Trust 143
Wajcman, Judy 32, 41, 113, 114, 116, 124, 127, 170
Wilmott, Peter 59, 62
Wilson, Amrit 45
Wilson, Harold 70
Wise, Audrey 37
Women and Employment Survey 32
Women's Industrial Union 126
women's liberation movement 1, 7–9, 13–14, 26, 36–42, 43, 45, 48, 57, 74–76, 84, 99–106, 112, 113, 126–134, 169–172
  Brighton WLM 126
  Colchester Women's Lib 126
  East Manchester and Stockport Women's Lib 126
  Glasgow Women in Action 126
Working Women's Charter 6, 34–35, 98, 100

EU authorised representative for GPSR:
Easy Access System Europe, Mustamäe tee 50,
10621 Tallinn, Estonia
gpsr.requests@easproject.com

www.ingramcontent.com/pod-product-compliance
Lightning Source LLC
Chambersburg PA
CBHW070238240426
43673CB00044B/1845